UNORTHODOX TACK

I couldn't see the color and insignia on the other aircraft, only the silhouette. So I chased him at high speed, pulled up, and at that moment saw the aircraft against the ground instead of against the sun. The red star was glaring back at me from his fuselage. I couldn't turn away, because otherwise he would just have turned, too, and shot me down like a duck.

I turned back from the left and down, pulled the trigger, and there was an earsplitting, terrifying crash. Collision! I bounced on this Russian from above. I cut his wing with my propeller, and he cut my fuselage with his propeller. He got the worst of it, because my propeller went through his wing like a ripsaw.

—German Ace Günther Rall
(275 shootdowns), from
Luftwaffe Fighter Aces

Books published by The Ballantine Publishing Group
are available at quantity discounts on bulk purchases
for premium, educational, fund-raising, and special
sales use. For details, please call 1-800-733-3000.

LUFTWAFFE FIGHTER ACES

The Jagdflieger and Their Combat Tactics and Techniques

Mike Spick

IVY BOOKS • NEW YORK

Ivy Books
Published by Ballantine Books
Copyright © 1996 by Mike Spick

http://www.randomhouse.com

Library of Congress Catalog Card Number: 97-93363

ISBN 0-8041-1696-2

Manufactured in the United States of America

First Ballantine Books Edition: September 1997

10 9 8 7 6 5 4 3 2 1

CONTENTS

ILLUSTRATIONS

Figures

PREFACE

Flying has no equivalent, while war is the second-oldest profession. Combined, they are the ultimate in human experience. The fighter pilot is the modern equivalent of the ancient single combat champion, whose worth was measured by the number of his victories. Yet no champion of old ever approached the number of victories attributed to the leading fighter pilots of the *Luftwaffe* in the Second World War. What sort of men were they?

The truth is that fighter pilots are an international fraternity, a brotherhood divided only by language and the national insignia on their aircraft. The German pilots of the Second World War may have been more successful, but in essence they were no different from those of any other nation or period. Many retained an innate decency in spite of the slaughter, under the banner of chivalry. As second-highest scorer Gerd Barkhorn once told Erich Hartmann, ". . . you must remember that one day that Russian pilot was the baby son of a beautiful Russian girl. He has his right to life and love the same as we do."

The war itself took a heavy toll, and the intervening years have not been kind. Even as this book was being written, the redoubtable Adolf Galland, Georg-Peter Eder—"Lucky 13"— and ace of aces Erich Hartmann all "went upstairs." For those remaining, fifty years has faded the memory. As my friend Julius Neumann, once a young Bf 109E pilot with *II/JG 27*, told me, "The heroes are getting tired." This being the case, entirely new material was virtually unobtainable.

I am therefore indebted to my friends Alfred Price and

Edward Sims for permission to quote extracts from their published works, and to Martin Middlebrook for permission to use two passages from his book *The Nuremberg Raid*. All sources used are listed in the Bibliography. My thanks are also due to my friends at Cranwell College Library and the Royal Aeronautical Society, and to Mr. Brian Cocks of Helpston, for their generous help in making information available.

The German fighter arm did not use the expression "ace," preferring *"Experte."* This expression I have used throughout. Nor have I anglicized the spelling of German names except for the few cases where this is already widely accepted. *Geschwader*, *Gruppe*, and *Staffel* have been left in their original forms, as English approximations are misleading. Ranks have for the most part been omitted: rapid promotion is a feature of war, and to go from corporal to colonel in the space of a paragraph or two is not only confusing but unnecessary. Finally, I have used the widely accepted "Bf" (Bayerische Flugzeugwerke) for early Messerschmitt fighters, changing to "Me" where the Germans themselves did so.

MIKE SPICK

 **PROLOGUE**

I had seen Tempests above me, I could see them beside me, and new Tempests were approaching from underneath. My only chance lay in evading them until I could reach the cloud layer. So I tore off at top speed toward the cloud, jinking to the left and right with the rudder. This deceived the enemy behind me as to my direction of flight, and the more rapidly I trod on the rudder pedal the more difficult it was for the reflex sights behind me to show the right deflection. As a result, the fire of the Tempests missed to the side, since the pilots relied on the views in their sights. The trick worked well. I reached the cloud and attempted a zoom climb, intending to come around into a head-on firing pass at the Tempests, breaking up their attack. This was not to happen, since a Tempest below me could see me in the thin cloud and reported my direction of flight to my pursuers. Thus a Tempest was waiting to attack me when I left the cloud, and struck my wounded bird in the tail area. After a sharp blow, which I could feel through the control stick, my elevators failed. It was time to get out.

I jettisoned the canopy at about 600km/hr, released my harness, and was sucked from the cockpit of my FW, which was now standing on its nose. I was hurled upside down along the fuselage, and the fin struck my left arm so hard that it broke it, ripping the sleeve from my leather jacket.

The fate of FW 190D pilot *Unteroffizier* Georg Genth of *12/JG 26* represents in miniature that of the *Luftwaffe* fighter arm itself, the once-proud *Jagdflieger*. Heavily outnumbered,

1

and for the most part with their aircraft outclassed, they were hunted down and shot from the skies over their own homeland. Genth survived this encounter, which took place on March 7, 1945, with injuries that were relatively minor but which were still enough to put him out of the war. Over the previous six years, tens of thousands of his comrades had not been so lucky. Although the cause for which they had fought was tarnished, their honor was redeemed by the luster of their deeds.

When the skies over Europe were finally still and the victorious Allies had overrun the Third Reich on the ground, the record of the *Jagdflieger* became available for inspection. It caused a sensation. The scores of the German fighter pilots totally eclipsed those of their Allied counterparts. Whereas a tally of 30 victories was exceptional among British and American fighter pilots, a mere 35 German pilots were credited with the destruction of no fewer than 6,848 aircraft in air combat— an average of almost 196! Two of them had actually topped the 300 mark! Even in the demanding scenario of night fighting, two pilots had recorded over 100 victories.

These figures were at first regarded with incredulity by the Allies: the Nazi propaganda department headed by Dr. Joseph Goebbels had long made all German pronouncements suspect. Then, as serious researchers investigated, it was found that while overclaiming is and always has been a feature of air warfare, regardless of period and nationality, the claims of the *Jagdflieger* had been made in good faith, and had been examined as rigorously as circumstances permitted before confirmation was issued.

The Fighter Ace

The fighter ace needs a unique combination of gifts to succeed. Physically he needs to be fit, and to have first-class vision, with a bias toward long-sightedness. He must be a good shot, with a flair for deflection shooting at fast-moving targets. His physical reactions must be fast and instinctive, as in fighter combat there is little time for reasoned action. He must be an accomplished aircraft handler, without necessarily being proficient in aerobatics—the latter merely serve to give confidence, and to allow the pilot to get used to functioning in unusual attitudes.

Courage is a term widely applied to fighter pilots, but self-control is a far more appropriate one. In war, the pilot functions under the threat of imminent extinction or maiming. One of the more usual ways for him to depart this vale of tears is in flames, trapped in the cockpit. Wounds are hardly better: there is no one to give immediate aid, and he is entirely dependent upon his own resources. Truly, no warrior is more alone than the pilot of a single-seat fighter. Fear must be channeled into action if he is to survive, let alone overcome the enemy, and this calls for the ultimate in self-control.

Aggression is essential, although it must be tempered with caution. The "fangs out, hair on fire" type rarely lasts long. In the confusion of a dogfight, it is all too easy to be lured into an irrecoverable situation, usually through target fixation at the expense of keeping a good lookout. As we shall see in a later chapter, Erich Hartmann, the ace of aces, was a very cagey individual in his methods and attitudes.

Finally there is the ability to survive. A really impressive score cannot be amassed overnight. It is therefore necessary to survive for long enough to make this possible. At first sight survival appears to be due to nothing more than luck. There is of course no doubt that luck—chance . . . call it what you will—plays a part in war. But there is more to it than that. Survival in air combat is largely dependent on a quality called situational awareness, or SA. This is basically the ability to keep track of events in a fast-moving, highly dynamic, three-dimensional situation, but there is a body of evidence to suggest that some sort of sixth sense is at work which warns a pilot of impending danger. It is unquantifiable, and it seems to work better on some days than others, but potentially SA is the fighter pilot's greatest asset.

By a convention established in the First World War, a fighter pilot with five confirmed victories becomes an ace. This standard was adopted by most combatants, although Germany was out of step in settling for ten! In the Second World War the same convention was applied by the Allies, whereas Germany dropped the expression altogether in favor of the term *"Experte."* To be regarded as such, a fighter pilot had to demonstrate his proficiency in combat rather than attain a set number of victories. By the five-victory convention, the *Luftwaffe* produced something like 2,500 aces in all; the number of *Experten* was far smaller. The *Ritterkreuz* (Knight's Cross) was awarded to just over 500 German fighter pilots.

Another area in which the *Luftwaffe* differed from the Allies was in the use of a points system for decorations, although this only applied from about 1943 for operations against the West. Half a point was awarded for the destruction of an already damaged twin-engine aircraft and one point for destroying a single-engine aircraft, damaging a twin-engine type or the final destruction of a four-engine bomber; two points were awarded for destroying a twin-engine aircraft or damaging a multi-engine bomber sufficiently to separate it from its formation; and three points were awarded for a multiengine bomber brought down. As we shall see later, the latter was an extremely difficult feat to accomplish.

From about 1943, the unprecedentedly high scores of the *Experten* resulted in a certain amount of standardization for decorations. On the Russian Front, the *Ritterkreuz* was awarded after 75 victories, with the *Eichenlaub* (Oak Leaves) to the *Ritterkreuz* due between 100 and 120 victories, the *Eichenlaub mit Schwerten* (Oak Leaves with Swords, irreverently known as the "cabbages, knives and forks") at 200, and finally the *Eichenlaub mit Schwerten und Brilliante* (Diamonds) above 250.

In the West, with the points system operating, a pilot could earn the *Ritterkreuz* with between 40 and 50 points; therefore fifteen heavy bombers, or between 40 and 50 fighters in the West, were equal to 75 Soviet aircraft—which were for the most part single-engine—in the East.

If we accept the enormous scores of the *Experten* as at least being in the right area, other questions spring to mind. Was their equipment in any way superior to that of the Allies? Were they better trained? Were their tactics better? To answer these, at least partially, we should start with a look at how the *Luftwaffe* itself came into existence.

The *Luftwaffe*

Following the Treaty of Versailles in 1919, military aviation was forbidden in Germany, as was the construction of any type of aircraft. The latter restriction was lifted in 1922, allowing the production of small civil machines. This in effect kept the German aviation industry in being—a factor that was to have far-reaching consequences.

Even in defeat, Germany was an air-minded nation. During the Great War the German fighter aces—Boelcke, Richthofen, Udet, and many others—had been household names. They became role models for the next generation. In 1920, the *Deutscher Luftsportsverband* was formed at the instigation of the Defense Ministry to encourage the population, and youth in particular, to take to the air. Mostly equipped with gliders, this organization had a membership of 50,000 by 1929—far more than in other countries, in which aviation of any sort was generally the exclusive preserve of the wealthy. With free or subsidized flying and gliding available, German youth became far more air-minded than that of other countries, providing a large pool of applicants with basic flying skills which could be drawn on when the time for expansion came.

In 1924, *General* Hans von Seekt moved one of his *Reichswehr* protégés into the Ministry of Transport as head of the Civil Aviation Department. Ernst Brandenberg was a former commander of the *England Geschwader*, and his appointment meant that the development of German civil aviation was henceforth conducted with future military needs in mind.

Shortly afterward, a secret treaty with the Soviet Union allowed the establishment of a clandestine military aviation training school at Lipetsk, some 230 miles south of Moscow. Equipped with unmarked Fokker D.XIIIs, German pilots once more trained for war. It was also in the closed area at Lipetsk that new German combat aircraft underwent weapons trials. A further development was the formation of the state airline

Deutsche Lufthansa in 1926. This had four flying schools, and, while ostensibly training civil airline pilots, it also formed a covert nucleus of military flyers.

When, in January 1933, Adolf Hitler became Chancellor, the pace was stepped up. One of his first appointments was that of Hermann Goering as *Reichskommissar* for Air. Goering, a First World War fighter ace with 22 victories and the final commander of the *Richthofen Geschwader*, was a charismatic figure guaranteed to catch the imagination of the masses. Although in those days a man of formidable energy and ability, he had many other duties, and the task of building the new *Luftwaffe* fell to his deputy, Erhard Milch, a former fighter pilot and previously chairman of *Lufthansa*.

One of Milch's first tasks was to increase Germany's aircraft production capability. With ample funds available, he did this by the simple expedient of placing large orders with several companies, on the strength of which they could build and equip new factories. Some idea of his success can be gauged from the fact that monthly aircraft output in 1933 was a mere 31, but by 1935 had risen by 854 percent to 265! Priority was given to the development of new military aircraft types, to the construction of new airfields, and to the establishment of more flying training schools.

This huge expansion could scarcely go unremarked abroad, and in March 1935 the existence of the new *Luftwaffe* was formally revealed. At its inception, its strength was 20,000 personnel and no fewer than 1,888 aircraft. In September of that same year, the first flight took place of a radically new fighter, the Messerschmitt Bf 109. Eventually built in greater numbers than any other fighter, the Bf 109 was a cantilever construction monoplane with an enclosed cockpit, retractable main gear, and automatic slots on the wing leading edge. At that time it represented the cutting edge of technology. The same period also saw the emergence of several other types of advanced military aircraft, among them the Bf 110 heavy fighter and the Junkers Ju 88 fast bomber. The expansion of the *Luftwaffe*, coupled with the development of advanced warplanes which were equal to anything produced anywhere in the world, in such a short space of time, was an achievement of no mean order.

Basic Fighter Maneuvers

In common with most other air forces of the period, the German fighter pilots were taught standard maneuvers for fighter-versus-fighter combat. Aerobatics played little or no part in these; in the main they involved hard turning to get on the tail of an opponent. But while turning ability was important to a fighter, it was not an absolute. Both radius and rate of turn are functions of speed: as the speed increases, so the radius of turn widens, while the rate of turn, measured in degrees per second, decreases (see Fig. 1). All else being equal (which it seldom is), the slower aircraft will generally out-turn the faster.

Attacks were generally launched from a higher altitude, often from the glare of the sun. Mostly these took the form of a curve of pursuit which brought the attacker in behind his opponent. If the attacker remained unseen and his shooting was accurate, a victory was very probable. If, however, the attacker was seen coming in, his opponent took evasive action and the fight was on. The basic evasion maneuver was the break (Fig. 2). In this, the defending aircraft turned as hard as possible in the direction of the attacker, who only rarely would be dead astern. This rapidly increased the deflection angle, giving the attacker the most difficult shot possible. If the turn capabilities of the two aircraft were fairly similar, and the speed difference was not too great, they would then enter the classic turning fight, with each trying to out-turn the other to achieve a firing position. As hard turning bled off speed, the circles turned into a downward spiral. This ended only when another aircraft intervened, or the lower one was forced to pull out by the proximity of the ground.

As the attacker was often moving considerably faster than his opponent in order to close the range quickly, he would frequently be unable to hold his position on the inside of the turn and would overshoot to the outside. This gave the defender a chance to turn the tables by reversing the direction of his turn back toward his opponent. At this point the original attacker

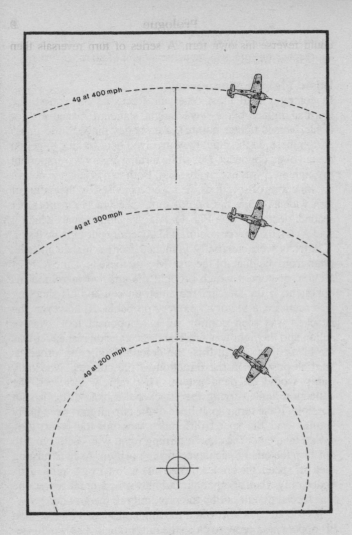

Fig. 1. Effect of Speed on Turn Radius
*Speed reduces turning ability markedly. Depicted here to scale are
the turn radii for the same fighter at three different speeds. Naturally, this influenced a pilot's options in the dogfight.*

could reverse his own turn. A series of turn reversals then ensued, known as the scissors (Fig. 3), in which both aircraft tried to gain a position astern, with the advantage going to the most maneuverable. In the scissors, a faster rate of roll was often a greater advantage than turning ability, as it allowed changes of direction to be made very quickly.

Once the attacker overshot, he had two alternatives to entering a scissors, both using his speed advantage: he could dive away out of range, or he could pull up, converting his excess speed into altitude. An aileron turn in the vertical climb allowed him to reposition himself, pulling out into level flight in any direction he chose, ready for another diving attack. The modern name for this is the Immelmann Turn (see Fig. 4). Alternatively he could stall-turn at the top of his climb and launch into another diving attack. These were the tricks on which all fighter combat was based.

The *Legion Kondor*

Preparation and training for war is a largely theoretical exercise. The trouble is that training is carried out in a sterile environment: rarely does anyone get killed, and then only by accident. Until the shooting starts, no one knows for certain what will happen, how either aircraft or individuals will perform, and what unforeseen problems lie in wait. In this respect the *Luftwaffe* was lucky: a civil war broke out more or less on Germany's doorstep which it was able to use as a proving ground for new ideas and theories.

The Spanish Civil War, which commenced in 1936, was a conflict between the Nationalists, who were thinly disguised Fascists, and the Republicans, who were less thinly disguised Communists. Hitler, who was inherently opposed to Bolshevism, naturally sided with the Nationalists and provided aid. In this he was not alone: Benito Mussolini sent a strong Italian contingent. To provide some balance, Stalin furnished a considerable amount of Soviet aid to the Republicans. Three nations thus stood to benefit from battle experience in Spain. However, circumstances conspired to see that, in the

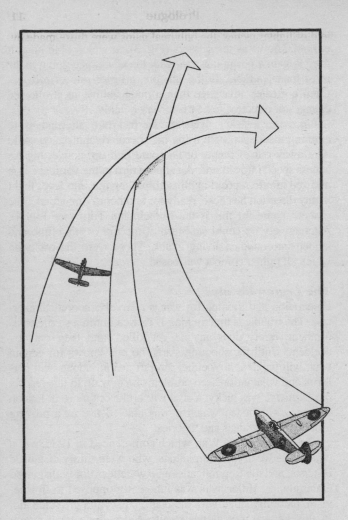

Fig. 2. The Break

The standard procedure when attacked from astern was to turn as hard as possible in the direction of the attacker. This gave a difficult crossing shot, and if the attacker had a speed advantage it frequently caused him to overshoot.

field of fighter tactics, the only real gains were those made by
the *Luftwaffe*.

To maintain the fiction of legality, the Germans were all
"volunteers" and arrived in Spain as "tourists" on a succession
of cruise ships. The first German fighters to arrive were
Heinkel He 51 biplanes. These were handed over to the
Spanish, who achieved little, a state of affairs which led to
German instructors taking over and flying operationally. All
aircraft bore Spanish Nationalist insignia, a practice which
continued even when the *Legion Kondor* expanded into a full-
scale miniature air force with its own fighter, bomber, and
reconnaissance units.

Air combat was at first very similar to that of the First World
War, with fighters flying in the *Kette*, a formation of three aircraft in either tight "Vic" or echelon. Standard tactics consisted
of a diving attack from the direction of the sun, after which the
battle degenerated into a series of individual turning fights.

Initially all went well for the Nationalists, who were
opposed by an international ragbag of volunteers flying a
variety of antiquated aircraft. Matters changed in October
1936 with the arrival of a large Soviet contingent equipped
with Polikarpov I-15 and I-16 fighters and Tupolev SB-2
bombers, to aid the hard-pressed Republicans. At that time the
I-16 was the most modern fighter in service anywhere in the
world. By using dive and zoom tactics the Russian monoplane
could more than hold its own against the agile Italian Fiat
CR.32s, and it totally outclassed the German He 51s. The I-15
was a biplane of superior all-around performance to the
German fighter, while the SB-2 bomber was too fast to be
easily caught by the Heinkel biplane.

The balance was partially redressed in the spring with the
arrival of the first Bf 109Bs. These were assigned to the 2nd
Staffel of *Jagdgruppe 88*, commanded by Günther Lützow.
Powered by a Junkers Jumo 210D or E engine, and armed with
three MG 17 7.9mm machine guns, the 109B was nowhere
near as potent as the models that were to follow, but in many
ways it was a better fighting machine than the I-16. It was at
this point that a quirk of fate determined the course of *Legion*

Fig. 3. The Scissors

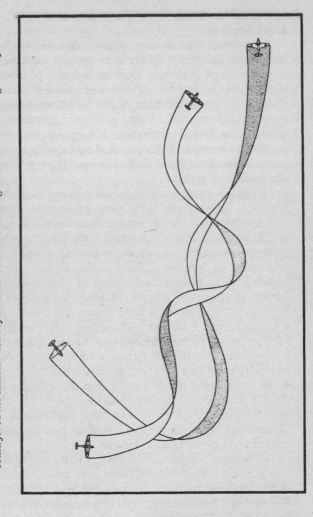

Once the break forced an attacker to overshoot, a series of turn reversals, known as the scissors, could force the attacker out in front. Not recommended against a better-turning aircraft.

Kondor, and eventually *Luftwaffe,* fighter tactics. The initial
delivery was a mere six aircraft, and further deliveries were
slow in arriving. This, coupled with the fact that the operational debut of any new fighter is beset with serviceability
and maintenance problems, kept the number of available
109s low for some considerable time. Lützow and his fellow
Staffelkapitän, Joachim Schlichting of *1/J 88,* were forced to
improvise.

Forming three-aircraft *Ketten* from the number of aircraft
available was difficult, and often wasteful of resources. Four
serviceable aircraft allowed a *Kette* of three and one spare. A
more convenient solution was to use the two-aircraft *Rotte,*
with two *Rotte* making up a *Schwarm.* In action it was found
that the pair gave far more operational flexibility than a three-
ship. Air-to-air radio was another advantage: with less need to
rely on visual signals, spacings could become wider. Trial and
error showed the optimum distance between aircraft to be
about 600ft. in line abreast. By concentrating his search
inward, each pilot could cover the blind spots below and
behind his fellow. Teamwork was made easy. If one aircraft of
a pair was bounced from astern and broke into the attack, his
Kacmarek (wingman: an old Silesian family name) turned in
the same direction. If the attacker followed his target around
the break, he soon found the wingman on his tail, sandwiching
him (see Fig. 5). If the leader launched an attack, his wingman
was well placed to drop back and cover him, thus allowing the
leader to concentrate entirely on attack, knowing that he would
be warned if danger threatened.

The He 51s remained in service with *3/J 88* in the ground
attack role until April 1938, when they were replaced by the
Bf 109C, which mounted four MG 17s but was in other
respects much the same as the B model. At the same time,
command of this unit passed from Adolf Galland to Werner
Mölders—two names that were to become famous in the
annals of air combat. To Mölders must go much of the credit
for refining the basic *Rotte/Schwarm* into a devastatingly effective combat system. The first step was to pull the wingman

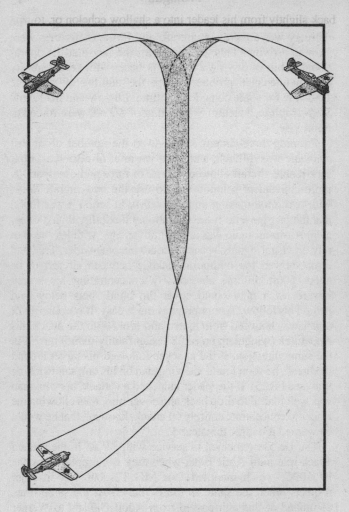

Fig. 4. The Immelmann Turn
Named after First World War ace Max Immelmann, this maneuver allows a fighter to reposition without too much horizontal displacement. The fighter pulls up vertically, aileron turns in the desired direction, then pulls out and rolls upright.

back slightly from his leader into a shallow echelon or, to use American terminology, a slightly sucked line abreast. The second *Rotte* making up the *Schwarm* was then staggered back even more, into what was to become the classic "Finger Four" formation, in which the fighters took up the positions represented by the fingertips of an outstretched hand. A further refinement was to stagger the pairs vertically, the second *Rotte* taking position higher on the down-sun side. This improved the chances of spotting an attacker coming out of the sun.

The wider spacings adopted, about 1,800ft. frontage for a *Schwarm*, made radical course changes a problem. Turning in the traditional manner caused the outside man to lag, even at full throttle, while the inside man was throttled back almost to the point of stall. Mölders solved this difficulty with the crossover turn (Fig. 6). In this, the leader would call the turn and the outside man would immediately pull hard in the required direction, crossing above his comrades. After a short delay he would be followed by the next in line and so on, until all aircraft had turned onto the new heading, swapping sides in the formation as they went. This allowed very rapid changes of heading without the necessity to juggle the throttles, with each aircraft turning at its maximum. Wide spacings minimized the chance of midair collisions and allowed a lookout to be maintained throughout. Necessary changes in vertical separation could be made as the formation rolled out on the new heading.

Werner Mölders is often credited with inventing the crossover turn, but in fact he did not. The origins of the maneuver are lost in the mists of time, but it seems probable that it was known to the Royal Air Force as early as 1918, and it was certainly shown in the first RAF Training Manual of 1922 as being used by a Vic of five aircraft. After this it seems to have fallen into disuse, probably due to the difficulty (and danger) of performing it in a multiaircraft formation with perhaps less than 100ft. spacing between them. Like many another good idea, its time had not yet come. It is probable that the wide lateral separation between aircraft introduced by *J 88* in the Spanish Civil War first made it a practical proposition.

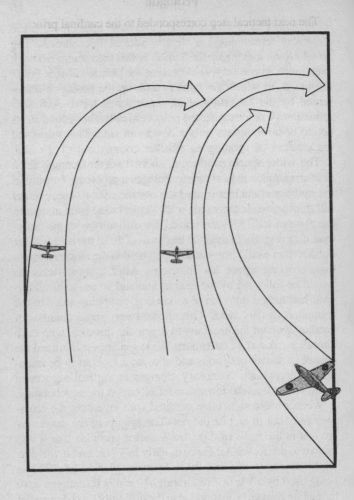

Fig. 5. The Sandwich
Any fighter attacking a German element of two was liable to be sandwiched as shown. This was made easy by the wide spacing and almost abreast positioning of the German Rotte, *or pair.*

The next tactical step corresponded to the cardinal principle of concentration of force. By this time there was no shortage of fighters, and it was often desirable to use the entire *Staffel* of twelve aircraft as a single unit. Formations adopted for this were three *Schwarme* either abreast or slightly sucked, stepped up away from the sun or stepped up in line astern. Standard attack tactics involved dive and zoom as initiated by the Soviet Republican units, as the Bf 109 was vulnerable in a turning fight against the agile Russian fighters.

The involvement of the *Legion Kondor* in the Spanish Civil War allowed basic German fighter tactics to evolve to a stage where only minor adjustments were necessary in the world conflict to come. By contrast, the Allies were to learn many hard lessons before they finally caught up. A further advantage was that personnel were rotated through Spain at frequent intervals, which allowed a large pool of combat-experienced pilots to be formed within the *Luftwaffe*. This, however, poses the question: why did the Italians and Soviets not learn equally?

From the Italians' viewpoint, their CR.32 fighters were outperformed by the Russian I-15s and I-16s. All too often, survival depended on the high agility of their Fiats, and they naturally came to look upon this as a cardinal virtue—an outlook easily adopted by such an aerobatically minded force. The Soviets did in fact learn much the same lessons as the Germans. It was they who had introduced dive and zoom tactics; they then copied the German pair and four as the *pary* and *zveno*. During 1938 they recommended this tactical system for adoption throughout the entire Soviet fighter force. That it was not put into effect was almost entirely due to Stalin's maniacal purges, which swept away many veterans of Spain.

The Spanish Civil War ended in March 1939 when Republican resistance collapsed. The *Legion Kondor* was disbanded, and its members returned to their units. Having experience of actual aerial combat influenced fighter training considerably. Not only were the Spanish lessons readily absorbed: training

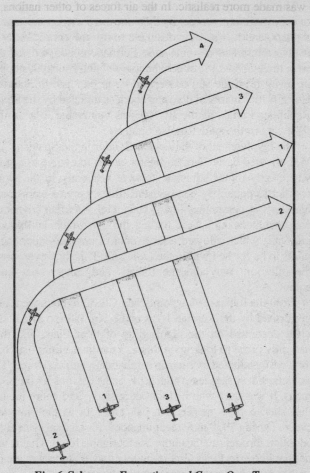

Fig. 6. Schwarm *Formation and Cross-Over Turn*
The typical Schwarm formation consisted of two elements of two with about 600ft. spacings between aircraft. This allowed all pilots to keep a lookout without fear of collision. To turn through 90 degrees, the fighter on the outside pulled up and turned above the one nearest to it. The others followed in sequence, rolling out onto the new heading with formation integrity intact.

was made more realistic. In the air forces of other nations, air combat training was generally a one-versus-one engagement, with both participants from the same unit and flying exactly the same type of aircraft. This reduced it to a contest of flying skill and experience. The *Jagdflieger* knew better. Much of their training consisted of multiaircraft combats—four versus four, even at times *Staffel* versus *Staffel*—accepting the increased risk of midair collision. This served them well in years to come.

1. THE LIGHTNING VICTORIES

I have done my best, in the past few years, to make our Luftwaffe *the largest and most powerful in the world. The creation of the Greater German Reich has been made possible largely by the strength and constant readiness of the Air Force. Born in the spirit of the German airmen of the First World War, inspired by faith in our* Führer *and commander-in-chief, thus stands the* Luftwaffe *today, ready to carry out every command of the* Führer *with lightning speed and undreamed-of might.*

—Hermann Goering, August 1939

The years preceding the Second World War saw Germany invade both Austria and what was then Czechoslovakia. Both operations were successfully carried out without bloodshed. Now it was the turn of Poland. The Poles were expected to resist, but, since they were outnumbered and outclassed both in the air and on the ground, a German victory was just a question of time. What Hitler did not reckon with was that Britain and France would undertake to guarantee Poland's sovereignty, and that war with these two great powers would become inevitable.

In the event, the Anglo-French guarantee proved worthless. With the *Luftwaffe* spearheading the attack, Poland was overrun in a matter of weeks, and the plan to provide military assistance in the shape of British and French squadrons could not be implemented in time. There followed the period of the "Phony War," which was broken in the spring of 1940 when, in a dazzling series of operations, the *Wehrmacht* invaded and overran Denmark, Norway, Holland, Belgium, and France in quick succession. In every case the *Jagdflieger* played a decisive role, sweeping the skies clear of enemy fighters to allow their bombers to operate with minimal interference, while inflicting devastating losses on Allied bomber formations when they tried to intervene in land operations.

The Invasion of Poland

Germany invaded Poland on the morning of September 1, 1939, opening an unbroken period of nearly six years during which the skies of Europe were never quiet. The operation was carefully planned in advance. The Polish Air Force was to be eliminated on the ground by a series of attacks on its airfields, leaving the way clear for the *Luftwaffe* attack and bomber units to support the ground troops.

It did not work out quite that way. The preceding period of international tension allowed the Poles to disperse their frontline aircraft to temporary strips. Then, in the event, early morning fog disrupted the German plan completely. The airfield assault, when it finally came, fell only upon obsolete and unserviceable combat aircraft and trainers. However, even with this initial setback, the odds were heavily in favor of the *Luftwaffe*. Not only did they have a sizable numerical advantage: their aircraft were qualitatively far superior to those of the Poles, while their fighter tactics and training were, thanks to the Spanish experience, ahead of those of any other nation in the world.

The Polish Air Force had been reorganized shortly before the war. On September 1, 1939, the fighter force consisted of a mere 161 aircraft, of which 30 were the obsolete PZL P.7, defending a frontage of approximately 350 miles. To make matters worse, centralized control was lacking. A relatively strong Pursuit Brigade of four squadrons and 45 fighters was based on Warsaw, plus a single understrength squadron far to the south at Krakow with ten obsolete fighters. The remainder were scattered around the various Polish army regions for air defense and bomber escort duties. See Table 1.

Table 1. Polish Fighter Strength, September 1, 1939

	Squadrons	Base	Aircraft
Pursuit Brigade	111 and 112	Warsaw-Okecie	23 PZL P.11c
Pursuit Brigade	113 and 114	Warsaw-Okecie	22 PZL P.11c
Pursuit Brigade	123	Krakow	10 PZL P.7
Army Lodz	161 and 162	Widzev	10 PZL P.11c, 2 PZL P.11a
Army Krakow	121 and 122	Igolomie	20 PZL P.11c
Army Modlin	152	Szpondowo	9 PZL P.11c, 1 PZL P.11a
Army Pomorze	141 and 142	Markowo	22 PZL P.11c
Army Poznan	131 and 132	Dzieznica	22 PZL P.11c/a
Army Group Narew	151	Zalesie	10 PZL P.7

This mere handful of fighters, obsolete by the standards of the day, operating from makeshift airfields and using tactics which had remained unchanged since 1917, faced the might of the *Luftwaffe*. It was backed by a primitive early warning system based on ground observers linked by a rather fragile communications network. Once the shooting started, all semblance of centralized control was lost. Ranged against them

Table 2. *Luftwaffe* Fighter Units Participating in the Polish Campaign

Unit	Strength	Aircraft type	Base
Luftflotte 1			
I/JG 21	29	Bf 109C and E	Elbing
I(Z)/LG 1	32	Bf 110B and C	Elbing
I(J)/LG 2	36	Bf 109E	Lottin/Malzkow
Luftflotte 4			
I/JG 76	45	Bf 109E	Vienna/Aspern
I/ZG 2	44	Bf 109D	Gross Stein
I/ZG 76	31	Bf 110B and C	Ohlau

were *Luftflotten 1* and *4*—about 1,500 aircraft in all. The sharp end consisted of 648 level bombers, 219 dive bombers, 30 attack (*Schlacht*) aircraft, and 217 single- and twin-engine fighters. To the small and scattered Polish fighter arm, the odds were overwhelming.

The destruction of German records at the end of the war makes it difficult to establish exactly which fighter units took part in the Polish campaign. However, those known to have participated are detailed in Table 2.

Qualitatively, the disparity between the Polish fighters and those of the *Luftwaffe* was great. Both the P.7 and P.11 were monoplanes, with high-set gull wings, fixed landing gear, and open cockpits. The P.7 first flew in October 1930, and, powered by a Skoda-built Bristol Jupiter radial engine, could just about exceed 200mph in level flight at 10,000ft. Its rate of climb was 2,047ft./min. and wing loading just under 17lb./sq. ft. Its armament was minimal—two 7.92mm Vickers E machine guns. The P.11 was basically a heavily modified P.7 adapted to take the much more powerful Bristol Mercury radial. The first prototype flew in August 1931 and the major variant in Polish service, the P.11c, could make 242mph at 18,045ft. Weight had inevitably increased, with wing loading rising to 20.5lb./sq. ft. The initial climb rate was 20 percent better at 2,440ft./min., and armament consisted of two KM Wz.33 7.7mm machine guns. It was planned to fit a further pair of machine guns in the wings, but at the outbreak of war only about one-third of all P.11s had been so adapted. Radio was another shortcoming: provision for its installation had been made, but it was not fitted to many aircraft.

The early 1930s were a watershed in aircraft design and engineering, and the few years between the advent of the Polish fighters and their German adversaries resulted in a tremendous difference in performance and capabilities. The Messerschmitt Bf 109 variants used against Poland were the C, D, and E models. The Bf 109D-1 was powered by the Daimler-Benz DB 600 liquid-cooled engine rated at 960hp, which gave the aircraft a maximum speed of 323mph and a higher ceiling and a greater rate of climb than previous models. Armament remained at four MG 17 machine guns; attempts to mount an MG FF 20mm cannon firing through the propeller hub were unsuccessful. Only a few Ds were produced: these were allocated to certain *Zerstörer* heavy fighter *Gruppen* as a stopgap until sufficient Bf 110s became available to equip them.

The D was followed by the E subtype, which became the first major mass-production machine. This was powered by the DB 601, which featured variable-speed supercharging, had fuel injection instead of a carburetor, and was rated at 1,100hp.

General Notes on Aircraft Data

Turning ability is dependent on two factors—wing loading and speed. If two fighters are co-speed, the more lightly wing-loaded one will generally be able to out-turn its opponent. However, if it is traveling significantly faster than its opponent, the opposite will often apply.

Rate of climb has a rough relationship to acceleration. The fighter with the better rate of climb will generally be able to out-accelerate its opponent in level flight.

When a fighter reaches its ceiling, maneuverability is considerably reduced. A ceiling advantage often indicates a maneuver advantage throughout the higher altitude spectrum.

What does comparison of basic performance figures tell us? First, the Polish fighters would be hard put to intercept even the German bombers unless they were exceptionally well placed at the outset. Given the rudimentary system of early warning, and the lack of radios in the Polish fighters, luck would have to play a large part in achieving this. Second, the low wing loadings of the P.7s and P.11s would allow them to turn more tightly than their adversaries, speed for speed, but their otherwise poor performance would not allow them to force battle on the *Jagdflieger*, nor would it allow them to disengage unless the German pilots were willing, for whatever reason, to break off the action.

This gave greatly improved performance—a maximum speed of 354mph at 12,300ft., an initial climb rate of 3,100ft./min., and a service ceiling of 36,000ft. Fuel injection meant that negative-g maneuvers could be made without the engine cutting—a tremendous advantage in combat. The two nose machine guns were retained, but the wing machine guns were replaced by 20mm MG FF cannon, to give a large increase in hitting power. Wing loading, at 32lb./sq. ft., was fairly high for a single-seat fighter at that time, and turning ability was comparatively modest.

The third *Luftwaffe* fighter type to see action in Poland was the Messerschmitt BF 110. Designed as a long-range escort fighter, it first flew in May 1936, a year later than the 109. Although this aircraft was far less maneuverable than, and had an acceleration inferior to, its single-engine sibling, trials in 1937 showed it to be appreciably faster than the BF 109B, which was currently in production. This, plus the perceived need for a long-range fighter to escort bombers deep into enemy territory, ensured its eventual adoption by the *Luftwaffe*.

The BF 110B-1 was powered by two DB 600A liquid-cooled inline engines and was very heavily armed, with a battery of two 20mm MG FF cannon plus four 7.9mm MG 17 machine guns in the nose. The need for long-range radio communications resulted in a second crew member being carried; in combat he provided a rearward lookout and gave a modicum of rearward protection with a swiveling 7.9mm MG 15 machine gun.

With the advent of the superior DB 601 engine, production of the B-1 was halted in favor of the C-1, which was powered by this unit. Other changes embodied extensive structural strengthening, and a slightly reduced wingspan. The maximum speed of the C-1 was 336mph at 19,686ft.; initial climb rate was 2,165ft./min., service ceiling 32,810ft., and wing loading at maximum all-up weight a moderate 33lb./sq. ft.

The first *Jagdflieger* action of the war occurred on September 1, when P.11cs and P.7s of the Pursuit Brigade encountered Heinkel bombers heading for their airfield at Okecie. The

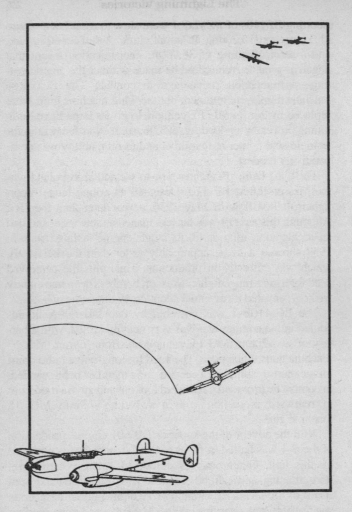

Fig. 7. The Decoy

The decoy, a solitary aircraft looking vulnerable in the presence of enemy fighters while covered by friends above, was widely used until late 1943. Large numbers of high-performance enemy fighters made it a suicidal maneuver after this time.

escorting Bf 110s of *I(Z)/LG 1* were slow to react but eventually accounted for two P.7s, although their *Kommandeur*, seven-victory Spanish Civil War veteran Walter Grabmann, was wounded in the action. This was hardly a promising combat debut for the *Zerstörer*.

That afternoon *I(Z)/LG 1* was again in action, this time while escorting bombers over Warsaw itself. Led in Grabmann's absence by *Hauptmann* Schlief, they tangled once more with the Pursuit Brigade. The initial bounce from above failed, but then the Germans tried the decoy trick, one of the oldest in the book (Fig. 7). A single 110 slipped away on its own, flying slowly and uncertainly. A P.11 pounced on it, only to fall to the lurking Schlief's guns. Four more Polish flyers were decoyed and shot down in this way before the action was broken off.

The correct tactics against the lightly wing-loaded Polish fighters were dive and zoom, or high-speed slashing attacks, but often the temptation to start turning with them proved too much. This was not a good idea. On the afternoon of September 2 about twenty Bf 110s of *I/ZG 2* clashed with six P.11s, two of which were shot down, one by future night fighter *Experte* Helmut Lent, but at a cost of three of their own. While the Polish fighters might be technically outclassed it was yet another matter to underestimate the skill of the man in the cockpit, and an error of the first magnitude to fight on his terms.

In a matter of days the air battle for Poland had been decisively won by the *Luftwaffe*. Most of the escort missions were carried out by the Bf 110 *Gruppen*: the shorter-legged Bf 109s were mainly employed on defensive duties. This apart, the German top scorer of the Polish campaign was Hannes Gentzen, *Kommandeur* of the Bf 109D–equipped *I/ZG 2*, with seven victories, consisting of two fighters and five bombers. No other German fighter pilot attained five victories.

The Polish campaign was notable for the number of future *Experten* who scored their first victories there. Among these were Bf 110 pilots Wolfgang Falcke of *I/ZG 76*, with three victories, and Gordon Gollob, later to become the first man to score 150 victories, of the same unit. Bf 109 pilots who later became famous were Hans Phillipp of *I/JG 76*, Erwin Clausen and Fritz Geisshardt of *I(J)/LG 2*, and Gustav Rödel of *I/JG 21*.

The Campaign in the West

Great Britain and France declared war on Germany shortly after the invasion of Poland had begun, and a British Expeditionary Force was deployed to France. This included an air component with bomber and army cooperation squadrons, and four fighter squadrons of Hurricanes. Little action could be undertaken by the Allied ground forces, but interception of reconnaissance aircraft of both sides over France and Germany, and clashes in the air along the border, became fairly frequent events.

The basic tactical unit of *l'Armée de l'Air* was the *Groupe de Chasse*, which consisted of two or three *Escadrilles* of about twelve fighters each. This was roughly equivalent to the *Luftwaffe Gruppe* and its constituent *Staffeln*, although the French unit had no counterpart to the German *Stab*. In turn, two or three *Groupes* combined to form an *Escadre de Chasse*, which, although similar to a *Geschwader* in composition, differed from it in being tied to a fixed base. Redeployment from one base to another thus involved a change of designation for the unit concerned. Abbreviations were commonly used: for example, *GC II/5* was the second *Groupe de Chasse* of the fifth *Escadre*.

Tactically, *l'Armée de l'Air* had continued where it had left off in 1918. The basic fighter element was the three-aircraft *patrouille* in Vic formation, spaced at about 600ft. laterally and 160ft. vertically with the low man on the sun side. The standard attack was from the beam, which in theory ended in a difficult full-deflection shot but more often resulted in a curve of pursuit to bring the fighter onto its opponent's tail. Early warning was by lookout, linked by the unreliable French telephone system. It was backed by a form of radio-location which, using alternate transmitters and receivers, could produce an approximate location for an aircraft, albeit with no indication of height, out to about 31 miles, but was unsatisfactory against a formation.

On the outbreak of war, the two main French fighter types were the Morane Saulnier MS.406 and the American-built Curtiss Hawk 75. First flown (as the MS.405) in August 1935, the former was powered by a Hispano-Suiza liquid-cooled engine rated at 860hp and armed with two wing-mounted 7.5mm machine guns and an engine-mounted 20mm cannon. Maximum speed was 304mph at 16,405ft. and initial climb rate 2,559ft./min. Wing loading at 33lb./sq. ft. made it a fairly agile aircraft. Although generally outperformed by the Bf 109E, if well handled it was a worthy opponent. Rather better was the Hawk 75. It was of comparable performance to the MS.406, but with a superior rate of climb and significant handling advantages, and its Pratt & Whitney Twin Wasp radial engine was less vulnerable to battle damage. Two-thirds of all confirmed *Armée de l'Air* victories up to May 25, 1940, were scored by Hawk 75 pilots.

The first fighter engagement over France came on September 8, when a *Schwarm* of Bf 109Es of *I/JG 53* clashed with five Hawks of *GC II/4*. Spanish *Experte* Werner Mölders was one of the victims, forced to land with a shot-up engine, although it was not long before he restored the balance. A more significant combat took place on November 6, 1939. Polish campaign top-scorer Hannes Gentzen, at the head of *JGr 102* (*I/ZG 2* was still equipped with Bf 109s), was patrolling the frontier between the Maginot and Siegfried Lines. Well below he spotted a French Potez 637 on reconnaissance, escorted by nine Hawk 75s of *GC II/5*. Everything was in his favor—altitude, combat experience, and a numerical advantage of 3:1. He dived to the attack.

The French fought back fiercely. During the ensuing dogfight four Bf 109s were shot down and another four force-landed. The sole French casualty was a Hawk 75 that belly-landed but was repairable. A German fighter unit had attacked with every advantage in its favor, yet had been thoroughly trounced. How could this happen?

Table 3. French Single-Seat Fighters in Service, May 1940

	Morane Saulnier MS.406	Curtiss Hawk 75A	Dewoitine D.520	Bloch MB.152
Wingspan	34ft. 10in.	37ft. 3in.	33ft. 6in.	34ft. 7in.
Length	26ft. 9in.	28ft. 8in.	28ft. 9in.	29ft. 10in.
Height	9ft. 4in.	11ft. 8in.	8ft. 5in.	9ft. 11in.
Wing area	172.22 sq. ft.	236 sq. ft.	172 sq. ft.	186.43 sq. ft.
Engine	Hispano-Suiza 12Y-31 inline rated at 860hp	P&W Twin Wasp radial rated at 900hp	Hispano-Suiza 12Y-45 inline rated at 930hp	GR 14N-25 radial rated at 1,000hp
Loaded weight	5,610lb.	5,730lb.	5,900lb.	6,173lb.
Wing loading	33lb./sq. ft.	24lb./sq. ft.	34lb./sq. ft.	33lb./sq. ft.
Maximum speed	304mph	311mph	332mph	316mph
Service ceiling	32,800ft.	32,700ft.	33,600ft.	c.31,000ft.
Rate of climb	2,559ft./min.	4.9 min. to 15,000ft.	5.8 min. to 13,125ft.	3.4 min. to 6,560ft.
Range	500 miles	603 miles	550 miles	335 miles
Armament	1 × 20mm cannon (60rpg), 2 × 7.5mm MG (300rpg)	1 × .50 and 3 ×.30in MG	1 × 20mm cannon (60rpg), 4 × 7.5mm MG (500rpg)	2 × 20mm cannon, 2 × 7.5mm MG

There were three main reasons. First, the alertness of the French pilots prevented *JGr 102* from achieving surprise. Second, the Hawk 75 was in some ways far superior to the Bf 109D. Although performance was slightly inferior, it was far more maneuverable, thanks to a lower wing loading combined with finely harmonized controls, which gave a smaller turning radius coupled with a much faster rate of roll, which allowed it to establish itself in a turn faster than the German fighter could manage. An automatic constant-speed propeller enabled the 1,200hp Twin Wasp to run at maximum efficiency throughout the speed range, unlike the manually adjusted propeller of the Messerschmitt, which in combat was more of a distraction than an asset.

The third reason is conjectural, but it seems probable that, Spanish experience notwithstanding, *JGr 102* used the wrong tactics! Almost certainly they stayed and mixed it with *GCII/5* instead of using the much safer dive and zoom. The reason for this was probably overconfidence, born of experience in Poland and the dogfighting tradition of the Great War. Gentzen, as the ranking *Luftwaffe Experte* (Spain was of course *Legion Kondor*, not *Luftwaffe*), would have zealously been trying to maintain his lead. The "fangs out, hair on fire" syndrome is widely known among fighter pilots of all nations and all periods and has led many a budding ace to overreach himself. In fact such rashness was not confined to the *Jagdflieger*: in both Poland and France there were several recorded instances of German bombers attacking enemy fighters!

A further factor was that, at this stage, many *Geschwader* were still led by "old eagles" of the Great War, men such as *Ritter* Eduard von Schleich and Theo Osterkamp, who imposed their own tactical ideas on their units and whose exploits were worthy of emulation. Certainly, from British and French accounts of the period, the *Jagdflieger* showed no disinclination to dogfight. Their first clash with the RAF came on December 22 when *III/JG 53* accounted for two Hurricanes of No. 73 Squadron, one of which fell to Mölders.

Flying was restricted that winter by particularly bad weather, and months passed with no more than occasional skirmishes in what had become known as the "Phony War" or *"Sitzkrieg."* But restricted opportunities or no, many future high-scoring *Experten* opened their accounts during this period. Among them were Heinz Baer (with a final total of 220 victories), who as an NCO pilot claimed his first victory, a Hawk 75, on September 29; Anton Hackl (192); Max Stötz (189); Wolf-Dietrich Wilcke (162); Joachim Müncheberg (135); and Erich Leie (118). The *Sitzkrieg* did, however, give

l'Armée de l'Air time to expand and reequip its fighter force.
By the beginning of May 1940 two new types were entering
service, the Bloch MB.151/152 and, best of all, the Dewoitine
D.520, although the latter appeared only in small numbers
before the surrender. See Table 3.

Blitzkrieg

The uneasy calm was broken on the morning of May 10, 1940.
To invade France, Germany had to circumvent the strongly
fortified Maginot Line, which protected the French border.
They bypassed it, violating the neutrality of Belgium and Holland with airborne forces and fast-moving armored columns.
Protected and preceded by the *Luftwaffe*, they streamed southwest. The numerically weak and poorly equipped Dutch and
Belgian air forces were overwhelmed and largely destroyed on
the ground. This treacherous attack was accompanied by
heavy bombing raids on French airfields at Dijon, Lyons,
Metz, Nancy, and Romilly, and against major communications
centers in France.

The *Luftwaffe* had 860 Bf 109s and 350 Bf 110s to clear the
way for their 1,680 level and dive bombers (see Table 4).
Against this armada *l'Armée de l'Air* could pit 552 modern
fighters—278 MS.406s, 98 Hawk 75s, 140 Bloch MB.151s
and 152s, and 36 Dewoitine D.520s. The French fighters (see
Table 5), ably supported by RAF Hurricanes, fought back
fiercely, but without an effective early warning system they
were unable to bring sufficient force to bear.

The essence of the *Blitzkrieg* was speed. The two biggest
natural obstacles to the advance of the *Wehrmacht* across Belgium were the Albert Canal and the River Maas (Meuse).
Bridges over these had been captured on May 10; it was only
to be expected that the Allies would make strenuous efforts to
cut them. The air defense of the bridges was assigned to *JG 27*,
a recently formed composite unit equipped with Bf 109Es.
Operations during the previous two days had reduced its
strength, but it still had about 85 fighters serviceable.

At dawn on May 12, *1* and *2/JG 1*, led by Spanish Civil War

Table 4. German Fighter Units, May 10, 1940

Geschwader	Gruppe	Aircraft	Bases
JG 27	I/JG 27, I/JG 11, I/JG 21	Bf 109E	Monchen Gladbach, Gymnich
JG 26	II and III/JG 26, III/JG 3	Bf 109E	Dortmund, Essen-Muhlheim, Hopsten
JG 51	I/JG 51, I/JG 26, I/JG 20, II/JG 27	Bf 109E	Krefeld, Bonninghardt
ZG 26	I and III/ZG 26, I and II/ZG 1	Bf 110C/D	Neidermendig, Krefeld, Kirchenhellen, Gelsenkirchen
JG 77	I/JG 77, I/JG 3	Bf 109E	Peppenhoven, Odendorf, Vogelsang
ZG 76	II/ZG 76, II/ZG 26	Bf 110C/D	Cologne-Wahn, Kaarst-Neuss

Note: Most of the *Geschwader* listed are composite units. This arose from the continued expansion of the fighter arm.

---

veteran Joachim Schlichting, intercepted a formation of nine RAF Blenheims over Maastricht and, in the ensuing battle, claimed six of them. *3/JG 1*, patrolling over Liége, encountered the survivors on their egress and accounted for two more. It was the pattern for the day. The small fighter escorts which were all the Allies could provide were brushed aside and the bombers were mercilessly hacked from the skies. During the course of the day *JG 27* mounted no fewer than 340 sorties, claiming 28 victories for the loss of four of its own aircraft.

The day was notable for another reason. German veteran Adolf Galland had led a Heinkel He 51 unit in Spain, flying ground attack missions. In Poland he had then commanded *2(Schlacht)/LG 2*, equipped with Henschel Hs 123 biplanes, in the same role. But air combat had so far eluded him. At last his longed-for transfer to fighters had come through, and he became the operations staff officer of *JG 27*, flying Bf 109Es. May 12, 1940, saw him freelancing near Liége in company with Gustav Rödel when he encountered eight Hurricanes about 3,000ft. below. His combat report reads:

> The enemy was attacked from a position of advantage above and astern. The first burst with machine guns and cannon hit the enemy aircraft. When I broke away *Leutnant* Rödel fired and scored hits. The enemy machine spiraled down and I followed, firing from a distance of between 50 and 70m. Parts of the aircraft were observed to break off and it spun down into the clouds. Ammunition used: 90 cannon shells; about 150 machine-gun bullets. The Hurricanes appeared poorly trained and failed to support each other.

The records of fighter-versus-fighter combat in all eras show that in something like 80 percent of all cases, the victim either never sees the one that gets him or only becomes aware of being under attack when his assailant has already reached a position of decisive advantage. Such was the case with Galland's first victory. Two more Hurricanes fell to his guns that day: the man whom many consider to have been the greatest fighter pilot of the war had opened his account.

The RAF quickly reinforced their four Hurricane squadrons with six more, and added two squadrons of Gloster Gladiator biplanes. However, it was now too late. Spearheaded by the *Luftwaffe*, the victorious *Wehrmacht* thrust past the end of the vaunted Maginot Line at Sedan and advanced rapidly across France toward the Channel ports, effectively severing the BEF and the northern Allied armies from the rest of France.

May 14 saw heavy fighting in the air as the French threw in everything they had to stop the German breakthrough at Sedan. Among the many German victories, Hans-Karl Mayer of *I/JG 53* claimed five on this day, while Werner Mölders of *III/JG 53*, who had ended the Spanish Civil War as top scorer with 14, shot down a Hurricane to bring his score in the French campaign to 11. By nightfall, the *Jagdflieger* had flown 814 sorties over Sedan, and the remains of 89 Allied aircraft were counted on the ground in this sector.

Table 5. *Armée de l'Air* **Fighter Units, May 10, 1940**

Groupement	Base	Units	Aircraft
Groupement 21	Chantilly	*GC I/1*	Bloch MB.152
		GC II/1	Bloch MB.152
		GC III/3	Morane MS.406
		GC II/10	Bloch MB.151
		GC III/10	Bloch MB.151
Groupement 23	Laon	*GC II/2*	Morane MS.406
		GC I/5	Hawk 75
		GC III/7	Morane MS.406
Groupement 25	Avie sur la Lys	*GC I/4*	Hawk 75
		GC III/1	Morane MS.406
		GC III/2	Morane MS.406
Groupement 22	Velein-en-Haye	*GC I/2*	Morane MS.406
		GC I/8	Bloch MB.152
		GC II/4	Hawk 75
		GC II/5	Hawk 75
		GC II/6	Morane MS.406
Groupement 24 (part)	Dijon	*GC II/7*	Dewoitine D.520
		GC III/6	Morane MS.406
Groupement 24 (part)	Lyon	*GC I/3*	Dewoitine D.520
		GC I/6	Morane MS.406
		GC II/3	Dewoitine D.520
		GC II/9	Bloch MB.151
		GC III/9	Bloch MB.151

As the aggressor, the *Luftwaffe* held the initiative, forcing the defenders to dance to their tune, and now this advantage was increased by an order of magnitude. As the speed of the German advance threatened to overrun the Allied airfields, the British and French air units were forced to retreat, often to emergency landing grounds with poor or nonexistent communications. The primitive French early warning system collapsed; spares, fuel, and ammunition ran short; and fighting effectiveness was greatly reduced. Morale was another factor with some French fighter units: as the French Army signally failed even to slow the German advance, so an atmosphere of defeatism spread. As Julius Neumann of *JG 27* once commented, he saw few French fighters during this period, and those he did see did not appear interested in engaging. This was not universal: the French fighter pilots had fought magnificently against overwhelming odds in the early stages, and many *Groupes* continued to do so to the bitter end. One of their victims was Hannes Gentzen, who went down on May 26, having added 10 victories in France to his Polish tally of seven.

This period showed one significant trend. The Bf 110 *Zerstörer* was even at this early stage found to be vulnerable in maneuver combat against the more agile Allied single-seaters and from May 1940 onward started to adopt the defensive circle when attacked by fighters. In this, the rear of each aircraft is covered by the guns of the one behind it. The defensive circle was of course still vulnerable to attacks from the beam or above, but these involved shooting at high deflection angles. Few pilots could muster the necessary level of accuracy to succeed at this. On the other hand, the Bf 110 units usually operated in *Gruppe* or even *Geschwader* strength; if a single *Staffel* went into a defensive circle, other *Staffeln* were at hand to brush their assailants off their backs. There were never enough Allied fighters in the air to put a whole *Zerstörergeschwader* on the defensive, but, while it passed largely unremarked at the time, the writing was on the wall for the Bf 110.

Table 6. Sorties and Losses, Dunkirk,
May 27–June 2, 1940

	Sorties	Losses
Luftwaffe		
Bf 109E	1,595	29
Bf 110C/D	405	8
Bombers (Do 17, He 111, Ju 88)	1,010	45
Dive bombers (Ju 87)	805	10
Totals	3,815	92
Royal Air Force		
Spitfire	746	48
Hurricane	906	49
Defiant/Blenheim	112	9
Totals	1,764	106

Dunkirk

The evacuation of the BEF and a fair portion of the French Northern Army from Dunkirk during late May and early June resulted in some of the hardest fighting the *Jagdflieger* had yet experienced. Even though many *Jagdgruppen* had moved forward into bases in Belgium and northern France, they were still operating at the limit of their effective range while simultaneously handicapped by a lack of fuel and spares, the supply organization having failed to keep up with the advance.

The *Jagdflieger* encountered Spitfires for the first time during the Dunkirk evacuation. The performance of the British fighter was generally identical to that of the Bf 109E, while its maneuverability was rather better, which came as a nasty shock to the German pilots. But generally the *Jagdflieger* had a numerical advantage, operating in *Gruppe* strength whereas the British initially flew in squadrons of twelve aircraft. But, like the Germans, the British fighters were also operating at

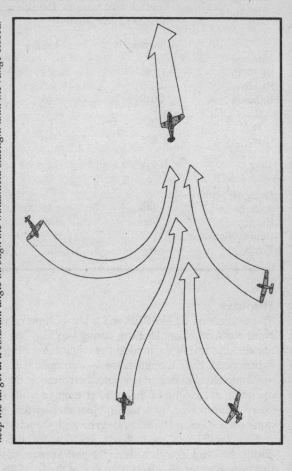

Fig. 8. Curve of Pursuit

The favored attack from astern almost invariably involved a curve of pursuit to take the attacker from his start point to a firing position. Usually done by keeping one's nose on the target, this normally resulted in a tail-chase, as seen here. A far better method was to keep the target at a constant angle through the windshield sidelight until the range closed.

extreme range, which meant that it was a matter of chance whether they were both over the area at the same time.

Statistics appear to indicate that the *Jagdflieger* had rather the better of things: during the seven days of fighting they flew 2,000 sorties, losing 37 of their number, whereas British fighters flew 1,764 sorties, losing 106 (see Table 6). It should, however, be remembered that the main target for the British fighters was the German bombers and in attacking these they often became vulnerable to the prowling Messerschmitts.

With Dunkirk no longer in Allied hands, the German forces turned their attention to the rest of France. *L'Armée de l'Air* and the remaining RAF units were driven ever westward. It was now that the adage was born: "the ultimate in air superiority is a tank in the middle of the runway!" Allied communications broke down, command chaos reigned, and effectiveness was eroded. Hard fighting still took place, but this became increasingly spasmodic. The final *Jagdflieger* victory of the campaign came on June 24 when a Bf 109 shot down a Potez 63 over Montelimar. Hostilities ceased the next day.

The *Experten*

Top scorer in the French campaign was Werner Mölders with 25, amassed in the course of 127 sorties. He was closely followed by Wilhelm Balthasar with 23. Trailing well behind, although both were relatively late starters, were Helmut Wick with 14 and Adolf Galland with 13.

WERNER MÖLDERS With 14 victories in Spain to add to his 25 in France, at the close of hostilities in June 1940 Werner Mölders was by far the most successful of the German fighter pilots. Progress had been slow at first, mainly due to lack of opportunity, and his first ten French victories had taken 78 sorties. They included two Hawk 75s, a Blenheim, three MS.406s, and four Hurricanes, one of which he misidentified as a Morane.

Once the *Blitzkrieg* commenced, opportunities increased and the next fifteen victories, one of which was a Spitfire, came in only 49 sorties. But on his 128th sortie, in the afternoon of June 5, 1940, came near-disaster. Mölders's own account appeared in *Der Adler*:

> There are aircraft overhead which we cannot identify; we climb to 7,000m. German Messerschmitts! So we lose altitude and turn toward home. Suddenly we encounter six Moranes. I line up for an attack from astern. As I approach I spot two other *Staffeln* of Messerschmitts who are engaging the same opponents from above and astern. They were in position first, so I pull away to see what happens.
>
> There is the usual dogfight while several Moranes stand their ground bravely and fight. A burning Messerschmitt crashes to earth; the pilot bails out. I watch for a while, then attack a Morane which keeps making steep turns as three Messerschmitts fire at it in vain. Briefly I get my enemy in my sights. He immediately swings away, but he has still not had enough. Suddenly he pulls up underneath me; I lose sight of him under my wing. There he is again, down below, behind me and off to one side. Damn it—he's still shooting, too, although very wide.
>
> I turn briefly, then pull sharply up into the sun. My opponent must have lost sight of me, for he turns in the opposite direction and disappears to the south.
>
> Below me, two Messerschmitts are still tangling with the last Morane. I watch the fight as the Morane tries to escape at low level, evading their fire by jinking. A backward glance, another above and behind me; the sky is still full of turning Messerschmitts. I am at about 800m. Suddenly there is a bang and a flash in my cockpit, and I black out. The engine is shot to pieces, the control column lurches forward; we're headed straight down. Get out now, otherwise you're finished.

Mölders had suffered the fate which he dealt out to so many: he had been surprised and bounced from out of the sun. His victor was *Sous-Lieutenant* Pommier Layrarges, flying a Dewoitine

D.520 of *GC II/7*. Cornered by three Bf 109s immediately afterward, the young French pilot did not survive to learn the identity of his eminent victim. Parachuting down into French territory, Mölders was taken prisoner, only to be freed at the armistice three weeks later.

"Vati" (Daddy) Mölders demonstrated an iron will to overcome motion sickness in his training days. He was also a tactical thinker of considerable ability and did much to get *Jagdflieger* tactics right in the early days. To him must go much of the credit for developing the four-aircraft *Schwarm* which was so superior to the three-aircraft Vic of other nations, although, as noted earlier, the initial steps were taken from necessity rather than preference. Perhaps his most important contribution to air combat was his care of the pilots under his command, in particular his credo: "The most important thing for a fighter pilot is to get his first victory without too much trauma." Virtually ignored by most other fighter leaders, this advice has an importance which cannot be overstressed. Fear in combat is entirely natural, but it has to be overcome. If in the early days it is allowed to build, it can destroy the confidence of a young pilot to such an extent that either he cannot continue to fly or he becomes so defensive-minded that he is easy meat for the opposition. If, however, he is allowed to gain confidence in easy stages, he will become an asset, but not before. We shall meet this proposition again and again in coming chapters, as we shall meet Werner Mölders himself.

Mölders flew throughout the Battle of Britain (apart from a brief interval as a result of being shot down and wounded), opposed RAF incursions over Occupied France in 1941, then flew during the early days on the Russian Front. Although a first-class marksman, he preferred to get in close when possible before shooting, and he had a tendency to use his machine guns only. With his score at 101 (not including his 14 Spanish victories), he was grounded in July 1941 and appointed General of the Fighter Pilots. He died in a flying accident in November of that year.

WILHELM BALTHASAR Whereas Werner Mölders was the highest scorer during the French campaign as a whole, he was eclipsed during the *Blitzkrieg* by Wilhelm Balthasar, *Staffelkapitän* of *7/JG 27*. Balthasar had early shown a talent for mass destruction: of his seven victories in Spain, four were gained in a single action. His best day in France came on June 6, when he was credited with nine French aircraft shot down, although these were not all in a single action. His total at the surrender was 23, with many others destroyed on the ground with strafing attacks.

Balthasar was a dedicated mentor of young fighter pilots, an example of his methods coming during the French campaign when he spotted a strange fighter below and to his right. Its camouflage scheme was unfamiliar, which caused him to identify it as English. At once opening a running commentary for the benefit of his young pilots, he announced that they should watch carefully as he shot it down. First turning right to allow the "bogey" to draw ahead, he then reversed his turn to take up a curve of pursuit (Fig. 8), dropping his nose to complete a classic bounce from above and astern.

Meanwhile Adolf Galland, flying in the vicinity, listened admiringly as Balthasar commented in unflattering terms that the Englishman seemed to be asleep. The only aircraft in his vicinity were a *Schwarm* of Bf 109Es high on his left. But suddenly he noticed that its leader had broken away and was making an attacking run on him! With a start, Galland realized that *he* was the "Englishman"! As he was on the same radio frequency, a quick transmission averted what could have been a disaster. Faulty aircraft recognition has always been a feature of air combat. In this case, matters were not helped by the fact that Galland's aircraft carried an experimental camouflage scheme, which misled Balthasar.

Balthasar went on to lead *III/JG 3* in the Battle of Britain but found that success over England was harder to come by. With his score at 31, he was wounded in combat with Spitfires of No. 222 Squadron and as a result was off operations for several months. In February 1941 he was appointed *Kommodore* of

JG 2 on the Channel coast, which he led with distinction until July 3 of that year. On that date he was air-testing a new Bf 109F near Aire when he was bounced by Spitfires and killed.

✠ 2. THE BATTLE OF BRITAIN

In its previous campaigns, the *Luftwaffe* had been used as an adjunct to the Army, with the *Jagdflieger* tasked primarily with gaining and maintaining air superiority in support of surface operations. Deep and rapid penetrations by armored forces had considerably eased their task by disrupting supply routes and communications and by threatening Allied airfields. But with the *Wehrmacht* now halted on the Channel coast, the *Luftwaffe* was forced to operate autonomously.

At first its brief was merely to keep up pressure on the recalcitrant islanders while peace terms were negotiated. When this failed, it was called upon to create conditions suitable for the invasion of southern England. Hitler's Directive of July 16, 1940, stated: "The English air force must be eliminated to such an extent that it will be incapable of putting up any substantial opposition to the invading troops . . ." The stage was set for the world's first solely aerial campaign.

The situation was totally unlike anything ever envisaged by the *Luftwaffe* High Command. They faced a numerous, well-trained, and resolute opponent equipped with fighters at least as good as their own. Moreover, that opponent possessed a fully developed detection and reporting system based on radar and ground observers, coupled with a sophisticated system of fighter control which would severely curtail the advantages of initiative and surprise traditionally held by the attacker.

At the start of the battle, RAF Fighter Command was organized into three operational areas or Groups, increased to four at a very early stage: No. 11 Group covered London and the southeast, No. 10 Group covered southwestern England and Wales, No. 12 Group was responsible for the defense of East Anglia and the Midlands, and No. 13 Group covered northern England and Scotland. Each Group was responsible for the defense of its own area, for which it exercised a centralized command system, although this was sufficiently flexible to allow squadrons from one Group to support its neighbors. Control of individual squadrons in combat was exercised from sector stations within the Groups. For technical reasons, only four squadrons could be handled by each sector station at any one time; however, the squadrons were not confined to their own sector, but could range freely anywhere in the Group area or, if requested, into adjoining Group areas. The keynote was flexibility.

The front line of the detection and reporting system was a chain of radar stations looking out to sea. These could detect raiders at considerable distances and give accurate positions for them, but were less accurate as to height and numbers. Once the raiders crossed the coast, they were tracked by observers. All reports were made to a filter room, where the situation was clarified and passed to Group Headquarters. Group then instructed the sector stations which squadrons to scramble and which raids to intercept. The most advanced system of its time, its only fault was a time lag of about four minutes—representing a distance of about twelve miles for the average bomber formation—between the initial sighting and the plot appearing on the operations room tables. Fighter controllers had therefore to allow for this lag when guiding their squadrons into action.

No. 11 Group deployed five Spitfire, thirteen Hurricane, one Defiant, and three Blenheim squadrons at the start of the battle, from seven sector stations. No. 10 Group contained three Spitfire and two Hurricane squadrons. This was slightly less than half Fighter Command's total strength: 28 more fighter squadrons were deployed in Nos. 12 and 13 Groups. By this time the Blenheim squadrons had largely been relegated to night fighting.

RAF fighter squadron tactics were inferior to those of the *Jagdflieger*. A typical squadron formation consisted of twelve aircraft made up of two Flights, each consisting of two sections of three which flew in tight Vics. Experience in France had led to the adoption of weavers, either a section or individuals, who flew above and astern of the formation to guard its tail, but experience showed that weavers were far too vulnerable and they were soon discontinued. As the battle progressed, some squadrons started to use pairs. A section of four in loose line astern and all aircraft weaving was favored. This was far better

Table 7. Fighter Data, Battle of Britain

	Messerschmitt Bf 109E-3	Messerschmitt Bf 110C-4	Supermarine Spitfire I	Hawker Hurricane I
Wingspan	32ft. 4in.	53ft. 5in.	36ft. 10in.	40ft. 0in.
Length	28ft. 4in.	39ft. 9in.	29ft. 11in.	31ft. 5in.
Height	11ft. 2in.	11ft. 6in.	11ft. 5in.	13ft. 2in.
Wing area	174 sq. ft.	413 sq. ft.	242 sq. ft.	258 sq. ft.
Engine	Daimler-Benz DB 601A inline rated at 1,100hp	2 × Daimler-Benz DB 601A inlines rated at 1,100hp	Rolls-Royce Merlin II rated at 1,030hp	Rolls-Royce Merlin II rated at 1,030hp
Loaded weight	5,523lb.	14,884lb.	5,784lb.	6,600lb.
Wing loading	32lb./sq. ft.	36lb./sq. ft.	24lb./sq. ft.	26lb./sq. ft.
Maximum speed	354mph	349mph	355mph	316mph
Service ceiling	36,091ft.	32,800ft.	34,000ft.	33,200ft.
Rate of climb	3,281ft./min.	2,165ft./min.	2,530ft./min.	2,300ft./min.
Range	412 miles	481 miles	575 miles	425 miles

Note: Range is a purely theoretical figure, given for comparison. What really matters is combat radius, which necessarily includes combat time at full throttle, and a margin for delay in landing. The effective combat radius of the Bf 109E was 125 miles—less than one-third of the stated range.

than the Vic, but the *Jagdflieger* were not impressed, referring to it as the *"Idiotenreihe,"* or "idiot's file"!

Officially the Battle of Britain opened on July 10, 1940, and terminated on October 31. In practice things were never this clear-cut, although four distinct phases are discernible. The first occupied the period when the *Luftwaffe* was moving to bases in France and the Low Countries, readying itself for an all-out assault. It consisted mainly of attacks on convoys in the Channel or Thames Estuary, coupled with *Frei-jagd* (fighter sweeps) over southeastern England to probe the defenses. The bulk of this effort fell upon *JG 51*, led by Great War ace and *Pour le Mérite* holder Theo Osterkamp. Only gradually was it reinforced by other fighter units.

Hitler's Directive No. 17, issued on August 1, stated that the *Luftwaffe* should "use all forces at its disposal to destroy the British Air Force as quickly as possible." This gave rise to the second phase of the battle, *Adlerangriff*, or Eagle Attack, an all-out attempt to destroy Fighter Command with a series of heavy raids on radar stations, airfields, and other military targets calculated to bring the RAF fighters to battle. Originally scheduled to commence on August 10, it was delayed by bad weather.

The third phase commenced in early September, when the full weight of the attack was switched to London in a last vain attempt to neutralize Fighter Command. When this failed, and with autumnal weather in the English Channel unsuitable for major seaborne operations, the planned invasion was called off. Raids on the capital continued until the end of the month. From this point on, the main accent was on the night blitz, and phase four consisted mainly of fighter sweeps and fighter-bomber raids, diminishing with the onset of winter.

Fighters of the Battle of Britain

How a fighter handles in combat cannot be assessed purely on absolute performance data, although the latter can give strong indications in certain areas. For example, the greater rate of climb of the Bf 109E added to its higher service ceiling

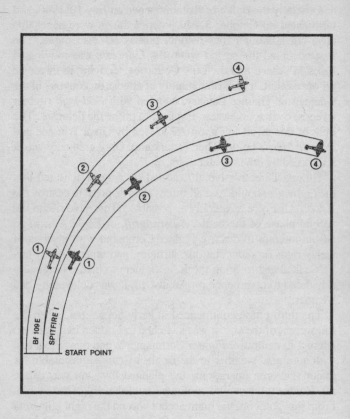

Bf 109 E

SPITFIRE I

START POINT

Fig. 9. Comparative Turning Abilities, Bf 109 vs. Spitfire I
*Seen here to scale are the comparative turning abilities of the
Bf 109E and Spitfire I, with both turning as hard as they can at the
same speed. However, rarely are the two fighters co-speed in
combat, and the advantage always lies with the attacker.*

indicate that at high altitude it handily outperformed the Spitfire I. It is less obvious that at low level the Spitfire generally
had the advantage. But most Battle of Britain combats took
place at medium altitudes, because that was where the German
bombers were, and at medium altitudes there was little to
choose between the two. The Hurricane was generally outperformed by the Bf 109, but below 20,000ft. it was far more
maneuverable. It was very resistant to battle damage, and was
a very stable gun platform.

After his return from captivity, Werner Mölders flew captured examples of the Spitfire and Hurricane at the Rechlin test
center. His comments were as follows:

> Both types are very simple to fly compared with our aircraft,
> and childishly easy to take off and land. The Hurricane is
> very good-natured and turns well, but its performance is
> decidedly inferior to that of the Bf 109. It has heavy stick
> forces and is "lazy" on the ailerons.
>
> The Spitfire is one class better. It handles well, is light on
> the controls, [is] faultless in the turn and has a performance
> approaching that of the Bf 109. As a fighting aircraft, how-
> ever, it is miserable. A sudden push forward on the stick will
> cause the motor to cut; and because the propeller has only
> two pitch settings (takeoff and cruise), in a rapidly changing
> air combat situation the motor is either overspeeding or else
> is not being used to the full.

Given that the wing loadings of both British fighters were
about one quarter less than that of the Bf 109E, Mölders's

The Spitfires showed themselves wonderfully maneuverable. Their aerobatics display—looping and rolling,
opening fire in a climbing roll—filled us with amaze-
ment. There was a lot of shooting, but not many hits.
—Max-Hellmuth Ostermann,
III/JG 54 (final score 102)

comments on the turning abilities of the British fighters are hardly surprising, although the reference to the "lazy" ailerons of the Hurricane indicate an altogether slower rate of acceleration into the roll needed to establish the aircraft in a turn. The relatively high wing loading of the German single-seater was to a degree offset by leading-edge slats to increase lift and improve turning ability at speeds approaching the stall, but in tight turns these had the embarrassing habit of opening asymmetrically, affecting lateral stability and making gun aiming difficult. See Fig. 9.

The description of the Spitfire as "miserable" stems from the fact that the fuel-injected engines of the German fighters allowed them to bunt into a negative-g maneuver without losing power. This provided the *Jagdflieger* with a last-ditch escape maneuver that the British fighters could not follow without their engines cutting. To follow a German fighter down, RAF pilots had to perform a time-consuming half-roll and pull-through, during which the 109, with its superior diving qualities, was usually able to pull away out of range. The comment on both British fighters being "childishly easy" to take off and land was very relevant. The Bf 109, of whatever model, was an unforgiving airplane. Many aircraft and pilots were lost as a result of takeoff and landing accidents. It suffered from incipient swings caused by torque from the engine, and if lifted off the ground too soon tended to roll onto its back. Landings were made power-on. The port wing tended to drop as speed decayed, and adding power at this stage simply made the problem worse. Matters were not helped by the narrow-track, rather flimsy undercarriage. Mölders's final comment, on the two-pitch propeller, was fast becoming irrelevant: a program was already under way to fit the British fighters with constant-speed units which would improve their performance, particularly in rate of climb.

> The Bf 110 was simply too heavy to contend with either
> the Spitfire or the Hurricane. You had to be lucky to
> survive.
>
> —Hartmann Grasser, *II/ZG 2* (7 victories
> with the 110, total victories 103)

One area where the opposing fighters differed widely was
armament. The *Luftwaffe* fighters mounted a mix of cannon
and rifle-caliber machine guns whereas the RAF relied almost
exclusively on the latter until the following year. While the
weight of fire of the Bf 109E was about 25 percent heavier than
that of the British fighters, the latter could put more than three
times as many projectiles in the air in a one-second burst.
Against an evading target, this was far more likely to score hits,
although, shell for shell, the destructive power of the cannon
was much greater. With both sides adopting self-sealing fuel
tanks and armor protection for the pilot, one big hit was generally better than three light ones.

The cockpit of the Bf 109 was cramped, and the Revi
reflector gunsight was offset to the right, unlike the centrally
mounted GM 2 in British fighters. The seat was very low, with
the pilot's legs stretched almost straight out in front of him.
This was no bad thing, as it gave added resistance to gray-out
in hard maneuvering. But the real difference lay in the view
"out of the window." The side-hinged canopy of the German
single-seater was claustrophobic, with heavy metal framing
obstructing vision. Rearward view was also poor. This con-
trasted with the sliding canopies of the British fighters, which
could be, and often were, pushed back in combat to afford
unobstructed vision.

Another point which exercised the *Jagdflieger* was instant
visual identification in a multibogey fight, with perhaps two
or three dozen fighters milling around in a relatively small
volume of sky. This was particularly important for units which
heavily outnumbered their opponents. Shooting opportunities
were often fleeting, and mistakes were all too easily made. To

minimize this, some units adopted the famous "yellow nose" to make friendly aircraft more easily identifiable.

Destroyer

The only twin-engine fighter to play a major role in the Battle of Britain was the Messerschmitt Bf 110. In all, nine *Gruppen* of these heavy fighters took part in the battle, while two *Staffeln* of Bf 110s flew with *Erprobungsgruppe 210* in the fighter-bomber role. Initially *Zerstörer* units were regarded as an elite, and many promising young pilots were posted to them. The type did well in Poland as a long-range escort fighter, and rather less well in France. Now it faced the British air defense system.

The Bf 110 was universally popular with its pilots. Entry was from the left by means of an integral ladder housed in the fuselage aft of the wing. The front canopy was rather complex; the top hinged backward and the side panels folded down. By German standards the cockpit was roomy. The reflector gun sight was centrally placed and the adjustable seat comfortable. The blind flying panel was adequate for the era, and two dials not found in British aircraft were indicators of cannon and machine gun rounds remaining. Propeller pitch indicators were also featured, and duplicated on the inboard side of the engine nacelles where the pilot could see them in flight.

The inertia starters could be operated from an onboard battery, a ground starter, or, if absolutely necessary, by hand. Taxiing was simple, with a good all-around view. The takeoff run was lengthy, even using flaps. At low speeds the rudders were blanketed by the engines and wings, making directional control poor, while the tail itself was slow to rise. Raising the flaps caused a strong nose-down change of trim, and for safety reasons this was not done until an altitude of 500 feet had been reached.

With the engines set at 2,300 revs, climbing speed was 149mph, a moderately steep angle giving a reasonable rate of climb. In flight the controls were well harmonized, and light up to about 250mph, after which they began to stiffen, particularly the elevator. Turn capability was unsurprisingly less than that of its single-seater stablemate, while rate of roll was considerably worse. In maneuver combat it was outclassed by the RAF single-seaters; its sole advantages were high speed at very low level, a rear gunner to guard against surprise, and heavier firepower than any other fighter in the battle. Like the 109, it had automatic leading-edge slats which were prone to open asymmetrically.

Landing presented few problems. The undercarriage was lowered before the flaps, the initial deployment of which caused the nose to pitch up. This was countered with forward stick, the pilot relaxing pressure as the flaps came fully down and trim returned to normal. The approach angle was steep, but the forward view from the cockpit was always adequate. Once the aircraft was on the ground, hard braking could be used without any tendency to nose over. This was the fighter in which the *Zerstörerflieger* went to war.

Table 8. RAF Fighter Command Order of Battle, August 13, 1940

Sector	Squadron	Type	Base
No. 11 Group (HQ Uxbridge)			
Biggin Hill	32	Hurricane	Biggin Hill
	610	Spitfire	Biggin Hill
	501	Hurricane	Gravesend
	600	Blenheim	Manston
North Weald	56	Hurricane	North Weald
	151	Hurricane	North Weald
	85	Hurricane	Martlesham
	25	Blenheim	Martlesham
Kenley	64	Spitfire	Kenley
	615	Hurricane	Kenley
	111	Hurricane	Croydon
	1 RCAF	Hurricane	Croydon
Hornchurch	54	Spitfire	Hornchurch
	65	Spitfire	Hornchurch
	74	Spitfire	Hornchurch
	266	Spitfire	Eastchurch

Table 8 continued

Tangmere	43	Hurricane	Tangmere
	601	Hurricane	Tangmere
	145	Hurricane	Westhampnett
Debden	17	Hurricane	Debden
	85	Hurricane	Debden
Northolt	1	Hurricane	Northolt
	257	Hurricane	Northolt
	303	Hurricane	Northolt

No. 10 Group (HQ Rudloe Manor)

Filton	87	Hurricane	Exeter
	213	Hurricane	Exeter
Middle Wallop	238	Hurricane	Middle Wallop
	609	Spitfire	Middle Wallop
	604	Blenheim	Middle Wallop
	152	Spitfire	Warmwell
St. Eval	234	Spitfire	St. Eval
	247	Gladiator	Roborough
Pembrey	92	Spitfire	Pembrey

No. 12 Group (HQ Watnall)

Duxford	310	Hurricane	Duxford
	19	Spitfire	Fowlmere
Coltishall	66	Spitfire	Coltishall
	242	Hurricane	Coltishall
Kirton-in-Lindsey	222	Spitfire	Kirton
	264	Defiant	Kirton
Digby	46	Hurricane	Digby
	611	Spitfire	Digby
	29	Blenheim	Digby
Wittering	229	Hurricane	Wittering
	23	Blenheim	Collyweston
Church Fenton	73	Hurricane	Church Fenton
	249	Hurricane	Church Fenton
	616	Spitfire	Leconfield

Table 8 continued

No. 13 Group (HQ Ponteland)

Catterick	41	Spitfire	Catterick
	219	Blenheim	Catterick
Usworth	607	Hurricane	Usworth
	72	Spitfire	Acklington
	79	Hurricane	Acklington
Turnhouse	253	Hurricane	Turnhouse
	602	Spitfire	Drem
	605	Hurricane	Drem
	141	Defiant	Prestwick
Dyce	603	Spitfire	Montrose
	263	Hurricane	Grangemouth
Wick	3	Hurricane	Wick
	232	Hurricane	Sumbergh
	504	Hurricane	Castletown
Aldergrove	245	Hurricane	Aldergrove

Note: No. 263 Sqn was converting to Whirlwinds.

Battle Overview

The so-called Battle of Britain was in fact a campaign, with major air battles on some days and small-scale skirmishes on others. The strategic aim of the *Luftwaffe* was to destroy RAF Fighter Command as an effective force. The strategic aim of Fighter Command was to stay in being to thwart the expected invasion, while inflicting unacceptably high levels of attrition on the *Luftwaffe*.

The short combat radius of the Bf 109 effectively restricted it to southeastern England, reaching inland only as far as north London when based in the Pas-de-Calais, and the south and southwest coast from the Cherbourg Peninsula. And not only were the German fighters thus restricted: if the bombers were to have fighter protection, then they also had to confine themselves to these areas.

While the number of single-engine fighters available to

either side was very similar, the British were able to deploy barely half of theirs in the most threatened areas. Although other airfields were available, these did not have the communications facilities to enable them to slot into the main fighter control system, and were discounted for that reason. On the other hand, the detection and control network was usually able to direct the RAF fighter squadrons to the right place at the right time, thus greatly increasing their effectiveness. At a lower operational level, the *Jagdflieger* generally operated in *Gruppe* strength of 30 to 40 fighters. Even when casualties reduced strength, this was easily enough to heavily outnumber the twelve-ship squadron formation used by the British.

The German fighter pilots enjoyed two further tactical advantages. The primary aim of the British fighters was to shoot down bombers. When concentrating on the latter, they were vulnerable to the escorting German fighters. In addition, the German top cover almost invariably had a considerable altitude advantage, which allowed them to swoop swiftly down from their high perches to intercept. Altitude was traditionally the greatest advantage that a fighter pilot could have, and the *Jagdflieger* made full use of it.

The advantages were not all one-sided. Flying over water in a single-engine fighter was a nerve-racking experience. A motor which ran smoothly over land often sounded rougher over the sea. As *Oberleutnant* Julius Neumann commented, "Either the Channel or the Spitfires: either was bad enough. But both together . . ." Flying with *JG 27* from Normandy, he and his comrades faced the longest sea crossing. But even those pilots based in the Pas-de-Calais flew with one eye on the fuel gauge, waiting for the warning light to flash. When this happened, they had but a few minutes to make good their return to base. Quite often they failed.

Finally, with much of the fighting taking place over England, any German pilot who force-landed or bailed out was destined for a prisoner-of-war camp. This imposed an extra psychological strain. By contrast, a British pilot in the same situation would soon be back with his unit.

Phase I: Early July to August 10

The first fighter actions of the battle took place on July 4, when, in a series of isolated skirmishes, one Hurricane was shot down and four Spitfires damaged, two of them severely enough to have to make forced landings. The Bf 109s involved emerged unscathed. The pattern was repeated three days later when Bf 109Es of *JG 51* bounced a section of three Spitfires of No. 54 Squadron near Deal, shooting down two and damaging the third. Later in the day, a *Frei-jagd* by *II* and *III/JG 51* clashed with Spitfires of No. 65 Squadron, shooting down three of them, again for no loss.

It was a promising beginning for the Germans, but it was not to last. On the following day four Bf 109s were lost and a fifth force-landed, its pilot wounded. British fighter losses were three shot down and one damaged. Then on July 10 came fighting heavy enough to allow this day to be formally identified (by the British) as the official opening of the Battle of Britain. A 26-strong *Gruppe* of Do 17s was launched against a convoy near Dover, escorted by about 20 Bf 109s of *III/JG 51*, led by Spanish veteran Hannes Trautloft, and 30 Bf 110s of *I/ZG 26*. The six Hurricanes patrolling above the convoy were heavily outnumbered but were soon joined by elements of three more squadrons, making a total of 30 British fighters.

The *Zerstörer*, well aware of their vulnerability to single-seat fighters, immediately entered a defensive circle in which each machine was protected by the front guns of the aircraft behind. This became a standard ploy of the 110 units and has often been denigrated on the grounds that the escort fighters were not even capable of defending themselves in open combat. The truth is rather more complex. By forming a circle, the *Zerstörerflieger* occupied a commanding position in the sky: thus not only were they difficult to attack, but they could at any moment launch an attack of their own if the opportunity arose. The circle was of necessity very large—rather over a mile in diameter—and threatened a considerable area around it. Just because the 110s were in a circle, they could not be ignored by British fighters unless the latter had a significant

altitude advantage. In the fierce fighting that followed, while
the Spitfires and Hurricanes outnumbered the German single-
seaters, they were forced to keep a wary eye on the 110s, which
thus exerted an indirect influence on the battle. It was difficult
to counter, although as the circles increased in size they
became rather easier to break up, as we shall see shortly. The
final factor was that the circle was not confined to one place:
by widening the turn, it could be moved in any direction!
To summarize, the defensive circle was valid given two pre-
conditions. The first was that it was not too large; the second
was that combats took place over the Channel or English coast.
Only when the fighting moved inland did it become a liability,
because once the *Zerstörerflieger* had to break off and head for
home they became vulnerable.

The convoy attack was a failure: only one small ship was
sunk, for the loss of two Dorniers and a third badly damaged.
III/JG 51 lost one aircraft, that of *Oberfeldwebel* Dau, Trautloft's *Kacmarek*, who got the worst of a head-on encounter
with a Hurricane of No. 56 Squadron. He later recalled:

> The coolant temperature rose quickly to 120 degrees. The
> whole cockpit stank of burnt insulation. But I managed to
> stretch my glide to the coast, then made a belly landing close
> to Boulogne. As I jumped out the machine was on fire, and
> within seconds the ammunition and fuel went up with
> a bang.

Another NCO pilot of *III/JG 51* belly-landed outside Calais;
and a Bf 110 of *III/ZG 26* was shot down into the sea and
another damaged. German claims during this action totaled
six, including two by future high scorer Walter Oesau. British
losses were actually minimal—one Hurricane destroyed in a
collision with a Dornier, two Spitfires heavily damaged, and
one Hurricane receiving minor damage. Further combats that
day saw seven more German aircraft lost, mostly reconnaissance types, but no further British losses.

This action set the pattern for the next few days—convoy

> Our mission was to provide close escort, which I loathed. It gave the bomber crews the feeling they were being protected, and it might have deterred some of the enemy pilots. But for us fighter pilots it was very bad. We needed the advantages of altitude and speed so we could engage the enemy on favorable terms. As it was, the British fighters had the initiative of when and how to attack. We needed to maintain speed, otherwise the Bf 109 would have taken too long to accelerate to fighting speed if we were bounced by Spitfires.
> —*Oblt* Hans Schmoller-Haldy, Bf 109 pilot, *JG 54*

attacks interspersed with raids on coastal targets and fighter sweeps thrown in for good measure. These last the British soon learned to leave well alone to suffer the attrition inevitable when flying from temporary airfields. By July 16, Hannes Trautloft's *III/JG 51* was down to fifteen serviceable aircraft, 40 percent below establishment. The other *Gruppen* were in a similar plight, and only later in the month were they reinforced by other *Jagdgeschwader*.

Table 9. *Jagdflieger* **Order of Battle, August 13, 1940**

Unit	Commander	Aircraft	Base
Luftflotte 2 *(based in France north of the Seine, Belgium and Holland; Commander* Oberst *Theo Osterkamp at Wissant)*			
Stab/JG 3	*Obstlt* Carl Viek	Bf 109	Samer
I/JG 3	*Maj* Günther Lützow	Bf 109	Samer
II/JG 3	*Hpt* Erich von Selle	Bf 109	Samer
III/JG 3	*Hpt* Wilhelm Balthasar	Bf 109	Desvres
Stab/JG 26	*Maj* Gotthard Handrick	Bf 109	Audembert
I/JG 26	*Hpt* Kurt Fischer	Bf 109	Audembert
II/JG 26	*Hpt* Karl Ebbinghausen	Bf 109	Marquise
III/JG 26	*Maj* Adolf Galland	Bf 109	Caffiers
Stab/JG 51	*Maj* Werner Mölders	Bf 109	Wissant
I/JG 51	*Hpt* Hans-Heinrich Brustellin	Bf 109	Wissant
II/JG 51	*Hpt* Günther Matthes	Bf 109	Wissant

Table 9 continued

III/JG 51	*Maj* Hannes Trautloft	Bf 109	St. Omer
Stab/JG 52	*Maj* Hans Trübenbach	Bf 109	Cocquelles
I/JG 52	*Hpt* Wolfgang Ewald	Bf 109	Cocquelles
II/JG 52	*Hpt* von Kornatzki	Bf 109	Peuplingues
Stab/JG 54	*Maj* Martin Mettig	Bf 109	Campagne
I/JG 54	*Hpt* Hubertus von Bonin	Bf 109	Guines
II/JG 54	*Hpt* Winterer	Bf 109	Hermelinghen
III/JG 54	*Hpt* Werner Ultsch	Bf 109	Guines
I(J)/LG 2	*Hpt* Herbert Ihlefeld	Bf 109	Calais-Marck
I/ZG 2	*Hpt* Heinlein	Bf 110	Amiens
Stab/ZG 26	*Obstlt* Friedrich Hüth	Bf 110	Lille
I/ZG 26	*Hpt* Wilhelm Makrocki	Bf 110	St. Omer
II/ZG 26	*Hpt* von Rettburg	Bf 110	St. Omer
III/ZG 26	*Hpt* Johann Schalke	Bf 110	Arques
II/ZG 76	*Hpt* Erich Gröth	Bf 110	Abbeville
EprGr 210	*Hpt* Walter Rübensdorffer	Bf 109/ Bf 110	Calais-Marck

Luftflotte 3 (*based in France, mainly south of the Seine; Commander* Oberst *Werner Junck*)

Stab/JG 2	*Obstlt* Harry von Bulow-Bothkamp	Bf 109	Evreux
I/JG 2	*Maj* Hennig Strumpell	Bf 109	Beaumont-le-Roger
II/JG 2	*Maj* Wolfgang Schellmann	Bf 109	Beaumont-le-Roger
III/JG 2	*Hpt* Erich Mix	Bf 109	Le Havre
Stab/JG 27	*Maj* Max Ibel	Bf 109	Cherbourg-Ouest
I/JG 27	*Maj* Eduard Neumann	Bf 109	Plumetot
II/JG 27	*Hpt* Lippert	Bf 109	Crepon
III/JG 27	*Maj* Joachim Schlichting	Bf 109	Carquebut
Stab/JG 53	*Maj* Hans-Jürgen von Cramon-Taubadel	Bf 109	Cherbourg
I/JG 53	*Hpt* Hans-Karl Mayer	Bf 109	Rennes
II/JG 53	*Maj* Günther von Maltzahn	Bf 109	Dinan
III/JG 53	None (KIA 12 Aug)	Bf 109	Brest
Stab/ZG 2	*Obstlt* Friedrich Vollbracht	Bf 110	Toussée-le-Noble

Table 9 continued

II/ZG 2	*Maj* Carl	Bf 110	Guyancourt
V(Z)/LG 1	*Hpt* Otto Leinsberger	Bf 110	Caen

Note: While main bases are given, many units stationed far from the battle moved to forward areas to refuel before starting out.

Two Fighter Command squadrons were equipped with the Boulton-Paul Defiant. This strange aircraft was a single-engine bomber interceptor, armed with a powered gun turret but no forward-firing weapons. Defiants achieved a certain amount of success over Dunkirk, where they were mistaken for Hurricanes and attacked from astern. The *Jagdflieger* soon recognized the type for what it was—a slow and unmaneuverable turkey—and did not make the same mistake twice. Their chance came on July 19, when Trautloft's men encountered twelve Defiants off Dover. A bounce from head-on out of the sun was followed by attacks from below and astern, to which the British two-seaters had no answer. Six were shot down and a seventh badly damaged. Only the intervention of a Hurricane squadron prevented the slaughter from becoming total. All the Bf 109s returned safely, although many had sustained damage: on the following day, only eleven were serviceable. Total British losses on the day were ten, to four German. At this rate it would not be long before air superiority was attained.

JG 26 "Schlageter," with the redoubtable Adolf Galland at the head of the third *Gruppe*, joined the fray on July 24. His first mission was to escort Dorniers attacking a convoy in the Thames Estuary. Weaving and crisscrossing high above the bombers, Galland saw a flight of Spitfires from No. 54 Squadron approaching the bombers. Hurtling down from his high perch, Galland engaged as they reached the Dorniers, hitting one which broke away. The five remaining British fighters were engulfed in 109s, and their survival was due in part to the German fighters' getting in one another's way. The fray was then joined by a flight of Spitfires of No. 65 Squadron.

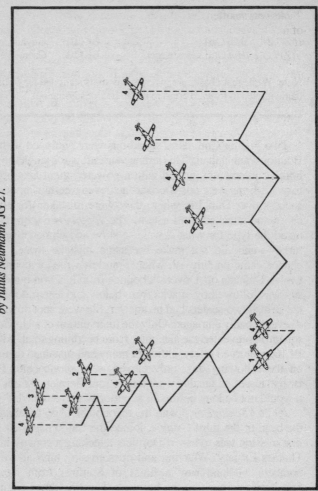

Fig. 10. Typical Staffel Formation, Summer 1940

1. Staffelkapitän; 2. Schwarmführer; 3. Rottenführer; 4. Rottenflieger. As described by Julius Neumann, JG 27.

As was so often the case, this intense dogfight produced a lot of maneuvering and shooting but few positive results. With the aircraft held in close combat for an extended period, fuel ran low and one by one the Messerschmitts disengaged with a half-roll and dive, engines smoking at full power. This led many British pilots to think they were going down with engine damage. In fact, only two were lost, in return for two Spitfires downed, one of which force-landed with its pilot wounded. The man whom many consider to be the greatest ace of the war was back in action.

Four days later Werner Mölders's return to combat was less happy. Appointed *Kommodore* of *JG 51* only that morning to replace Osterkamp, in the early afternoon he led elements of *I* and *II/JG 51* to escort a bomber raid. As they approached Dover they were engaged by Spitfires of No. 74 Squadron, led by the man widely considered to be the "British Mölders"—Adolph "Sailor" Malan. A vicious dogfight developed, in the course of which Mölders's aircraft was badly damaged and he was wounded in the leg, putting him out of action for several weeks. It is possible that the victor was Malan, but, as Richard Leppla of *I/JG 51* (eventual score 68) claimed to have immediately shot down the Spitfire responsible, some doubt exists. Certainly two Spitfires were lost in this engagement, although one pilot survived. German losses numbered four, including Mölders's aircraft (which had to be written off after a belly landing), plus two more damaged, one of which force-landed.

One thing the Germans noted during this period was the ability of the British fighters to show up when and where they were least wanted. Naturally they monitored Fighter Command's radio transmissions, and from these they deduced that an extremely advanced ground detection and control system was in operation. But exactly how it worked, they were not certain. This was to become crucial in the next phase.

From below we looked up at the bright blue bellies of the Tommy planes. Mostly they waited there until our bombers made their turn. Then they would swoop down, pull out briefly, fire their guns, and at once dive on down. All we could do was to shoot off short nuisance bursts while at the same time watching out that there was no one nibbling at our tails. Often we pulled madly on the stick until the ailerons shook, but were then unable to turn around quickly enough and could only watch as the Tommies knocked hell out of one of the bombers. . . .
—Max-Hellmuth Ostermann, *III/JG 54*,
flying close escort

Phase 2: August 11 to September 6

The assault which was supposed to destroy Fighter Command was scheduled for August 10, but bad weather forced a postponement. August 11 saw ferocious fighting. Fighter sweeps over southern England were followed by a huge raid on the Royal Navy base at Portland. About 75 bombers, strongly escorted by 61 Bf 110s of *I* and *II/ZG 2*, and 30 Bf 109s of *III/JG 2*, were intercepted by seven RAF fighter squadrons.

The BF 110s immediately formed a huge defensive circle, but this time it was a failure. The first Spitfires to arrive swept across the top of it, taking full deflection shots at the *Zerstörer* on the far side. Five Bf 110s fell to this initial attack: with the circle broken the remainder were embroiled in the general melee in which one more was lost and five damaged.

Beset on all sides, the *Jagdflieger* desperately tried to keep the fiercely battling Spitfires and Hurricanes away from the bombers; in this they only partially succeeded, even though they were reinforced on the withdrawal by *JG 27*. Six bombers were lost, and seven Bf 109s, making a total of nineteen for this single action. The RAF fighters paid a heavy price, however: sixteen Hurricanes and a Spitfire were destroyed.

The opening attacks of *Adlerangriff* actually took place on

August 12, when the fighter-bomber *(Jabo) Gruppe EprGr 210* launched a concerted attack on British coastal radar stations. This was followed by a large raid on the radar station at Ventnor. That afternoon also saw the first attacks on British fighter airfields.

The British radar stations were soon back on the air with the exception of Ventnor, the loss of which was concealed and the gap plugged with a mobile unit. The *Luftwaffe* High Command deduced that radar stations were particularly difficult targets to knock out, and from then on left them pretty much alone. Nor did they ever concentrate on the sector stations with their vulnerable operations rooms. This was an error of the first magnitude, as it greatly reduced the chances of catching the British fighter squadrons on the ground. However, the *Jagdflieger* took an optimistic view, regarding anything that drew enemy fighters up and into combat as an advantage.

In the event, the opening day proper, *Adler Tag*, was an anticlimax owing to bad weather. The score that day was adverse: nine Bf 109s and 18 Bf 110s were lost or force-landed, while twenty bombers were written off. British losses were thirteen fighters, although overclaiming—always such a pernicious feature of air combat—concealed the unpalatable truth from the *Jagdflieger*.

Poor weather restricted operations on August 14, but the next few days saw an all-out assault directed mainly at airfields. This was less effective than expected. Faulty reconnaissance revealed which airfields were in use, but not the aircraft types based on them. Consequently a great deal of effort was wasted raiding bases not used by Fighter Command.

Heavy fighting saw the scores of the *Experten* rise. Galland gained his twentieth victory on August 15, closely followed by Walter Oesau *(III/JG 51)* and Horst Tietzen *(II/JG 51)*, although the latter was shot down and killed by Hurricanes near Whitstable on the 18th. Werner Mölders returned to action, and after ten fruitless missions notched up his 27th victory, a Spitfire, on August 26. Two days later he is recorded as having downed a Hurricane and, rather surprisingly, a

Hawk 75, a type not in RAF service. A trio of Hurricanes on the last day of the month put him back in the lead ahead of Balthasar. He need hardly have bothered: the latter was seriously wounded by Spitfires near Canterbury on September 4 and, his score at 31, Balthasar was out of the battle.

Bomber losses in the first six days of *Adlerangriff* totaled 125. Of these, no fewer than 43 were the vulnerable Ju 87 dive bombers, which were withdrawn from operations after a terrible beating on August 18. The *Jagdflieger* had fought hard to protect them, as witnessed by the loss of 56 Bf 109s and 63 Bf 110s. RAF fighter losses in combat came to just under 100 for this period, although overclaiming fooled *Luftwaffe* intelligence into thinking they were far higher. This notwithstanding, the hard fact was that *Luftwaffe* combat losses were averaging an unacceptable 49 aircraft a day for the first five full days (bad weather on August 17 restricted operations and there were no combat losses on either side).

The German bomber crews complained bitterly about the lack of fighter protection, and instructions were given that in future the majority of the fighters would fly close escort, tied to the bombers to ward off the British interceptors. A further measure taken at about this time was to replace several fighter leaders with young and successful pilots. Adolf Galland, promoted to command *JG 26*, was one of the first to benefit from this change, which took effect right down the line. He was replaced as *Kommandeur* of *III/JG 26* by Gerhard Schöpfel, and Heinz Ebeling took over *9/JG 26* from Schöpfel. Other new *Kommodoren* appointed were Günther Lützow to *JG 3*, Hans Trübenbach to *JG 52*, and Hannes Trautloft to *JG 54*.

The infusion of new leadership in the air appears to have made an almost immediate difference. Although the *Jagdflieger* did not like being tied to the bombers as close escort, claiming with some justification that their advantages of speed, altitude, and initiative were being wasted, the fact remains that combat attrition fell to an average of 21 aircraft a day over the final fortnight—a reduction of 60 percent. Bombers and Bf 110s benefited most: average combat losses for the single-seaters remained at eleven fighters a day! The average loss rate of British fighters remained unchanged at nineteen aircraft a day during this period.

Werner Mölders saw himself as the successor to Oswald Boelcke, the Great War ace generally acclaimed as the "father of air fighting." Galland, on the other hand, regarded himself as the Richthofen of the Second World War. Both were concerned to improve their tactics. The Bf 109 was at a disadvantage in the dogfight against the better-turning Spitfires and Hurricanes. They came up with the only possible solution, which was to fight in the vertical, using initial altitude advantage to plummet down, fire, then, using their accumulated speed, climb away again. But often the situation did not allow this: Galland twice found Spitfires on his tail which he was unable to shake off. His unorthodox ploy on both occasions was to fire his guns into the blue. Seeing gun smoke coming back, and perhaps showered with spent cases, his pursuers, possibly thinking that they had encountered a fighter with rearward-firing guns, broke off the chase.

Phase 3: September 7 to 30

By early September it had become increasingly obvious that Fighter Command had not been defeated in the air, nor were its aircraft being destroyed on the ground in significant numbers. If airfield attacks had not worked, a new target was needed. London! Surely the British would throw in every last fighter to defend the capital. Many fighter units from *Luftflotte 3* were redeployed to the Pas-de-Calais to give a massive numerical advantage.

In the midafternoon of September 7, a massive armada of 350 bombers, escorted by more than 600 fighters, set course for the metropolis. Caught out of position by this change of targets, the defenders offered little resistance. The huge raid steamrollered its way through and inflicted massive damage on the Dockland area. German losses were a mere ten bombers and 22 fighters; RAF losses were 29.

London was again the target on September 11, then came a

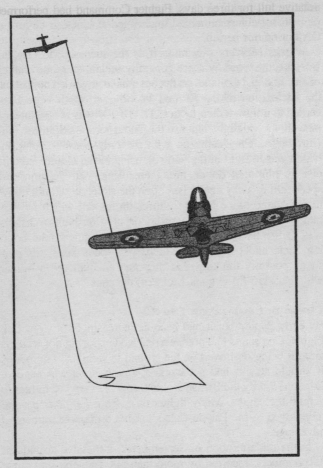

Fig. 11. Galland's Favored "Up and Under" Attack
The vast majority of Adolf Galland's victories came by this means. A steep plunge from astern was followed by an attack coming up in the blind spot astern and below. While not specifically stated, this was best made from a few degrees to the right: the average fighter pilot, his left hand on the throttle and his right on the stick, could look over his left shoulder more easily than his right.

relative lull for three days. Fighter Command had performed unimpressively since early September. For some while the German parrot cry had been that the British were "down to their last 50 Spitfires." Now it really seemed possible.

Sunday, September 15, saw a resumption of the offensive. About 150 Bf 109s drawn from several *Gruppen* set course for the capital. In their midst was the bait—a mere 25 Dorniers drawn from *I* and *III/KG 76*. Fighter Command scrambled 23 squadrons, and the wished-for fighter battle began. The first encounters took place near Maidstone and continued all the way to the outskirts of London. The *Jagdflieger* tried hard to protect their charges but, in spite of their best efforts, were peeled away and run short of fuel, leaving the bombers defenseless. Fighter combat often operates on a law of diminishing returns. The more aircraft in the dogfight, the lower the percentage that become casualties. And so it proved on this occasion in which honors were even—nine 109s lost against the same number of British fighters. Two Hurricanes fell to bombers, one in a collision, but the latter paid a terrible price: six of the 25 were shot down and two more damaged beyond repair.

Launched in the early afternoon, the second raid followed the track of the first. The "bait" was larger—some 114 bombers drawn from four different *Kampfgeschwader*, protected by 361 fighters! As before, the British fighters reacted in force and a running battle commenced which lasted from the coast to London itself.

The fighting was fast and confused: with so many aircraft around, it was unwise to concentrate on one for more than a few seconds, for this rendered the attacker vulnerable to surprise in his turn. Surprise was, and still is, the dominant factor in air fighting, whereas maneuver combat rarely produces decisive results. Adolf Galland, at the head of *JG 26* on this day, later recalled his 33rd victory:

After an unsuccessful dogfight with about eight Hurricanes, during which much altitude was lost, with the Staff flight I attacked two Hurricanes about 800m below us. Maintaining surprise, I closed on the wingman and opened fire from 120m as he was in a gentle turn to the left. The enemy plane reeled as my rounds struck the nose from below, and pieces fell from the left wing and fuselage. The left side of the fuselage burst into flame.

It was fairly typical that dogfights against well-trained and mounted opponents were fruitless, even for a "honcho" like Galland. Surprise attacks were far more likely to be effective, and it is significant that, even though Galland started out with a considerable altitude advantage, he ended attacking from the blind area below (Fig. 11). Finally, the range was fairly short at 120m: too often pilots opened fire at 300m or more and failed to connect. Galland himself often closed to what he described as "ramming distance."

The running battle continued all the way to the target and back to the coast, where 50 Bf 109s, the "reception committee," met the returning raiders. And still fresh British squadrons arrived to do battle! The afternoon action cost them fifteen fighters, while *Luftwaffe* losses amounted to 21 bombers and at least twelve fighters, possibly more.

September 15 was a bad day for the *Jagdflieger*. It showed clearly that they were nowhere near gaining ascendancy over the British fighters. In fact the enemy seemed stronger than ever, notwithstanding the weeks and months of heavy fighting. The invasion was postponed indefinitely. The night Blitz took on increasing importance, and after heavy losses in major raids on London on September 27 and 30 the daylight assault on the capital was quietly terminated.

Phase 4: October 1 to December 31

The experimental *EprGr 210* had used Bf 109s and 110s as fighter-bombers from July, with a fair degree of success. Encouraged by this, *Reichsmarschall* Goering ordered in early September that up to one-third of all fighters must be equipped for the *Jagdbomber (Jabo)* role. Twenty-one Bf 109Es of *II/LG 2* had taken a minor part in raiding London on September 15.

Flying high and fast, the *Jabos* were difficult to intercept, but their pilots were for the most part resentful of being relegated to the role of bomb truck. Not as well trained as the specialists of *EprGr 210*, they achieved little. Other daylight activity, such as fighter sweeps, continued, albeit at a much-reduced pace. As autumn progressed, poor weather not only restricted flying: it turned the temporary landing grounds of the *Jagdflieger* to mud. As 1940 drew to a close, it became obvious to all of them that they had suffered a defeat, although the full implications of this would not be apparent for some considerable time.

The *Experten*

Fighter pilots differ from most other warriors in that there is a practical, as opposed to a subjective, yardstick by which their deeds can be measured. This is the number of aerial victories they score. To preempt comments about overclaiming, the author wishes to stress that a victory is not necessarily a kill: it is a combat in which an enemy aircraft appears to be hit, and goes down in such a manner as to make the successful pilot believe that it is a total loss.

The heavy fighting during the Battle of Britain provided many combat opportunities, and the scores of the *Experten*—who, it must be said, were a small proportion of the whole—almost took on the aspect of a race. Mölders, the leader at the end of the French campaign, was wounded and out of action for about three weeks from late July, during which time Balthasar passed his score. Only when the latter was wounded early in September did Mölders recover his lead. Meanwhile Galland and Helmut Wick had been catching up fast.

Mölders's score reached 40 on September 20, followed by Galland five days later and Wick on October 6. Wick managed to edge into the lead on November 28 but was shot down that same day, his final score at 56. The last day of the year saw Galland in the lead with 58, three ahead of Mölders. Then came Walter Oesau with 39, while Hans-Karl Mayer reached 38 before his death in action on October 17. Among many

Fig. 12. Schöpfel's Combat, August 18, 1940

Gerd Schöpfel, leading III/JG 26 in Galland's absence, spotted the Hurricanes of No. 501 Squadron near Canterbury. Waiting until they had their backs to the sun, and leaving his Gruppe on high, he plummeted down and picked off both weavers and two others without being spotted. Only when hit by wreckage and oil from his fourth victim did he break off the attack.

others were Hermann-Friedrich Joppien (31, of which five were in France), Joachim Müncheberg (23), and Gerhard Schöpfel (22). The least successful of the *Jagdgeschwader* was *JG 52*, surprisingly as it contained Gerhard Barkhorn (later to score 301 victories in the East but whose Battle of Britain score was nil) and Günther Rall (who achieved little over England but whose final score was 275, also in the East).

The leading Bf 110 pilots were Hans-Joachim Jabs of *II/ZG 76* and Eduard Tratt of *1/EprGr 210*, both of whom claimed 12 victories in the battle. Jabs, possibly the greatest Bf 110 pilot of all, had previously scored six in France, while Tratt's feat was remarkable in that he was flying *Jabo* sorties at the time. With an eventual score of 38, Tratt became the top-scoring *Zerstörerflieger* of the war.

HELMUT WICK Apart from natural ability, Helmut Wick had other advantages. His instructor during advanced training had been the great Werner Mölders, who was also his *Staffelkapitän* in *1/JG 53* from March 1939. Shortly after the beginning of the war he was transferred to *I/JG 2*, and he scored his first victory on November 22, 1939. But only with the *Blitzkreig* did his score start to mount. He early showed a talent for multiple victories, with two French aircraft on May 22, 1940, two British Swordfish torpedo bombers later that month (although these were unconfirmed for lack of a witness) and four Bloch 152s on June 5, and two more the next day. He ended the campaign in third place behind Mölders and Balthasar with a total of 14. He became *Staffelkapitän* of *3/JG 2 Richthofen* in July 1940; thereafter his rise was rapid. He reached 20 victories on August 27, then on September 7 he was appointed *Kommandeur* of *II/JG 2*.

Wick was a remarkable natural marksman, with a gift for keeping track of events around him. If he had a fault, it was impetuosity, which often led him to tangle with the better-turning Spitfires and Hurricanes. His personal creed was:

As long as I can shoot down the enemy, adding to the honor of the *Richthofen Geschwader* and the success of the

Fatherland, I am a happy man. I want to fight and die fighting, taking with me as many of the enemy as possible.

Wick got his wish. He was promoted to *Kommodore* of *JG 2* on October 19, 1940, and his score mounted. He claimed three victories on November 5 and five more the following day. On November 28 he finally passed Mölders's score to become the top-ranking *Experte*. Later that same afternoon he led his *Stab-schwarm* out over the Channel on a *Freijagd*. A skirmish with Spitfires near the Isle of Wight saw his 56th victim go down, then Wick was bounced from astern by a Spitfire. His Bf 109 mortally hit, he bailed out but was never found. His attacker, John Dundas of No. 609 Squadron, was almost immediately shot down by Wick's *Kacmarek* Rudi Pflanz (eventual score 52).

GERHARD SCHÖPFEL One of the lesser-known *Experten*, Schöpfel started the war as *Staffelkapitän* of *9/JG 26*. His first victory was a Spitfire over Dunkirk in May 1940, and he scored 21 more during that year. His greatest day came on August 18 when he personally accounted for four Hurricanes of No. 501 Squadron within minutes (Fig. 12). This multiple claim is fairly unusual in that each of his victims can be identified beyond doubt and in that all were destroyed in the air— there were no forced landings:

> Suddenly I noticed a *Staffel* of Hurricanes underneath me. They were using the English tactics of the period, flying in close formation of threes, climbing in a wide spiral. About 1,000m above I turned with them and managed to get behind the two covering Hurricanes, which were weaving continuously. I waited until they were once more heading away from Folkestone and had turned northwestward and then pulled around out of the sun and attacked from below.

The influence of Schöpfel's *Kommandeur* Adolf Galland can be strongly felt here. The spiral climb had two failings: first, it was aerodynamically inefficient; and second, sooner or later the formation would have its back to the sun. Schöpfel waited until this happened, then launched a solo attack, reasoning that whereas the *Gruppe*, which he was leading in Galland's absence, was sure to be seen, a single aircraft might well reach an attack position unobserved. It will also be noticed that, even with the initial altitude advantage, Schöpfel chose to attack from below. Two short bursts accounted for the two weavers, and, closing to short range on the nearest Vic, Schöpfel shot down a third:

> The Englishmen continued on, having noticed nothing. So I pulled in behind a fourth machine and took care of him, but this time I went in too close. When I pressed the firing button the Englishman was so close in front of my nose that pieces of wreckage struck my windmill. The oil from the fourth Hurricane spattered over my windscreen and the right side of my cabin so that I could see nothing. I had to break off the action.

Schöpfel succeeded Galland as *Kommandeur* of *III/JG 26*, then again as *Kommodore* of *JG 26* late in 1941, a command he held until January 1943. He survived the war, his final score 40, all in the West.

✠ 3. BARBAROSSA TO ZITADELLE

Hitler's Directive No. 21, dated December 18, 1940, opened with the words "The German armed forces must be prepared to crush Soviet Russia before the end of the war against England." From this moment the die was cast. *Reichsmarschall* Goering, Supreme Commander of the *Luftwaffe*, did his best to dissuade the *Führer* from this course of action, which would leave Germany fighting on two fronts—a situation which had proved disastrous in the 1914–18 war. But to no avail.

Following the campaign of 1939, Poland had been partitioned between Germany and Russia on a line stretching from East Prussia in the north, past Bialystok, Brest-Litovsk (now in Belorus) and Lwow (now in the Ukraine), southward to the Romanian border. At the same time the Baltic states of Latvia, Lithuania, and Estonia were incorporated into the USSR. Stalin, always suspicious of Hitler's intentions, moved large forces into the territory so gained, close to the new border. The Red Air Force was in the throes of a massive modernization program, and in 1941 work began on more than 200 airfields in the region, many of them new.

The Soviet Air Force could muster some 12,000–15,000 operational aircraft in all, of which about 7,000, over half of them fighters, were concentrated in the west of the country and in the occupied territories. Front-line combat aircraft were disposed in 23 air divisions, each with three air regiments, although this could vary. The basic flying organization was the regiment, with an establishment of 60 aircraft. These were made up of squadrons, each with about 9–12 aircraft, making a Russian squadron roughly equivalent to a German *Staffel*.

What were the Russian combat formations worth? In the Winter War against Finland they had showed up very poorly—brave, but lacking both skill and initiative. In part this was due to Stalin's purges of 1938, which swept away many able commanders on the grounds of political unreliability. Among these were flyers who had gained experience in the Spanish Civil War, and who, having watched the *Legion Kondor* at work, had recommended the adoption of the pair and four (*pary* and *zveno*) formations for fighter operations. Their recommendations died with them. In consequence, Russian fighter pilots were stuck with the three-aircraft Vic, and learned that individualism and innovation could be politically dangerous commodities. Pilot quality was on the whole poor, due to inadequate training. But whatever the shortcomings of individuals, the Soviet Air Force was a dangerous opponent by virtue of sheer weight of numbers.

The same could be said of the Soviet Army. Numerically strong, it outnumbered the German Army in tanks alone by about 5 to 1. Defeating it depended heavily on the *Blitzkrieg* form of armored warfare, proven in Poland and France, which in turn was reliant on close air support. To have any chance at all, Germany had to gain air superiority immediately, then retain it for the duration of the campaign. The war had to be won quickly, before Russia could mobilize her vast manpower and industrial resources. If this were allowed to happen, it was doubtful whether Germany could bring the war to a successful conclusion. And so it proved.

Prior to the attack, German intelligence concluded that Russian strength was 5,700 combat aircraft in the European area, of which 2,980 were fighters. This was a serious underestimate, as aircraft in reserve parks were not included. Against this horde, the *Luftwaffe* could deploy fewer than 2,000 combat aircraft, amounting to nearly two-thirds of total effectiveness. The Reich Air Defense could not be weakened, but many units were quietly redeployed eastward from the Channel coast, leaving only *JG 2* and *JG 26* to hold the British in play. A single *Gruppe, I/JG 27,* was in the Mediterranean.

The plan was to make three armored thrusts, each in Army Group strength, deep into Soviet territory. When the defending armies had been bypassed, the German forces would wheel in to encircle them as a preliminary to their total destruction. To provide air support each Army Group had an Air Fleet (*Luftflotte*) attached. *Luftflotte 1* was allocated to Army Group North, based in East Prussia. Its fighter component was a single *Geschwader, JG 54,* equipped with the Bf 109F. More or less central, based on Warsaw, Army Group Center was supported by *Luftflotte 2*. This disposed eight *Gruppen* of single-engine fighters—*II* and *III/JG 27* with Bf 109Es, and *JG 51* and *JG 53* equipped with the Bf 109F. In addition, two *Gruppen* of twin-engine Bf 110s, *I* and *II/ZG 26*, gave long-range cover. Southern Poland to the Romanian border was the domain of *Luftflotte 4* attached to Army Group South with eight *Gruppen* of fighters. Of these, *JG 3* and *I* and *II/JG 52* were equipped with Bf 109Fs, while *II* and *III/JG 77*, plus *I(J)/LG 2*, flew Bf 109Es. In addition, there were two peripheral Bf 109 units available for action: *III/JG 52* was based in Romania just outside Bucharest, while a single *Staffel, 13/JG 77*, was in northern Norway near the Russian border. Taking into account unserviceability, plus the fact that some units were below establishment, barely 500 fighters were available.

First Strike

The invasion of the Soviet Union, code-named "Barbarossa," took place shortly before dawn on June 22, 1941. Surprise was total. With many airfields unusable due to construction work, those that were operational were crammed with aircraft, lined up wingtip to wingtip as though for inspection. They made a wonderful target. So many were they that some *Luftwaffe* pilots felt certain that the Russians had planned a mass attack, which they themselves had preempted. This was of course to ignore the fact that air bases on a war footing would have had their aircraft dispersed and camouflaged. As it was, there was

> We hardly believed our eyes. Row after row of recon-
> naissance aircraft, bombers, and fighters stood lined up
> as if on parade. We were astonished at the number of air-
> fields and aircraft the Russians had ranged against us.
> —Hans von Hahn, *Kommandeur I/JG 3*
> (total victories 34)

little opposition from flak, and virtually none from fighters. When the bombers had finished their work, the *Jagdflieger* strafed anything that was left.

The destruction was enormous, but the huge number of Russian airfields ensured that they could not all be attacked by the first wave. The second attack, launched as soon as the German aircraft were refueled and rearmed, found Russian fighters in the air and ready. Savage dogfights erupted, in which the slow but maneuverable Soviet fighters caused the *Jagdflieger* many problems. Franz Schiess of *Stab/JG 53* (total score 67 victories) later recalled: "They would let us get almost into an aiming position, then bring their machines around a full 180 degrees, till both aircraft were firing at each other from head-on!"

Against the Polikarpov I-16 Type 24, armed with two 20mm ShVAK cannon, this was not a good place to be. Compared with the German 20mm MG FF, the Russian weapon had a muzzle velocity nearly 50 percent greater, well over double the rate of fire and a rather heavier projectile. Given accurate aiming, the greater effective range and weight of fire were to the advantage of the Russians, but poor training and in many cases the absence of a proper gun sight (some Russian aircraft carried only a painted circle on the windshield) redressed the balance.

What the Russian fighter pilots lacked in finesse they endeavored to make up in sheer doggedness. On many occasions German aircraft were destroyed by ramming, and frequently the Soviet pilot survived to fight again. It was a different matter with their bombers and attack aircraft, which, in the early days, came again and again in small formations with no fighter escort. They were mercilessly hacked from the skies.

Luftwaffe claims for the first day were 1,489 aircraft destroyed on the ground and 322 in air combat or by flak. The Soviet Official History admits 1,200 lost, of which 800 were on the ground. That the Soviet Air Force was far from wiped out on the ground is evident from the number of air victories claimed, added to which they flew over 6,000 sorties on the first day—hardly the sign of a beaten force.

There can be no doubt that the first day of Barbarossa was a victory for the *Luftwaffe*. Nevertheless, it carried within it the seeds of defeat. While the destruction of aircraft on the ground was important, their pilots were untouched. In the final analysis, this was critical. A surplus of trained pilots made the task of forming new units, equipped with new and better fighters, a simpler matter than might otherwise have been the case.

Advance to Moscow

The months that followed were a "happy time" for the *Jagdflieger*, and many *Experten* began to run up enormous scores. Werner Mölders exceeded Richthofen's First World War score of 80 victories on June 30 and went on to reach his century by July 15, the first fighter pilot ever to do so. Lagging him by three months were Günther Lützow, who achieved this mark on October 24, followed two days later by Walter Oesau.

Fighter pilots are by nature competitive, and in some units the race for victories during this period almost amounted to a fever. Several factors influenced this. The poor quality of the opposition, both pilots and aircraft, plus a high volume of Russian sorties, combined to form a target-rich environment.

The Germans had mobile radar sets and an ad hoc reporting system; the Russians had virtually nothing. The result was a series of encounter battles as one or the other tried to support their respective ground forces. Generally these took place at medium and low levels, as opposed to the "ever higher" trend evident during the Battle of Britain the previous year. Moreover, many of the lessons of that conflict were promptly "unlearned." The poor quality of most Soviet pilots bred contempt. Whereas most German pilots would have hesitated before trying to out-turn a British-flown Spitfire, they now entered into dogfights against numerous opponents without a second thought. It was an attitude that bred carelessness that eventually cost them dear.

Four other factors played a part. The first was that, as the penetration into Russia deepened, so the front widened. There was more ground to cover—fewer fighters per hundred miles of front. Second, difficulties in North Africa caused units to be detached there at the expense of the Eastern Front. These two factors resulted in the *Jagdwaffe* being increasingly used as a fire brigade and rushed to wherever the need was greatest. Third, as the advance continued, lines of communications lengthened, increasing logistics problems. Fuel and spares were often in short supply and serviceability declined. The inevitable result was a dilution of effort, while the Soviet Air Force was daily growing stronger. The final factor was "General Winter," who halted the German advance just short of Moscow and, far to the south, short of the Caucasian oil fields.

With the onset of winter, accidents caused by poor weather and icing proliferated, while the piercing cold froze engines and made flying almost impossible. This last problem was solved by captured Soviet personnel. The Russians were used to extreme conditions, and had overcome most difficulties with measures that by Western standards were unduly hazardous. The freezing of engine oil was countered by adding neat petrol to the mixture to thin it; this quickly evaporated when the engines were warmed up. Warming the engines to prevent them from freezing solid was done by lighting open petrol fires beneath them. Surprisingly, this caused few disasters.

There and Back Again

The spring of 1942 saw the Germans advancing once more, east toward Stalingrad and south toward the Caucasus oil fields. After some early successes they were halted by Russian counterattacks and finally driven back, while the 6th Army under von Paulus was encircled outside Stalingrad and eliminated early in 1943. It was the beginning of the end. After enduring another harsh winter, the German armies were driven back in the first six months of 1943, the summer of which climaxed with the decisive Battle of Kursk.

German fighter pilots generally admit that aerial victories were easy to come by in 1941, rather more difficult in 1942, and even harder by 1943. The reasons are obvious. The Russian fighter arm underwent a tremendous improvement over these years, both in quantity and quality. The qualitative improvement was not just in aircraft but also in pilots. The first year of the Great Patriotic War was a learning time for the Russians. Not only were they quick to adopt the "Finger Four" formation, but, with ace pilots like Alexsandr Pokryshkin analyzing and improving tactics, they became far more effective. Nor was that all. A close air support aircraft, the Ilyushin Il-2, was introduced. Heavily armored, it gained a reputation for being difficult to shoot down. On one notable occasion a *Jagdgeschwader Kommodore*, seeing an entire *Schwarme* attack an Il-2 with no visible result, asked "Whatever is going on down there?," only to draw the classic reply, *"Herr Oberst,* you cannot bite a porcupine in the arse!"

While the Russians grew stronger, the *Jagdflieger* grew weaker. By 1943 only four *Jagdgeschwader* were deployed on the 2,000-mile (3,200km) Eastern Front, and of these *JG 5* had only two *Gruppen*. This amounted to one fighter approximately every five miles! Pilot quality also declined. Death, wounds, or simply fatigue reduced the number of "old heads," and their replacements were no substitute. For each *Experte* piling up victories, dozens of young pilots arrived at the Eastern Front, flew a handful of fruitless missions, and then vanished as though they had never existed. For example, one *Jagdgeschwader* lost 80 pilots over quite a short period and, of these, 60 had failed to score.

Fighters of the Early Eastern Front
German fighters of this period differed little from those used in the Battle of Britain a year earlier. The Bf 109E and the twin-

engine Bf 110C were still in service, supplemented by the much-improved Bf 109F. This last was an extensively revamped 109E fitted with the Daimler-Benz DB 601E-1 engine rated at 1,300hp, housed in a completely redesigned symmetrical cowling. A larger spinner covered the boss of the propeller, which was six inches (15cm) smaller in diameter than that of its predecessor. On the left side of the cowling was a very prominent supercharger intake, so positioned to increase ram air effect. At the other end of the aircraft, a cantilevered tailplane eliminated the need for the bracing which had been one of the distinctive features of previous 109s. The tailwheel was made retractable and the wings and flying surfaces

Table 10. Fighter Data, Early Russian Front

	Messer-schmitt Bf 109F-3	Polikarpov I-16 Type 27	Mikoyan & Gurevich MiG-3	Lavochkin LaGG-3	Yakoviev Yak-1
Wingspan	32ft. 6in.	29ft. 6in.	33ft. 6in.	32ft. 2in.	32ft. 10in.
Length	29ft. 1in.	20ft. 1in.	27ft. 1in.	28ft. 11in.	27ft. 10in.
Height	11ft. 2in.	8ft. 5in.	10ft. 10in.	11ft. 9in.	8ft. 8in.
Wing area	173 sq. ft.	161 sq. ft.	188 sq. ft.	188 sq. ft.	185 sq. ft.
Engine	Daimler-Benz DB 601E rated at 1,300hp	Shvetsov M-62 radial rated at 1,000hp	Mikulin AM-35 inline rated at 1,350hp	Klimov 105PF inline rated at 1,310hp	Klimov 105PA inline rated at 1,310hp
Loaded weight	6,063lb.	4,215lb.	7,385lb.	7,032lb.	6,382lb
Wing loading	35lb./sq. ft.	26lb./sq. ft.	39lb./sq. ft.	37lb./sq. ft.	34lb./sq. ft.
Maximum speed	391mph	326mph	398mph	348mph	360mph
Service ceiling	39,370ft.	29,530ft.	39,400ft.	31,495ft.	32,810ft.
Rate of climb	4,291 ft./min.	c.3,200 ft./min.	c.3,700 ft./min.	c.3,900 ft./min.	c.3,900 ft./min.
Range	440 miles	248 miles	510 miles	404 miles	530 miles

underwent extensive revision, including increased span and rounded tips.

The armament of the Bf 109F was controversial—a single 20mm (15mm in the F-2) MG 151 firing through the propeller boss and two rifle-caliber MG 17s in the wings. While the higher rate of fire and greater muzzle velocity made it far superior to the MG FF, a single cannon was regarded as a retrograde step in many quarters. Werner Mölders favored the lighter armament but Adolf Galland was strongly against it. Be that as it may, the Bf 109F was faster and more maneuverable than its predecessor, making it more suitable for conditions at the Russian Front.

The Russians used several different fighter types during this period. Numerically, the most important in service was the Polikarpov I-16, but at the time of Barbarossa the Mikoyan MiG-3, Lavochkin LaGG-3, and Yakovlev Yak-1 were all entering service. While large numbers of British and American fighters were supplied to Russia, notably the Hurricane and Airacobra, these four indigenous types bore the brunt of the early fighting.

First flown on the final day of 1933, the I-16 was a world leader in fighter design. Conceived in the biplane era, it was a low-wing cantilever monoplane with an enclosed cockpit and a retractable undercarriage. Powered by a nine-cylinder radial engine, by 1941 it was hopelessly outclassed in performance by the German fighters, but it had other virtues. It was small and basically unstable; in combat this added to its agility. Its heavy armament has already been mentioned.

The MiG-3 was designed as a high-altitude interceptor. Powered by a twelve-cylinder inline engine, it was a very sleek machine, able to combat the Bf 109 at medium and high altitude, although less so lower down due to its high (for the time) wing loading. Armament was on the light side—a single 12.7 and two 7.62mm machine guns. Soviet ace Alexsandr Pokryshkin gained the majority of his 59 victories with the MiG-3.

The LaGG-3 bore a vague external resemblance to the American P-40 Tomahawk. It was largely of wooden construction, including birch ply skinning. Its acceleration was poor, and it had a tendency to stall and spin during hard maneuvering. This inhibited its pilots in the dogfight, although it was later found that lowering a few degrees of flap countered this tendency. Armament varied, but the usual fit was a single 20mm cannon and two 12.7mm machine guns, all mounted in the nose.

Best of all was the Yak-1. An aerodynamically clean design, it differed from its contemporaries in having a steel tube fuselage, although much of the skinning was of birch ply. Fast and very maneuverable, it was the ancestor of a whole family of successful Yakovlev single-seat fighters. Like most Soviet aircraft of the period, it was lightly armed, the usual fit being one 20mm cannon and two 12.7mm machine guns in the nose.

The *Experten*

The leader in the early days of the Russian campaign was Werner Mölders, who, after a short time at the front during which he became the first pilot in history to achieve 100 victories, was promoted to command the *Jagdwaffe*. This threw the race wide open. Many future high scorers were prominent at this time, but the first man to achieve 150 victories, on August 29, 1942, was former *Zerstörer* pilot Gordon Gollob. Of these, no fewer than 144 were on the Russian Front. Gollob, an Austrian with a Scottish father (McGollob), was then promoted to become a Fighter Leader in the West, and did not return to operations. He finally succeeded Adolf Galland as General of the Fighters in January 1945.

HERMANN GRAF Gollob's record was passed six days later by Hermann Graf, who, on October 2, reached 202. Graf's record was remarkable. After serving as a flying instructor, he was posted to *9/JG 52* as a *Feldwebel* in July 1941. His first victory came on August 3, and from that time he never looked back. The four weeks prior to passing the 200 mark saw him account for no fewer than 75 Russian aircraft. This was his high-water mark. Wounded shortly afterward, he returned to fly in the air defense of the Reich, where he accounted for ten

heavy bombers. Toward the end of the war he returned to
JG 52 as *Kommodore* but failed to add to his score.

The names that really stand out during this period are Gerhard Barkhorn and Günther Rall, both of *JG 52*. This pair survived the war as the second- and third-ranking fighter pilots of
all time, with 301 and 275 victories respectively, but the bulk
of their victims came in the first half of the Russian campaign.

GERHARD BARKHORN Gerhard Barkhorn's combat
debut, in the Battle of Britain, was singularly inauspicious. He
not only failed to score but was shot down twice, on one occasion bailing out into the Channel. Not until his 120th sortie, on
July 2, 1941, did he open his account. Once started, his progress
was steady. His hundredth victory came on December 19, and
his best-ever single sortie, on July 20, 1942, yielded four victories. After this his scoring rate slowed, and the two hundred
mark was not reached until November 30, 1943. Barkhorn's
comments on his opponents are revealing:

> Some of the Russian pilots flew without looking to either
> side of them, or back behind their tails. I shot down a lot of
> them like this who didn't even know I was there. A few of
> them were good, like other European pilots, but most were
> not flexible in their response to aerial fighting.

While not explicitly stated, it can be inferred from this passage
that Barkhorn was a master of the surprise bounce, the diving
attack from the sun, or the fast closure from astern and slightly
low. At the same time, he did not eschew the classic maneuver
combat, especially when flying the Bf 109F which he favored,
even the variant with the single 15mm cannon. But not all Russian pilots were easy:

> Once I had a forty-minute battle in 1943 with a hot Russian
> pilot and I just couldn't get him. Sweat was pouring off me
> just as though I had stepped out of the shower, and I won-
> dered if he was in the same condition. He was flying a
> LaGG-3, and we both pulled every aerobatic maneuver we

knew, as well as inventing some new ones as we went. I couldn't nail him, nor could he get me. He belonged to one of the Guards Regiments, in which the Russians concentrated their best pilots . . .

A one-versus-one combat lasting forty minutes must be something of a record. Usually other fighters would be in the vicinity, and they would intervene, or, on the rare occasions that singletons chanced to meet, one would normally have a decisive advantage in height or position. The inference here is that both pilots fought defensively, careful not to get into a false position. That Barkhorn tempered aggression with caution (possibly ingrained by his experiences of flying against the RAF) can be assumed from two facts. First, sorties in which he scored multiple victories were fewer than those of many other *Experten*, and second, in 1,104 sorties he was downed only nine times.

But in May 1944, his score at 273, very tired and rather careless, Barkhorn was jumped by a Russian fighter and put out of action for four months. On his return to *JG 52* he brought his score to 301, then was transferred to the West as *Kommodore* of *JG 6*. No further successes followed, and he then joined Galland's *JV 44*, flying the Me 262. Engine failure on his second sortie in the jet resulted in a crash landing in which he was once more badly injured.

Postwar, Barkhorn returned to flying with the new *Luftwaffe*. In the mid-1960s he "dropped" a hovering Kestrel (forerunner of the Harrier) which he was evaluating. As he was helped out of the battered jet, he is reported to have muttered *"Drei hundert und zwei* [302]!"

GÜNTHER RALL Of all the *Experten*, Günther Rall was probably the best marksman, able to score hits from extreme ranges (although he preferred to get in close) and crossing angles. His mastery of deflection shooting was instinctive, and it amazed those who saw it (Fig. 13). His first victory was a French Hawk 75 on May 12, 1940, but, like Barkhorn, he flew during the Battle of Britain with little success. It is a strange

Fig. 13. Deflection Shooting

Bullets took a second or so to cover the distance to the target, by which time it was no longer there. Deflection shooting was the art of aiming ahead of the target, so that it arrived in the same place and the same time as the bullets. Russian Front Experte Günther Rall was widely considered the best deflection shot in the Jagdwaffe.

fact that the top-scoring *Jagdgeschwader* of the war, containing such luminaries as Barkhorn and Rall, Beisswenger, Dickfeld, Grislawski, Dammers, and Eichel-Streiber, who racked up over 1,000 victories between them, failed to produce an *Experte* of note during this period. But in the early days of Barbarossa things changed radically.

Rall, by now *Staffelkapitän* of 8/JG 52, started the war at Constanza, Romania, his task to protect the oil refineries. His first encounter was with a formation of Soviet DB-3 bombers:

When they saw us coming out to meet them—we were still below them climbing—they turned back east, some dropping their bombs. They were silver-colored or white, and now the chase was on. We attacked from below and behind and shot many of them down. I aimed at the right engine of one and set him afire. He went into a spin. We continued our attacks until we were about out of fuel, and had to turn back toward the base. Since they had no fighter escort it was simple.

Over the next few days Rall's unit accounted for between 45 and 50 Russian bombers. They then returned to the *Gruppe*, *III/JG 52,* and took part in the offensive in southern Russia. The budding *Experte* soon increased his score to 36, shooting down a Soviet fighter in flames late on November 28. In the near-darkness the temptation to watch it go down proved irresistible. Distracted by the sight, and dazzled by the comet-like trail, he was shot up from behind by another Russian. In the ensuing crash landing, Rall broke his back.

It was eight months before he returned to the front, and he quickly made up for lost time. In a little over two months, Rall accounted for 64 Russians to reach the century mark. By August 1943 he reached 200 and, after knocking down 40 Russians in October, reached 250 the following month, only the second pilot to do so, just six weeks later than Walter Nowotny (final score 258 victories).

While Rall's incredible gunnery skills have already been mentioned, one of his victories came as the result of a midair collision. Uncertain whether a bogey was a Russian or an FW 190, which was new at the front at that time, he closed with it to make sure:

> I couldn't see the color and insignia on the other aircraft, only the silhouette. So I chased him at high speed, pulled up, and at that moment saw the aircraft against the ground instead of against the sun. The red star was glaring back at me from his fuselage. I couldn't turn away, because otherwise he would just have turned, too, and shot me down like a duck.
>
> I turned back from the left and down, pulled the trigger, and there was an earsplitting, terrifying crash. Collision! I bounced on this Russian from above. I cut his wing with my propeller, and he cut my fuselage with his propeller. He got the worst of it, because my propeller went through his wing like a ripsaw.

Mortally damaged, the Russian spun down, leaving Rall to pull off a belly landing from which he was able to walk away.

His score at 273, Günther Rall was transferred to the West in March 1944 as *Kommandeur* of *II/JG 11*. It was not a lucky move. Like so many of his Eastern Front comrades, he was able to achieve little against the hordes of American bombers and fighters and on May 12 he was shot down by a P-47, losing his left thumb in the process. Infection from his wound kept him hors de combat until November of that year, and a staff job followed. His final combat appointment was as *Kommodore* of *JG 300* in March 1945. He was shot down five times in the course of 621 sorties, and his final score was 275, making him the third-highest scorer of all time.

GÜNTHER SCHEEL No work on fighter pilots can afford to pass without at least a mention of *Leutnant* Günther Scheel. For sheer sustained mass destruction he is unrivaled. A few high-scoring *Experten* went through purple patches in which they matched his strike rate, but only after they had spent time playing themselves in and learning the game.

Not so Scheel. He joined *3/JG 54* in the spring of 1943 and almost immediately started scoring consistently, so much so that in just 70 sorties he notched up 71 confirmed victories —a record that was never surpassed. His luck ran out on July 16 when he rammed a Yak-9 near Orel at low level and his aircraft crashed and burned.

4. WESTERN FRONT, 1941–43

With the onset of winter 1940/41, the daylight battles over southeastern England had gradually fizzled out, leaving the German bomber force to continue the air war against the island fortress by night. Combatants on both sides expected the daylight assault to be renewed with the coming of better weather in the spring of 1941, but this was not to be. As noted in the previous chapter, Hitler was by now looking eastward.

Generalleutnant Adolf Galland later commented that the campaign against England was never one of Hitler's original war aims. It was merely a stone which had rolled in his way and it had either to be removed or to be bypassed. In any case, it was something which could not be allowed to interfere with the main objective, the destruction of Bolshevism. Having failed to remove the stone in the summer of 1940, he now chose to bypass it. If, after the conquest of the Soviet Union was complete, the islanders were still recalcitrant, they could then be dealt with by a Germany enriched, in the words of Hermann Goering, by the inexhaustible strategic resources of Russia.

Following heavy losses sustained in the Battle of Britain (*III/JG 52*, for example, had only four of its original complement of pilots left by October 1940), each *Jagdgeschwader* in turn withdrew to Germany to reequip and to train the youngsters. The Bf 109F-2 entered service with *III/JG 26* in May 1941, and other units soon converted to this model, which in some ways was superior to the newest British Spitfire, the Mk V.

Offensive action on the Channel coast during the first half of 1941 amounted to little more than skirmishing, with penny packets of German fighters carrying out sweeps in *Staffel* or even *Schwarm* strength. The RAF was of similar mind, putting a cautious toe in the water and probing the strength of the German air defenses. Meanwhile many *Jagdgeschwader* were unobtrusively transferred to the East, leaving only *JG 26 "Schlageter,"* commanded by the redoubtable Adolf Galland, and *JG 2 "Richthofen,"* commanded from July 1941 by Walter Oesau, to hold the ring on the Channel coast.

The air weapon must be used if it is to keep its cutting edge, and so RAF Fighter Command instituted a policy of "leaning forward into France." This took several forms. "Rhubarbs" and "Rangers" were incursions by small numbers (typically a pair) of fighters at low level, seeking targets of opportunity. Far more important were "Rodeos" and "Circuses." These differed only in whether they accompanied bombers. A Rodeo was a pure fighter sweep, typically by one or two wings of three squadrons (36 fighters) each. Provided it was identified as such in time, a Rodeo was left strictly alone by the *Jagdflieger*. This followed the pattern of the previous year, when the *Frei-jagd* of the *Luftwaffe* over southern England had been largely ignored by RAF Fighter Command. The Circus contained bombers, and this fact was enough to force the *Jagdgeschwader* to intercept. Even though only a handful of bombers was involved, and damage to their targets was often minimal, Circuses could not be ignored. To do so would simply have encouraged the RAF to step up the weight of attack, with consequent heavier damage.

The composition of a Circus was typically up to 24 Spitfire and Hurricane squadrons, each of twelve aircraft, protecting a few bombers. Preceding the main formation were three target support wings at high altitude, each three squadrons strong. Their task was to sweep the sky clear of opposition along the route of the main force and over the target. To make life difficult for the defenders, all three wings closed on the target from different directions and at different times.

The main force usually consisted of half a dozen Blenheim or Stirling bombers flying at about 12,000ft., surrounded by nine or ten squadrons of Spitfires and Hurricanes. The composition varied from time to time, but in the early days was more or less as follows. The close escort squadron was split on either side of the bombers, about 3,000ft. out and either level or a little higher. Beneath came the low escort squadron, split like the close escort squadron on both sides but 1,000ft. lower than the bombers. Behind and about 1,000ft. above the close escort squadron was the medium escort squadron, which in turn was covered by the high escort squadron, astern and a further 1,000ft. higher. These four squadrons made up the escort wing. Still higher came three squadrons of the escort cover wing, astern of and stacked up to 4,000ft. above the highest squadron of the escort wing, stepped up into the sun. Still higher were the three squadrons of the high cover wing, again stacked up into the sun over 7–8,000ft. The entire formation ranged from 11,000ft. up to between 25,000 and 26,000ft.

Nor was this all. Two or three squadrons of the forward support wing met the bombers at the French coast on the way out, while the rear support wing, generally two squadrons strong, provided a reception committee over mid-Channel. The total number of British fighters in a typical Circus often exceeded the combined strength of *JG 2* and *JG 26*. It was a difficult and dangerous nut for the defenders to crack.

Not that the German fighters ever attempted to match strength with strength. As previously noted, the *Gruppen* rather than the *Geschwader* were the primary fighting units, and these were widely scattered. The three *Gruppen* of Galland's *JG 26* were based at Moorseele (later Wevelghem) in Belgium, and at St. Omer and Abbeville in France. *JG 2,* commanded from February to July 1941 by Wilhelm Balthasar, basically covered the area south of the Seine although one *Gruppe* was occasionally used to reinforce the north. Among other things, it was responsible for protecting the German naval bases at Cherbourg and Brest. The latter in particular was beyond Circus range, but it was often the target for serious daylight bombing raids escorted by Spitfires with long-range tanks, especially when German capital ships were in harbor.

Circus No. 1 was flown on January 10, 1941, but the buildup was slow and by mid-June the tally had reached only fourteen. This gave the Germans time to piece together a radar detection and reporting system in the area. It was neither as good nor as comprehensive as the British network, but it did its job in a generally workmanlike manner. British radar already reached a considerable distance into France provided the aircraft under surveillance were at high altitude, and consequently this became the first air campaign in which radar tracking and ground control were available to both sides.

The task of the *Jagdflieger* on the Channel was to provide a modicum of air defense while remaining in being as an effective force. One or sometimes two *Gruppen* would be sent against a Circus, with the remainder held back to cover contingency situations. Inevitably the defenders were heavily outnumbered by the teeming hordes of British fighters in almost every case.

Some commentators have likened Circus operations to the Battle of Britain in reverse, citing the German defensive fight against odds. In point of fact there is little similarity. The German fighters were not defending their homeland against devastating attacks by swarms of bombers. While the targets chosen by the British were relatively important to the Germans, they were hardly vital to the future conduct of the war. The bomb loads carried by the British were never enough to inflict really serious damage, nor were any German civilians killed on the ground. While the air fighting itself was a deadly affair, the *Jagdflieger* could afford to be fairly circumspect about the manner in which they engaged.

The general principle was to inflict maximum damage at minimum risk. Whenever possible (and on most occasions it was, owing to the relative lack of defensive urgency), the *Jagdflieger* sought the advantage of height before attacking. Small formations nibbled at the flanks of the Circus as a distraction before other units launched steep diving attacks. It was not expected that the bombers could be attacked every time: only the most skilled leaders could succeed in breaking through the massed Spitfires and Hurricanes, and then not always.

In practice the huge number of British fighters was often a disadvantage, as they got in each other's way, adding greatly to the confusion. By contrast, once a few Germans became embroiled in the melee, they could take shots of opportunity without having to worry overmuch about positive identification. Aircraft quality was also a factor. The Hurricane, by now completely outclassed at the high altitudes where most combats took place, remained in service for some time, although it was gradually withdrawn in favor of the Spitfire. The superb Bf 109F outperformed the Spitfire I and II in certain areas, although it could still not match the British aircraft in a turning fight and was thus forced to continue the hit-and-run tactics developed during the previous summer. A more formidable opponent was the Spitfire VB, which entered service from February 1941. Armed with two 20mm Hispano cannon and four .303in. machine guns, the Mark VB was essentially a Spitfire I with a more powerful engine.

Focke-Wulf FW 190A

Commentators on the formative years of the *Luftwaffe* often give the impression that, once selected, the Bf 109 was to be the only single-engine fighter in that service. This is far from the truth. Design work on the FW 190 commenced in 1938 and the first prototype flew on 1 June 1939—well before the outbreak of war.

Powered by a 14-cylinder BMW radial engine, the FW 190 was an extremely rugged aircraft, far more so than the rather delicate Bf 109. Unlike the Messerschmitt fighter, it had a single-piece sliding canopy, giving a first-class all-around view from the cockpit, while the slightly nose-down level-flight attitude gave a good view forward. The seat was semireclining, with a high heel-line which gave the pilot good g-resistance.

Other good points were an ingenious gadget called the

Table 11. Fighter Data, Channel Coast, 1941–43

	Focke-Wulf FW 190A-3	Supermarine Spitfire VB	Supermarine Spitfire IX
Wingspan	34ft. 5½in.	36ft. 10in.	36ft. 10in.
Length	29ft. 0in.	29ft. 11in.	30ft. 6in.
Height	13ft. 0in.	12ft. 7in.	12ft. 7in.
Wing area	197 sq. ft.	242 sq. ft.	242 sq. ft.
Engine	BMW 801 Dg radial rated at 1,700hp	Rolls-Royce Merlin V-12 rated at 1,440hp	Rolls-Royce Merlin V-12 rated at 1,710hp
Loaded weight	7,652lb.	6,650lb.	7,500lb.
Wing loading	39lb./sq. ft.	28lb./sq. ft.	31lb./sq. ft.
Maximum speed	399mph	374mph	408mph
Service ceiling	33,800ft.	37,000ft.	44,000ft.
Rate of climb	c.4,100ft./min.	c.3,650ft./min.	c.4,150ft./min.
Range	644 miles	470 miles	434 miles

Note: The development of the FW 190A was a continuing process and many further subtypes entered service before the end of 1943. The same applied to the Spitfire, which was developed into high- and low-altitude variants. Therefore, the figures in this table are no more than a guide.

Kommandgerät, which automatically controlled propeller pitch, fuel, mixture, boost, and engine revs and which thus reduced the pilot's workload, as did the absence of any necessity to retrim for different flight conditions. Beautifully balanced ailerons gave a rate of roll significantly faster than that of the aircraft's main opponent, the Spitfire. Directional stability was good, longitudinal stability was neutral, while lateral instability contributed to its phenomenal agility in the rolling plane. At low and medium altitudes acceleration and climb rate were good, while the aircraft was exceptional in a dive.

Like any fighter, the FW 190 had its weak points. Wing

loading was a trifle on the heavy side, giving the German fighter an unexceptional turn radius and rate. It was difficult to fly on instruments, and stalling characteristics were unforgiving. British test pilot Eric Brown, who flew a captured example, commented:

> The stalling speed of the FW 190A-4 in clean configuration was 127mph and the stall came suddenly and without warning, the port wing dropping so violently that the aircraft almost inverted itself. In fact, if the German fighter was pulled into a g-stall in a tight turn, it would flick out onto the opposite bank and an incipient spin was the inevitable outcome if the pilot did not have his wits about him.

The figure of 127mph was the indicated airspeed. The true air speed would be a good deal more in the thin air at high altitude. Stalling speed in a 6g turn would be 311mph true airspeed at sea level. The nature of the high-speed stall was embarrassing enough at high altitude; at low level, where there was insufficient room to recover, it could be lethal, as many German pilots found to their cost. Consequently it constrained many from hard maneuvers near the ground.

The first FW 190s to enter service were received by II/JG 26 in July 1941, but the demands of conversion onto a new type, coupled with persistent engine problems, delayed its combat debut to September. Even then, it was not until the early months of 1942 that the new fighter really began to make its presence felt, while not until April did I/JG 26 trade in its Bf 109Fs for FW 190As. That same month also saw JG 2 complete its reequipment with the new fighter.

The British Response

So formidable was the Focke-Wulf fighter that the RAF was forced onto the tactical defensive. As a stopgap, the Spitfire IX was rushed into service. Basically it was a Spitfire V powered by the latest and more powerful Merlin engine with a two-speed, two-stage supercharger which gave it comparable performance to the FW 190A below 25,000ft. and a margin of superiority above this level. The German fighter retained its advantage in rate of roll, in the zoom climb and in the dive, but was generally equaled in all other departments. Leaving aside the surprise bounce, pilot skill became the deciding factor in any dogfight between the two. One major difficulty remained for the *Jagdflieger* pilot: externally the two Spitfire types were virtually indistinguishable. Until combat was joined, he was hard-pressed to tell whether he was up against the inferior Mk V or the more potent Mk IX. See Figs. 14 and 15.

The Campaign

In the first six months of 1941 air action on the Channel coast was desultory. Then, on June 21, two Circuses were flown in a single day. Weather permitting, this was the shape of things to come, and from then on the pressure was unrelenting. Bitter fighting on this day saw British losses of five fighters and one bomber. This was a poor return for the *Jagdflieger*, who lost nine Bf 109s and six pilots. However, it was not long before the pendulum swung in the other direction.

The fact was that, judged purely on the grounds of attrition, the campaign on the Channel coast was a minor victory for the *Jagdflieger*, whose victory-to-loss ratio often exceeded 3:1. With so many aircraft milling around in the air, the confusion was great, and this inevitably led to overclaiming. It was partly this that led Fighter Command to continue what was a costly policy, as it obscured the fact that they were actually losing more aircraft than they shot down. For example, between June 14 and July 4, 1941, RAF Fighter Command claimed 214 victories. Actual German losses were 48 fighters destroyed and 33 damaged, with 32 pilots killed or taken prisoner and six wounded. Over the same period, British losses were 80 aircraft and 62 pilots. This general trend was perpetuated through 1941 and 1942, and well into the following year.

Reasons for the German success are not hard to find. The hard core of pilots in the two *Jagdgeschwader* were veterans: the leavening of new flyers from the training schools was a

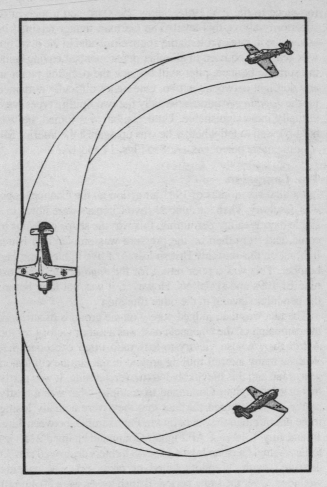

Fig. 14. The Abschwung
*Known to the British as the Half-Roll and the Americans as the
Split-S, the Abschwung was a widely used method of breaking off
action. It consisted of rolling inverted, followed by a hard pull into
a vertical dive and a low-level pull out in the opposite direction.
Not recommended against a better-diving opponent.*

fairly small proportion of the whole, and these few were introduced to combat gradually. By contrast, Fighter Command had undergone a massive expansion. While to a very high degree the squadron and flight commanders were old hands, the proportion of novices was far higher than in the German units. This was not helped by the RAF habit of resting their aces—a policy which, while it paid dividends in the long run, lowered fighting efficiency in the short term.

Finally, there was the question of tactics. Fighter Command did not take its first steps toward adopting the Finger Four formation as used by the Germans until the late summer of 1941. It took time to develop, and even then it was slow to catch on. The inferior *Idiotenreihe* fours in line astern of 1940 vintage was more often used, and this persisted even into 1943. Meanwhile the *Jadgwaffe* started flying in fours abreast, which offered advantages even over the Finger Four.

It was not readily apparent, but the *Jagdflieger* were paying a high price for what was to prove a transitory success. Many *Experten* added to their already impressive scores, but others melted away in the crucible of battle. Gustav Sprick (31 victories) was shot down by Spitfires near Holque on June 28. Wilhelm Balthasar also fell to Spitfires over Aire on July 3; as *Kommodore* of *JG 2* he had added a further 11 to his total, bringing his final score to 40, plus seven in Spain. Rolf Pingel, who had scored four in Spain, was taken prisoner on July 10, his total at 26. Fast-scoring Walter Adolph, with 28 victories in just 79 sorties, was shot down in his FW 190 on September 18. Men such as these were not available for the crucial battles that lay ahead. Their loss in what was to a large degree a sideshow was a tragedy for the *Luftwaffe*.

Winter weather was hardly conducive to large-scale air operations, and Circus No. 110, flown on November 8, was the last of 1941. By this time Adolf Galland had brought his score to 93, Joachim Müncheberg his to 59 (25 of which had been scored while on detachment to the Mediterranean), and Josef Priller his to 58. In the same month Galland was promoted away from the front line to become *General der Jagdflieger*,

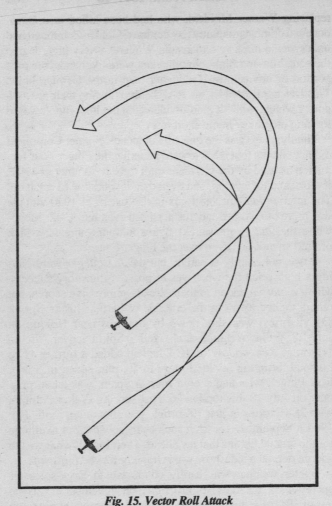

Fig. 15. Vector Roll Attack
Superiority in the rolling plane could be used to defeat a better-turning opponent. Rolling away from the direction of the turn allowed the pursuing fighter to cut the corner. This was, however, a double-edged sword. American Thunderbolts often used the vector roll against Bf 109s.

replacing Werner Mölders, who had been killed in a flying accident. He was replaced at the head of *JG 26* by Gerhard Schöpfel.

It was almost exactly five months before Circus operations were resumed, by which time the *Gruppen* equipped with the FW 190A had become really familiar with their new mount. This was just as well. Whereas previously the *Jagdflieger* had sought the advantages of height and position before attacking, nibbling at the fringes of the massive Circus formations, they were about to be thwarted by a change of tactics.

Instead of telegraphing their intentions by forming up at high altitude in full view of the German radar, the British now took to crossing the Channel at low level, then climbing flat out just before they reached the coast. At the same time, increasing use was made of low-level penetrations by light bombers, which called for a different approach to the fighter escort mission. For the *Jagdflieger*, the leisurely wait at cockpit readiness, followed by a calculated climb to altitude, was now eliminated: the Spitfires, rocketing skyward at full throttle, were often already above.

With the advent of the FW 190A, this was not as critical as it once had been. The aircraft was a superb dogfighter, and its pilots used it as such. The previous summer, faced with slashing attacks by the 109s, the constant complaint of RAF pilots was that "Jerry" didn't stay and fight, totally ignoring the fact that in the 109 this was tactically correct. Now they were repaid in spades: in his new FW 190A, "Jerry" stayed and fought as never before.

One of the Germans' more successful actions took place on June 2, when No. 403 Canadian Squadron, an inexperienced outfit but led by New Zealand veteran Al Deere, flew as top cover on a Rodeo. The intercepting *Jagdflieger*, *I/JG 26*, led by Johannes Seifert, and *II/JG 26*, led by Müncheberg, waited until the Rodeo was homeward bound before, taking advantage of cloud cover, they moved into position.

The opening ploy was a high-speed run from astern by a single *Staffel*. Deere saw them coming and called a complicated three-way break and reverse to meet the attackers

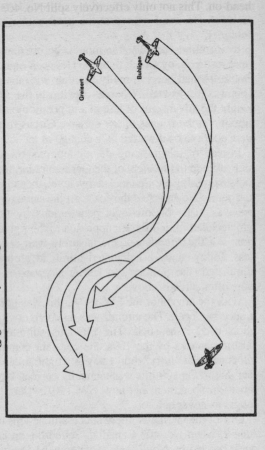

Fig. 16. Bühligen's Victory, June 13, 1941

Bühligen's leader, Heinrich Greisert, attacks a Spitfire, misses, and overshoots. Passing above, he commences a hard turn to port. The Spitfire pilot tries to turn inside Greisert, only to find Bühligen on his tail. Despite his excess speed, Bühligen manages to pull lead and open fire, scoring hits. This is a typical dogfight victory, lasting mere seconds from start to finish.

head-on. This not only effectively split No. 403 Squadron off from the rest of the Wing but disrupted its formation integrity—not that there was a lot of choice. As the Spitfires pulled around, they were assailed from the flank by two more *Staffeln*, which had taken full advantage of cloud cover. A fraction of a second for a head-on burst at the original formation of FW 190s, then they were hit again from the other flank by a whole *Gruppe*. No. 403's Spitfire Vs, outclassed and heavily outnumbered, were decimated. Deere later wrote of this encounter:

> I twisted and turned in an endeavor to avoid being jumped and at the same time to get myself into a favorable position for attack. Never had I seen the Huns stay and fight it out as these Focke-Wulf pilots were doing.

Of the original twelve Spitfires, eight were lost, one of which was written off after crash-landing at Manston, as were six pilots. German losses were nil. In this encounter Müncheberg claimed two aircraft, bringing his score to 81, and Seifert notched up the 35th of the 57 he scored before colliding with an American P-38 Lightning some seventeen months later.

After this, air activity eased considerably. The Spitfire IX started entering service, although it was some time before its numbers were sufficient to redress the Focke-Wulf threat. Then, on August 19, came the large-scale amphibious raid on Dieppe. The British, supported by the USAAF, put up a massive air umbrella over the beachhead, with no fewer than 2,462 fighter sorties during the day. The Germans reacted in force, throwing in not only every fighter in the area but bombers as well. A massive battle for local air superiority ensued, after which both sides claimed victory. RAF losses totaled 106, of which 88 were fighters. Eight Spitfires of the USAAF also failed to return. German losses amounted to 48, of which only 20 were fighters. The most successful *Jagdflieger* on this day was Josef Wurmheller of *III/JG 2*, who claimed seven victories, despite flying with a broken leg and concussion.

By the late summer of 1942 the Circus was rapidly falling into disuse. The superiority of the FW 190A over the Spitfire V made it a losing proposition for the British, while low-level penetrations by light and medium bombers were far more damaging than the "bait" bombers had ever been. In any case, a new factor was fast emerging. The USAAF had long been determined to carry out precision daylight attacks with massed formations of heavy bombers. By August the first units were operational. Two days before the Dieppe raid, with a close escort of four squadrons of Spitfire IXs, a dozen B-17 Flying Fortresses attacked the marshaling yards at Rouen. All returned safely.

It was the shape of things to come. At first the American heavy bombers rarely ventured beyond the range at which Spitfires could escort them, but, as they gained experience, they became more confident. Finally they ranged deep into Germany without fighter escort, and, while they suffered heavily, they set the *Jagdflieger* new and very difficult problems. But that is another story.

The *Experten*

Many of the leading *Experten* of the two years of the Channel campaign were "old heads," blooded in France and the Battle of Britain. Experienced in flying against the RAF, they continued from where they had left off the previous summer. Others were posted to the Eastern Front for Barbarossa and returned to the West later. Conditions in the East were so different, and the quality of the opposition so low, that they became careless. Flying against Fighter Command this was potentially disastrous, and often they failed to last long.

Although the established *Experten* continued to add to their scores on the Channel coast, hardly any really high scorers emerged from this theater, probably because conditions were not conducive to the survival of novices. Siegfried Lemke (96 victories) joined *I/JG 2* in the autumn of 1942. Wilhelm-Ferdinand (Wutz) Galland, brother of Adolf, scored 55 victories with *II/JG 26* between July 27, 1941, and his death in action at the hands of American ace Walker Mahurin in August 1943. Gerhard Vogt of the same unit amassed 48 victories between November 6, 1941, and January 14, 1945, when he was caught at low level by Mustangs. As an aside, the third Galland brother, Paul, was shot down by a Spitfire on October 31, 1942, his score a respectable 17.

KURT BÜHLIGEN Bühligen joined *II/JG 2* as a humble *Unteroffizier* in July 1940. Success was a while coming: his first victory was not until September 4. His score mounted slowly until June 13, 1941, the day he found his "shooting eye." Flying a Bf 109F with the *Gruppe Stab* as *Kacmarek* to the *Kommandeur*, Heinrich Greisert, he intercepted a Circus near Boulogne:

> I came down and then up fast with the *Kommandeur* and we each selected a Spit. I watched my sight ring fill with the wingspan and came on still closer. I aimed below, the Spitfire was fast, and when I was very close I opened fire. The *Kommandeur* was doing the same. A big dogfight now developed but I managed to stay behind this one and my shells poured into him. Pieces started to fly backward, then there was black smoke. He started down. There was no 'chute. The *Kommandeur*, I think, got a Spitfire also, but we had by then become separated. I saw my victim go down and then looked around. I saw the *Kommandeur* trying a pass on another Spitfire. He was closing too fast and instead of going under the Spit he pulled up and passed over his tail and continued up to the left, as if to come round for another pass. But the Spitfire pilot turned left too, to come up and around behind him. I was in position to curve in from behind and follow the Spit and I turned as sharply as I could on his tail. He was intent on shooting down the *Kommandeur*. I managed to gain, and hung on in the turn. When very close I opened fire again and almost immediately saw hits. White smoke began to trail backward and I kept firing. Then half his tail came off.

There are several points of interest in this account. The leader did not even attempt to attack the bombers, which, given the strength of the escort, would have been very hazardous. The opening attack consisted of a fast dive to below the Spitfires, followed by a pull-up into the blind spot astern and underneath. It appears that the recommended method of breaking off an attack was downward, keeping in the blind spot, rather than pulling up and over, although had Greisert pulled up more steeply he would not have ended with the Spitfire on his tail. Finally, Bühligen managed to turn briefly with his second victim. While the Spitfire could, speed for speed, handily out-turn the Bf 109F, the fact that the latter was positioned astern allowed it to keep its sights on for a brief space of time without turning so tightly, and to shoot across the circle, albeit at a rapidly increasing deflection angle. Only when a maximum-rate turn had been established for a few seconds would the Spitfire's superior turning ability have become decisive. See Fig. 16.

Shortly afterward Bühligen pulled off a successful bounce against a Hurricane, again coming up and under, for his third victim of the sortie. His score now climbed rapidly, reaching 21 on September 4, 1941. A trick from his personal bag was to have his aircraft trimmed tail-heavy. While it needed a slight forward pressure on the stick to hold it in level flight, it responded better to a backward pull, pitching up rapidly without mushing.

Having converted to the FW 190A, *II/JG 2* was transferred to Tunisia in November 1942 where, in the face of overwhelming numbers, Bühligen scored 40 victories in five months. Returning to the West in 1943, he reached the century mark in June 1944, by which time he had risen to *Kommodore* and had established a reputation as a slayer of heavy bombers. He was shot down only three times in over 700 missions, and his final total of 112 Western-flown victims was exceeded by only two other pilots.

WALTER OESAU "Gulle" Oesau was one of the great *Jagdwaffe* leaders of the war. He combined fighting ability, leadership, and the ability to impart his methods to others with great mental and physical stamina. Johannes Steinhoff, whom we will meet in a later chapter, called him the toughest fighter pilot in the *Luftwaffe*—high praise indeed from the man who rose to command the postwar German Air Force.

Starting the war with eight victories in Spain, Oesau continued scoring in France and the Battle of Britain. As *Kommandeur* of *III/JG 51* from August 1940, he attained his twentieth victory of the war on the 18th of that month, the fifth pilot to do so. On February 5, 1941, he became the fourth pilot to reach 40.

Transferred to *III/JG 3* as *Kommandeur* for Barbarossa, he accounted for 44 Russians in five weeks before being recalled to the West to replace Balthasar as *Kommodore* of *JG 2* in July, and he became the third German pilot to reach 100 victories (after Mölders and Lützow) on October 26. As previously noted, many Eastern Front *Experten* failed to make the transition.

Back in the West, Oesau's scoring rate slowed, but this did not prevent him from becoming the third *Experte* to reach the century mark, on October 26, 1941. But further victories were now few and far between, and he was given a staff post in June 1943. In October of that year he returned to combat at the head of *JG 1*, tackling the huge fleets of American bombers and sending down at least ten of these aircraft. On May 5, 1944, his luck ran out and he was shot down and killed by USAAF Lightnings over the Eifel. His final score was 123, amassed in just over 300 sorties.

ADOLF GALLAND Galland is considered by many to have been the greatest *Experte* of all. His final total of 104 was not exceptional by *Jagdwaffe* standards, even though all were gained against the Western Allies, the vast majority of them before November 1941. He was one of the great characters of the *Luftwaffe*. By nature a showman, he liked the good things of life, including the company of glamorous women, and flew the only Bf 109F to have a cigar lighter installed. Painted beneath the cockpit was his personal insigne, a cigar-smoking Mickey Mouse brandishing a revolver and a hatchet. His view of the fighter war was:

> Their element is to attack, to track, to hunt, and to destroy the enemy. Only in this way can the eager and skillful fighter pilot display his ability. Tie him to a narrow and confined task, rob him of his initiative, and you take away from him the best and most valuable qualities he possesses: aggressive spirit, joy of action, and the passion of the hunter.

At the start of the year his score stood at 58. For months opportunities were few, and only nine more had been added by mid-June, three of them on April 15 when, with typical Galland bravura, he and his *Kacmarek* made an unscheduled detour to the English coast with a crate of champagne and a basket of lobsters stowed in the fuselage.

On June 21, Galland led his *Stab* and a *Staffel* of *JG 26* to intercept a Circus near Arques:

> From a greater height I dived right through the fighter escort onto the main bomber force. I attacked the lower plane of the lower rear row from very close. The Blenheim caught fire immediately. Part of the crew bailed out.
>
> In the meantime my unit was struggling with Spitfires and Hurricanes. My wingman and I were the only Germans attacking the bombers at that moment. Immediately I started my second attack. Again I managed to dive through the fighters. This time it was a Blenheim in the leading row of the formation. Flames and black smoke poured from her starboard engine.

It is what is not said in this account that makes it interesting. Not only was the first attack made without hindrance from the escorts, but Galland was apparently able to distance himself from the melee sufficiently to gain enough altitude for a repeat performance. Certainly four minutes elapsed between attacks, and this is a long time in air combat. It seems probable that, after his first attack, Galland broke away in a shallow high-speed dive to gain separation before pulling back up to reposition. By this time he had lost the factor of surprise and the Spitfires were waiting. Although his second attack was successful, his Bf 109 was so badly shot up that he was forced to belly-land. Hegenauer, his wingman, was badly hit and bailed out. As if this were not enough excitement for one day, Galland took off alone (Hegenauer had not yet returned) that afternoon against another Circus and picked off a Spitfire with a surprise bounce. This was his seventieth victory. But moments later he was hit from behind by another Spitfire and his aircraft set on fire. Slightly wounded, he barely succeeded in bailing out of his stricken fighter.

Ordinarily a devotee of the fast plunging attack from an altitude advantage, Galland could be more subtle on occasion. When cloud cover was suitable, it was not unknown for him to ease his way into a Circus as though he had every right to be there. In a sky filled with aircraft, four Messerschmitts were easily mistaken for friendlies, especially if they were making no overtly hostile moves. On November 13, 1941, Galland flew with Peter Goering, the *Reichsmarschall*'s nephew, against

> . . . a formation of Blenheim bombers which were heavily protected by fighters. On our climb we passed near this hellish "goods train." We were overtaking British fighters right and left. This was so incredibly impertinent that it succeeded.

This apparently innocuous approach was the air combat equivalent of sauntering with hands in pockets and whistling! Even climbing, the two 109s were able to overtake because the escorts were throttled back and weaving to stay with the bombers. But on this occasion it all went badly wrong. As he opened fire Peter Goering was shot down and killed by the Blenheim's turret gunner.

Between June and November 1941, when he was taken off

operations, Adolf Galland increased his tally by 27, bringing his total to 94. As *General der Jagdflieger* he made occasional operational sorties to see the situation for himself, and in January 1945, when he was relieved of his command, he formed the jet fighter unit *JV 44*, with which he added to his total.

5. NORTH AFRICA

Initially neutral, Italy joined the war on the side of Germany in June 1940 but in the final month of that year suffered a spectacular reverse in Libya at the hands of the British. From the German viewpoint, her ally was strategically vital inasmuch as the Italian Fleet and Air Force could, in theory, deny the British passage through the Mediterranean. If the Italians were unceremoniously bundled out of North Africa, this would no longer be the case. In this event, there could be no guarantee that Italy would not make a separate peace, or, even worse, change sides (as, indeed, was to happen later). The Germans' presence in North Africa was at first little more than a move to keep their southern partner in the war. From there the logical next step was to conquer Egypt, thus sealing the Mediterranean at its eastern end while opening the way to the Middle East oil fields. But as Axis ambitions increased, so did their logistics problems. This inevitably highlighted Malta.

Malta was a small island some sixty miles from the southern coast of Sicily. The home of British air and naval bases, it was ideally situated to interdict Axis sea and air supply routes to Libya, while at the same time giving local air support to British naval units in transit between Gibraltar and Alexandria. It soon became obvious that success in North Africa was largely dependent on eliminating Malta as a British base.

The North African theater divides into three dissimilar campaigns. The first two, operations against Malta and the fighting in the Libyan/Egyptian desert, ran in parallel from 1941 to 1943. The third arose from the massive Allied landings in

French North Africa late in 1942 and continued until the final collapse of Axis resistance a few months later.

One factor was consistent throughout 1941 and 1942. The best British fighters were retained for home defense. Malta and the Desert Air Force had to make do with second-rate equipment. In the early days this consisted of Gloster Gladiator biplanes and war-weary Hurricane Is. Curtiss P-40 Tomahawks and Kittyhawks were introduced from June 1941 and April 1942 respectively. Considered inadequate for the fighter role in Europe, they were sent to the desert, where they were a match for most Italian fighters of the period, although considerably inferior to the German Bf 109E and F. The same can be said of the Hurricane IIC, which, despite its more powerful Merlin engine and exceptionally heavy armament of four 20mm Hispano cannon, lacked the performance to match the German fighters. Not until March 1942 did the first Spitfire Vs arrive, first in Malta and then shortly afterward in the desert squadrons. But by this time the even more potent Bf 109G was starting to equip the *Jagdgruppen*.

Malta

The *Jagdflieger* had greater advantages over the defenders of Malta than anywhere else in the theater. They could gain altitude at leisure on the long climb out from their Sicilian bases, arriving over the island at 20,000ft. or more, where the tired Hurricanes were no match for them. They could accept or decline battle as they chose. Often they accompanied German or Italian bombers, frequently with Italian fighters also in attendance. Invariably they had both position and a superior aircraft.

Incessant bombing and strafing took its toll of the RAF defenders. Even when replacement aircraft were flown in, the fact could not be concealed from the Axis and their arrival was the signal for a concerted airfield attack. On such a small island there was little chance of effective dispersal, and many were destroyed on the ground shortly after arrival. Spares were in short supply, and the number of serviceable British fighters frequently sank to single figures.

The first *Jagdwaffe* unit to operate against Malta was 7/*JG 26*, which took up residence at Gela in Sicily on February 9, 1941. Led by Joachim Müncheberg, who had flown as Galland's *Kacmarek* in the Battle of Britain and had adopted the same dive and zoom tactics, this single *Staffel* quickly gained the ascendancy. With the exception of a brief excursion to the Balkans, 7/*JG 26* operated against Malta until late May, during which time it claimed 41 victories, mainly Hurricanes. Of these, Müncheberg accounted for eighteen, plus one more in the Balkans. Underlining the measure of *Jagdflieger* superiority at this time, not one pilot was lost.

The *Luftwaffe*'s absence from Sicily from June allowed Malta to recover its strength. The interdiction of Axis sea lanes was so successful that Rommel's army in the desert, starved of supplies, came close to defeat by the end of the year. Reinforcements from the Russian Front were rushed to the area, arriving in December. The fighter element consisted of four *Gruppen*—*JG 53* in its entirety plus *II/JG 3*. All were equipped with the new Bf 109F. *Luftwaffe* operations reached a new pitch of intensity during the spring. Many defenders were lost when, short of fuel, they needed to land, only to find pairs of Messerschmitts patrolling the airfield approaches. But, just when the battle seemed won, victory was thrown away. The demands of other fronts saw *II/JG 3* and *I/JG 53* depart for the East, while *III/JG 53* left for North Africa, leaving only *II/JG 53* in Sicily. This coincided with wholesale reinforcements of Spitfires to the island. Almost overnight the situation was reversed.

The rest of 1942 saw further *Luftwaffe* fighter movements. *I/JG 77* arrived from the East in July; *I/JG 53* returned in September. Very heavy fighting took place, but the time had passed. The Battle of Malta had been lost at the very moment that victory was in sight.

During 1942 three *Jagdflieger* surpassed Müncheberg's score over Malta. Gerhard Michalski of *II/JG 53* counted 26 of his eventual total of 73 victories, closely followed by Siegfried

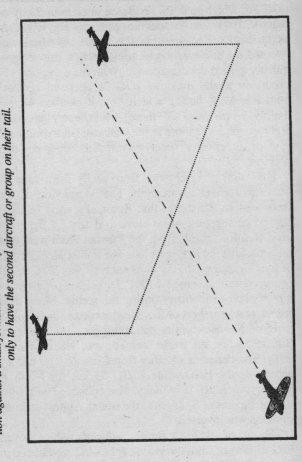

Fig. 17. Boxing
Boxing was standard whenever the Germans had greater numbers in an engagement, notably over Malta. It could be done two-versus-one, as shown here, or by a large formation against a small formation. Directly the attack went in, the defenders broke into it, only to have the second aircraft or group on their tail.

Freytag of *I/JG 77* with 25 (final score 102). Herbert Rollwage of *II/JG 53* claimed 20. Rollwage later transferred to home defense, where he became the champion slayer of American heavy bombers with 44 Fortresses and Liberators out of his final total of 102. Only 11 of his victories were gained in Russia.

Desert Song

The campaign in the desert was a war of movement over vast areas of featureless terrain. Advances and retreats of hundreds of miles followed each other with monotonous regularity. While advancing was a sign of success, it stretched supply lines to breaking point, causing shortages of fuel, ammunition, and spares, the lack of which often resulted in a headlong retreat. So often was this the case that the ebb and flow of battle became known to the irreverent British as the "Benghazi Handicap"!

Air operations in desert conditions were not easy. Sand got in everywhere, causing excessive engine wear, even though filters were fitted, which, combined with the ferocious heat,

Table 12. Fighter Data, Western Desert, 1941–42

	Tomahawk II	Kittyhawk III
Wingspan	37ft. 4in.	37ft. 4in.
Length	31ft. 9in.	31ft. 2in.
Height	10ft. 7in.	10ft. 7in.
Wing area	236 sq. ft.	236 sq. ft.
Engine	Allison V-1710-33 rated at 1,040hp	Allison V-1710-81 rated at 1,600hp
Loaded weight	7,459lb.	8,500lb.
Wing loading	32lb./sq. ft.	36lb./sq. ft.
Maximum speed	345mph	362mph
Service ceiling	29,500ft.	30,000ft.
Rate of climb	2,650ft./min.	2,800ft./min.
Range	730 miles	700 miles

materially reduced performance. Frequent sandstorms reduced visibility to nil, making flying impossible. Rather surprisingly, so did rainstorms, which turned airfields to mud. Both sides had mobile radar sets, although the range of these was so short as to result in a heavy reliance on radio monitoring systems for advance warning of enemy air movements.

With few strategic targets available, the majority of air activity by both sides was dedicated to supporting the ground forces. This in turn dictated that the bulk of the air fighting took place at medium and low altitudes. The superior performance of their Messerschmitts generally allowed the *Jagdflieger* to obtain an altitude advantage for their initial attacks.

As previously noted, the British, with their South African and Australian allies, were forced to make do with whatever fighters could be spared from Europe. Spitfires and Hurricanes have been covered previously; the other main fighter type in the theater was the Curtiss P-40. A direct development of the Hawk 75 used by the French in 1939–40, with a liquid-cooled Allison engine, it retained that aircraft's pleasant handling traits. Its main shortcoming was that its engine was not high altitude–rated, and above 20,000ft. the P-40 was totally outclassed by Messerschmitts.

The first *Jagdwaffe* unit in North Africa was *I/JG 27*, which arrived in Libya in April 1941, led by Edu Neumann. By *Experten* standards, Neumann had a very modest personal score, but he was renowned throughout the *Jagdwaffe* as one of the great fighter leaders. In this he paralleled the American Don Blakeslee. In his *Gruppe* was the man who was to become the greatest of them all, Hans-Joachim Marseille—of whom more later.

In order to make the best use of limited resources, *I/JG 27* was allowed a "roving commission," with the object of reducing the enemy's strength, rather than flying in direct support of the Army. With most Hurricane and Tomahawk units doubling in the attack role, it was hardly surprising that the majority of combat was fighter-versus-fighter, although

Blenheim, Boston, and Maryland light bombers were also encountered.

The outnumbered *I/JG 27* was reinforced by the 2nd *Gruppe* in September 1941. The Allied offensive at the end of the year also resulted in *III/JG 53* being deployed from Sicily in December, although this unit was in North Africa only for a matter of days before returning, its place taken by *III/JG 27*. This was in time for Rommel's counterattack, which regained the territory lost in previous weeks. On February 8, 1942, Marseille raised his score to 40 to become top scorer in the desert, a position he never lost, although Gerhard Homüth (final score 63) reached the same figure a day later.

III/JG 53 returned to the desert on May 20. Operations continued at a fast pace. Marseille, who had by then perfected his almost unique style, claimed his 101st victim on June 17 and was ordered home to be decorated. On this same day Otto Schulz went down near Sidi Rezegh, his score of 51 including 42 desert victories.

Marseille returned to Africa late in August and was at once caught up in a flurry of action. In the final five weeks of his life he accounted for a further 57 Allied aircraft, including a well-publicized 17 on September 1 alone. This figure was only once exceeded, by Emil "Bully" Lang of *III/JG 54*, who claimed 18 Russian aircraft on one day in December 1943. Marseille was killed on September 30 when his parachute failed to open after his aircraft caught fire. He was the third *Experte* of the *Gruppe* to die that month. Günther Steinhausen (40 victories) had been shot down on September 6 and Hans-Arnold "Fifi" Stahlschmidt (59 victories) on the following day. Demoralized by these losses, *I/JG 27* was transferred to Sicily.

The Second Battle of El Alamein began on October 23, with unrelenting air attacks by the Desert Air Force, by now heavily reinforced with Spitfire Vs. Four days later *I/JG 27* returned to the fray, accompanied by *III/JG 77*, replacing *III/JG 53*. The remaining *Gruppen* of *JG 77*, now led by *Kommodore* Joachim Müncheberg, followed shortly afterward. But now the

Axis retreat was irreversible, and defeat only a matter of time.
The remnants of *JG 27* were withdrawn completely.

"Torch"

The Allied invasion of French North Africa signaled the end.
As usual the *Jagdwaffe* was used as a fire brigade and rushed
to the scene of the latest conflagration. First to arrive in Tunisia
was *II/JG 51*, followed by *II/JG 2* with FW 190As. A few
fighter-bomber FW 190As had been used in the theater previously, but this was the first fighter unit equipped with the type.

The Axis forces were caught between the jaws of a vise and
were gradually compressed into Tunisia. In the air they were
not only totally outnumbered but had to face new types of
Allied fighters—Mustangs, Lightnings, and Spitfire IXs.
Gradually they were ground down. But a heavy price was paid.
On March 23, 1943, Joachim Müncheberg shot down a Spitfire. It was his 135th and last victory. A devotee of close-range
firing, he apparently collided with his victim. In May Axis
resistance collapsed. *JG 77*, now under the command of
Eastern Front *Experte* Johannes Steinhoff, were evacuated to
Sicily with their mechanics stuffed into the fuselages of their
aircraft. It was the end of an era.

The *Experten*

By comparison with the Russian Front, the scores of the
Experten over Malta and North Africa were, with one notable
exception, modest. The exception was of course Hans-Joachim
Marseille, the "Star of Africa." Once he began to demonstrate
the art of the possible, he naturally had his imitators, but even
the most gifted of them failed to match his final score, the
highest ever against Western-flown aircraft.

HANS-JOACHIM MARSEILLE "Jochen" Marseille arrived
in North Africa with seven victories to his credit, all British
fighters, and with a debit account of having been shot down
four times. His *Staffelkapitän* during the Battle of Britain,
Johannes Steinhoff, had him transferred out of *4/JG 52* for

insubordination. His next unit was *I/JG 27*, where his new *Kommandeur*, Edu Neumann, recognized his potential and took a lenient view of his failings. This posting eventually sent him to North Africa and ensured him a place in the pantheon of *Experten*. Such are the quirks of fate.

Marseille left no firsthand accounts of his actions. However, many witnesses of his flying and shooting skills survived the war, and from their recollections it is possible to piece together a fairly comprehensive picture of his methods. From an early stage Marseille was an outstanding aerobatic pilot. While aerobatics as such can have no place in the combat repertoire of a fighter pilot, they do improve his confidence and his familiarity with his machine, enabling him to function effectively no matter what altitude he finds himself in.

Marseille made an unimpressive start in the desert: within days of his arrival he was shot down by a Hurricane flown by a Free French pilot. But gradually he found his feet. The clear skies and unlimited visibility of the desert made the surprise bounce difficult to achieve. Most attacks ended in a swirling dogfight at medium and low level in which the favored no-deflection shot from astern could rarely be attained. Marseille reasoned that, to be successful, he had to be able to shoot from any angle. He began to practice dummy attacks on his comrades, seeking snap-shooting opportunities. Standard *Jagdwaffe* procedure in combat was to use full throttle all the time in order to make oneself a difficult target, and quickly to regain speed bled off in hard maneuvering. Here again Marseille was unorthodox. Often he not only throttled right back in order to gain an attacking position, but lowered his flaps to decrease his radius of turn.

Gradually his feel for the game grew, and he started to put his theories into practice. One of the great difficulties in deflection shooting is to judge how far to lead the target in order to hit it. He finally developed a technique in which he closed to very short range, then opened fire at the moment the target disappeared beneath the nose of his Messerschmitt. With experience, he perfected his methods and his score climbed. He reached 50 on February 22, 1942 (43 in forty weeks); 75 on

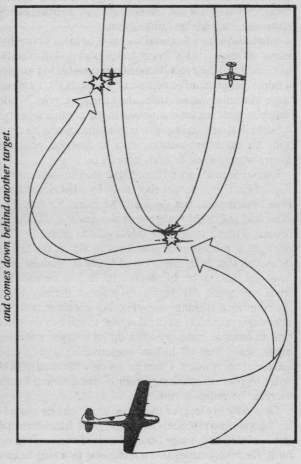

Fig. 18. Marseille Against the Defensive Circle, North Africa

Marseille dives below the circle, then comes up and under, opening fire from very close range as his target vanishes beneath his nose. He then continues his climb, rolls inverted, and comes down behind another target.

(left) Gerd Schöpfel (40 victories), who twice succeeded Adolf Galland, first as *Kommandeur* of *III/JG 26* in August 1940 and then as *Kommodore* in December 1941.

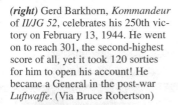

(right) Gerd Barkhorn, *Kommandeur* of *II/JG 52*, celebrates his 250th victory on February 13, 1944. He went on to reach 301, the second-highest score of all, yet it took 120 sorties for him to open his account! He became a General in the post-war *Luftwaffe*. (Via Bruce Robertson)

(below left) Hermann Graf (212 victories) was one of the fastest scorers in the early years of the Russian Front. On October 2, 1942, he became the first pilot to achieve 200 victories. Returned to home defense in 1943, he was less successful, with only ten victories against the West. (Via Bruce Robertson)
(below center) Günther Rall was the third-highest scorer of the war with 275. Arguably the best marksman in the *Jagdwaffe*, he reached 250 on November 28, 1942, the second man to do so. Injuries kept him away from the front for long periods. Like Barkhorn, he became a General post-war. (Via Bruce Robertson)
(below right) Kurt Bühligen spent the entire war with *JG 2 Richthofen*, and rose to become its last *Kommodore*. All his 112 victories were scored against the West, 40 of them in Tunisia. In more than 700 sorties he was shot down only three times.

June 5 (25 in fifteen weeks); then 101 on June 18 (26 in thirteen days), this rapidly accelerating progress demonstrating his improved prowess.

At this time, if Allied fighters and particularly fighter-bombers were caught at a tactical disadvantage, they went into a defensive circle for mutual protection, as had Bf 110s in the Battle of Britain. The usual approaches from astern left the attacker vulnerable to the guns of the next fighter in the circle, while few were sufficiently adept to get results with full deflection shots from above. Marseille's approach to the problem was typically unorthodox: a short dive to gain speed, then up and under from outside the circle, using the blind spot under the adversary's wing; close to 150 feet, a brief burst of fire, then up and away, using the accumulated speed of the dive to soar high above the circle; down again once more on the outside of the circle but this time coming from above at a moderate deflection angle of perhaps 30 degrees; ease the stick back, then, as the target disappears beneath the nose, a brief burst of fire, then up and outward once more, or maybe down and outward, ready for another climbing attack (Fig. 18). So swift and certain were these assaults that often more than one victim was going down at a time. Marseille's wingman did not attempt to follow him through these evolutions but stayed high, keeping a lookout, ready to intervene if it became necessary. It was also his task to count and record the times of the crashes.

As with most air combat techniques, the method was simple. Only the execution, the incredibly precise timing, the judgment of distance, and the accurate aiming necessary were difficult. Using these methods, Marseille accounted for six Tomahawks of No. 5 Squadron SAAF in just eleven minutes on June 6, 1942. The rest of his *Staffel* achieved virtually nothing. Marseille's marksmanship also rates a mention. Combat reports analyzed in Berlin showed that, at the height of his powers, he expended an average of fifteen shells and bullets per victory. More than one wingman has described the first shells hitting the nose of the enemy aircraft, then "walking" back to the

cockpit area. His final total of 158 included 151 in the desert—
101 P-40s, 30 Hurricanes, sixteen Spitfires, and four twin-
engine bombers.

JOACHIM MÜNCHEBERG Müncheberg started the war
with *7/JG 26* and his first victory, a Blenheim, came on
November 7, 1939. On his arrival in the Mediterranean in February 1941 his score was 23. When he departed four months
later, after seeing action over Malta, the Balkans, and North
Africa, it had risen to 48. His penchant for fast diving attacks
with hard pull-outs stood him in good stead over Malta, where
frequent haze limited visibility and aided surprise bounces.
Returned to the Channel coast, he soon converted to the FW
190A and brought his total up to 83. At this point he was transferred to the Eastern Front. Over the course of eight weeks he
accounted for 33 Russians but was himself shot down three
times. In October 1942 he became *Kommodore* of *JG 77* and
led it to Tunisia, where he claimed another 19 victories against
appalling odds. Müncheberg's final total of 135 included 102
against Western-flown aircraft, making him the equal-fifth-
ranking ace in the West. Of these, 43 were scored over Malta
and North Africa. He appears to have been unique in that he
took part in all three Mediterranean subcampaigns.

WERNER SCHROER The second-highest scorer in North
Africa was Werner Schroer, with 61 victories. A combat debu-
tante in the Battle of Britain, and a member of *I/JG 27* when
that unit arrived in the desert in 1941, he was made a *Staffelkapitän* in *II/JG 27* at about the same time as Marseille.
Impressed by the latter's success, Schroer became one of Marseille's tactical imitators. In fact, in some ways he exceeded the
master: although for various reasons he flew far fewer sorties,
his strike rate was significantly better. In fact, the only
Jagdflieger (as opposed to *Nachtjagdflieger*) to score faster
was Günther Scheel, who flew solely against the Russians.
Schroer equaled Müncheberg's tally against the West,
including 24 four-engine bombers, and knocked down a dozen

(above left) The strain of battle showing clearly on his face, Werner Mölders emerges from the cockpit of his Bf 109. Top scorer in Spain with 14 victories, Mölders had amassed 115 before his death in a flying accident in 1941. (Via Bruce Robertson)

(above right) Mölders boards his Bf 109E in France in 1940. At the time he was *Staffelkapitän* of *8/JG 51*. The side-hinged canopy is clearly seen from this angle. (Via Bruce Robertson)

(above left) Wilhelm Balthasar, center, seen in the closing stages of the Battle of Britain, October 7, 1940. To the left is Spanish veteran Günther "Franzl" Lützow (108 victories), the son of the famous German Admiral and *Kommodore* of *JG 3 Udet*. He flew throughout the war but went missing while flying an Me 262 on April 24, 1945. To the right is Egon von Troha, *Staffelkapitän* of *9/JG 3*, who was shot down over Kent on October 29, 1940, and taken prisoner.

(above right) Helmut Wick, *Kommodore* of *JG 2*, center: "I want to fight and die fighting, taking with me as many of the enemy as possible." He paid for his hubris over the English Channel on November 28, 1940, his score 56. On the right of the picture are budding *Experten* Rudi Pflanz (52 victories), shot down by Spitfires near Abbeville on July 31, 1942, and Erich Leie (118 victories), killed in a collision with a Yak-9 on March 7, 1945.

(left) Gerd Schöpfel (40 victories), who twice succeeded Adolf Galland, first as *Kommandeur* of *III/JG 26* in August 1940 and then as *Kommodore* in December 1941.

(right) Gerd Barkhorn, *Kommandeur* of *II/JG 52*, celebrates his 250th victory on February 13, 1944. He went on to reach 301, the second-highest score of all, yet it took 120 sorties for him to open his account! He became a General in the post-war *Luftwaffe*. (Via Bruce Robertson)

(below left) Hermann Graf (212 victories) was one of the fastest scorers in the early years of the Russian Front. On October 2, 1942, he became the first pilot to achieve 200 victories. Returned to home defense in 1943, he was less successful, with only ten victories against the West. (Via Bruce Robertson)
(below center) Günther Rall was the third-highest scorer of the war with 275. Arguably the best marksman in the *Jagdwaffe*, he reached 250 on November 28, 1942, the second man to do so. Injuries kept him away from the front for long periods. Like Barkhorn, he became a General post-war. (Via Bruce Robertson)
(below right) Kurt Bühligen spent the entire war with *JG 2 Richthofen*, and rose to become its last *Kommodore*. All his 112 victories were scored against the West, 40 of them in Tunisia. In more than 700 sorties he was shot down only three times.

(above left) Adolf Galland, *General der Jagdflieger* and, in the opinion of many, the greatest fighter pilot of the war, with a tremendous grasp of tactical problems. Like Montgomery, he combined the common touch with a flair for showmanship, of which his idiosyncratic high-buttoned tunic collar was but one manifestation. (Via Bruce Robertson)

(above center) Spanish veteran Walter "Gulle" Oesau (123 victories) was the third pilot to reach 100 victories (on October 26, 1941). After a brief spell on the Eastern Front, he returned to the West to lead *JG 2*, then *JG 1*. He was shot down by Lightnings on May 11, 1944.

(above right) Haggard with fatigue, "Jochen" Marseille looks at least ten years older than his 22 summers. He was a brilliant aircraft handler and his 158 victories were all against Western-flown machines, 151 of them in the desert. On September 30, 1942, the engine of his Bf 109G caught fire. Marseille bailed out but his parachute failed to open. (Via Bruce Robertson)

(above left) Joachim Müncheberg, right, flew with *JG 26* and *JG 51* before becoming *Kommodore* of *JG 77* in Tunisia, where he was shot down and killed on March 23, 1943. Only 33 of his 135 victories were on the Eastern Front, and he was a major ace over Malta.

(above right) Helmut Lent commenced the war as a *Zerstörer* pilot with *I/ZG 76*, with whom he gained eight victories by day. He then turned to night fighting, claiming his first victim on May 12, 1941. A steady rather than spectacular scorer, he reached 100 on June 15/16, 1944. On October 5 of that year, he was killed in a landing accident in daylight, his total 110.

(above left) Walther Dahl scored heavily on the Eastern Front before being transferred to home air defense as *Kommodore* of one of the new *Gefechtsverbände*. This view shows armor plating added to the roof of his cockpit canopy for extra protection. Of his 128 victories, 77 came in the East, while, of the rest, 36 were American heavy bombers.

(above center) Pioneer night fighter Ludwig Becker returns from a sortie. He persevered with tight ground control, then later with airborne radar, and it was largely due to his efforts that the latter was accepted. His life was squandered in a daylight mission against the U.S. "heavies" on February 26, 1943, his score at night 46.

(above right) Heinz Knoke pioneered air-to-air bombing. His 44 victories were all against the West and included 19 heavy bombers. To evade escort fighters, the climbing spiral was his preferred maneuver. Late in 1944 he was badly injured when his car struck a mine. He never returned to combat.

(above left) The doyen of night fighters was Heinz-Wolfgang Schnaufer with 121 victories, who developed an uncanny "feel" for the presence of the enemy. His usual method was to head for where the radar jamming was heaviest, there to search visually. Between 20 and 30 of his attacks were made with *Schräge Musik*, the remainder with forward-firing armament. Schnaufer survived the war, only to die in a car crash in July 1950.

(above right) The *Führer*, disrespectfully known to the *Jagdwaffe* in the later stages of the war as the *"Gröfaz"* (*Grösster Feldherr aller Zeiten*— Greatest Military Commander of All Time), seen here with Goering, presents the Oak Leaves to the Knight's Cross. Left to right: Alfred Grislawski (133 victories, 109 in the East); Emil "Bully" Lang (173 victories, 148 in the East), shot down by Thunderbolts on September 3, 1944; Günther Schack (174 victories, all in the East); Otto Kittel (267 victories in the East), the fourth-highest scorer but killed in combat with Il-2s on February 14, 1945; and Anton Hafner (204 victories, 20 in the West), who hit a tree during combat with a Yak-9 on October 17, 1944. (Via Bruce Robertson)

(above left) Heinrich, *Prinz* zu Sayn-Wittgenstein was one of the great characters of the *Nachtjagdflieger*. Starting the war as a bomber pilot, he transferred to night fighters in August 1941. His first 29 victories were in the East. Later in the war he developed strong anti-Nazi feelings but fought compulsively on to defend his country. His score at 83, he was shot down by a Mosquito on January 21, 1944.

(above center) Walter Nowotny was the top-scoring Austrian pilot of the war with 258 victories, all but three in the East. His first victories came on July 19, 1941, and the 250th on October 14, 1943. After several months commanding a fighter school he returned to operations with the Me 262 and was killed in a battle with Mustangs in November 1944. (Via Bruce Robertson)

(above right) *Experten* of *JG 26*. On the left is *Kommodore* Josef "Pips" Priller, just 5ft. 4in. tall but with 101 victories, all in the West. Of these, 85 were fighters, eleven were four-engine bombers, and five were twin-engine bombers. To the right is Adolf "Addi" Glunz (71 victories, 68 in the West, including 20 four-engine bombers and three Mosquitos). In 574 sorties Glunz was never shot down or wounded. (Via Bruce Robertson)

(below left) Erich "Bubi" Hartmann of *JG 52*, the highest-scoring fighter pilot of all time. His 352 victories were achieved between October 1942 and the last day of the war, during which time he flew more than 1,350 sorties apparently without experiencing combat fatigue. After the war he became a Colonel in the new *Luftwaffe*. (Via Bruce Robertson)

(below center) Johannes "Macky" Steinhoff, seen here as a young *Leutnant* in 1939. Of his 176 victories, 148 were scored in the East. In the final weeks of the war he became an ace with the Me 262. Badly burned in a takeoff accident in the jet in April 1945, he survived to command the new *Luftwaffe* post-war. (Via Bruce Robertson)

(below right) Heinz "Pritzl" Baer, one of the few "first-to-last" *Experten*. His score of 220 was fairly evenly divided over all fronts, which puts him among the all-time greats. The top-scoring NCO pilot in the Battle of Britain, he ended as the top-scoring jet ace of the war. Ironically, he was killed in a light aircraft crash in April 1957. (Via Bruce Robertson)

Many different models of the Messerschmitt Bf 109 saw action. This is the Bf 109B, first used in the Spanish Civil War by *J 88*. The next few years saw it progressively upgraded into a far more potent machine. (Via *FlyPast*)

(above) A Bf 109G-4 in Russia, showing the sleeker lines of the cowling. This aircraft was flown by Wolf-Dietrich "Fürst" Wilcke (162 victories) when he was *Kommodore* of *JG 3*. Returned to the West, he was shot down by Mustangs on March 23, 1944. (Via Bruce Robertson)

(below) The Focke-Wulf FW 190A gave British pilots nightmares when it was first introduced. This particular machine is an A-3, flown by Armin Faber of *III/JG 2*, who on June 23, 1943, landed in error in South Wales. (Via *FlyPast*)

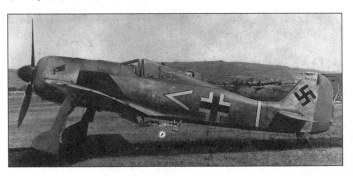

(above) The Messerschmitt Bf 110C *Zerstörer* enjoyed moderate success in Poland but was outclassed by the RAF single-seaters in the Battle of Britain. (Via *FlyPast*)

(below) Numerically the most important *Luftwaffe* night fighter was the Bf 110G, even though the antler-type radar antennae, engine exhaust shrouds, and the need for a third crewman all reduced its performance significantly. (Via *FlyPast*)

(below) The Messerschmitt Me 163 *Komet* rocket fighter. Operational limitations were such that few pilots scored even one victory with the type. (Via *FlyPast*)

The Heinkel 162A *Volksjäger* was another German wonder weapon that did not work out. Although about 275 were completed, the type is believed to have accounted for just one Allied aircraft in the course of the war. (Via *FlyPast*)

(above) The Messerschmitt Me 262 *Schwalbe* was the only successful German jet fighter of the war, but it entered service too late and in too small numbers. (Via *FlyPast*)
(below) The world's first effective jet night fighter was the Me 262B two-seater trainer fitted with radar and with the operator in the backseat. (Via *FlyPast*)

Ghosts! Two ex-*Luftwaffe* aircraft seen at the Champlin Fighter Museum some fifty years on. Nearest the camera is a FW 190D; farthest is a Bf 109E. (Via *FlyPast*)

Russians toward the end of the war for a grand total of 114 victories, achieved in the amazingly low number of 197 sorties. And, unlike so many others, he survived the war, his final command being *Kommodore* of *JG 3*. The little-known Werner Schroer must be rated one of the greatest of all the *Experten*.

6. THE NIGHT AIR WAR, 1940–42

Johannes Steinhoff started the war as *Staffelkapitän* of the specialized night-flying *10/JG 26* based at Jever. The *Staffel* was equipped with single-engine Bf 109Ds from which the canopy had been removed, first to eliminate annoying reflections from the cockpit instruments and second to reduce searchlight dazzle. The pilots had received little training in instrument flying, and the aircraft had no effective navigational aids.

British and French aircraft carried out leaflet raids in the first weeks of the war, and although Steinhoff's men were ordered to intercept, success eluded them. Even if ground control knew the position of an intruder, the information was of little value to a fighter pilot who was only vaguely aware of his own position. And even if he could have been brought close, near-perfect visibility was needed to gain visual contact.

Late in September, Steinhoff was ordered to Berlin to attend a conference on night fighting. That the *Luftwaffe* High Command had little idea of current conditions became apparent when *Reichsmarschall* Goering in person treated the assembly to a diatribe on how things were in France in 1918. Steinhoff later recalled:

> He enthused about flying in bright moonlight, about the stalking missions they flew along the roads of Flanders so as to spot the enemy's silhouette against the paler night sky overhead, how they had then increased speed and commenced the attack from below . . .

The young officer tried to explain that conditions were now different, that the British flew at much higher altitudes from which landmarks on the ground could not be seen and that the cloudy autumn skies over northern Germany were a far cry from Flanders in summer. What was needed were new methods of location and tracking, and better navigational aids to enable operations to be carried out in bad weather. Goering's reaction was a foretaste of what was in store for the entire *Jagdwaffe* in the coming years: "Sit down on your little bottom [possibly a less polite anatomical term was used], young man. You've still a long way to go before you can join in the discussion here."

It was a classic error. Had Goering used his tremendous influence and undoubted energy to further the night-fighting program at this stage, the course of the night air war might conceivably have been altered. But nothing was done at the time, and the British went on to establish a commanding lead in airborne radar and countermeasures which they were never to lose, despite the best efforts of the *Luftwaffe*. Shortly afterward, Steinhoff, unhappy with his lot, transferred to day fighters.

With the invasion of France, the RAF commenced bombing raids against mainland German targets. The new radar-laid gun defenses proved less competent than predicted, and the handful of night-flying Bf 109Ds were ineffective. Something better was needed, both aircraft and detection and reporting system, and urgently.

The choice of a new night fighter fell by default on the Bf 110. It was fast enough to overhaul the British bombers in an extended chase, it was relatively heavily armed, and its endurance was adequate. It was large enough to accommodate the extra systems required without undue problems, and its benign handling made it well suited to night operations. Best of all, it carried a radio operator/gunner who could assist with navigation.

The greatest difficulty with night fighting is finding the target—"like trying to catch flies in a dark room," as the early

Nachtjagdflieger succinctly put it. The best hope seemed to be to work in conjunction with searchlight batteries, attacking bombers that were illuminated by the latter. This was undesirable for several reasons. Most searchlights were concentrated around industrial areas, which meant that interceptions could only be made when the bombers were already over the target. Then, even if a bomber was caught by searchlights, it remained invisible from above. The night fighter pilot could only see it if he was at a lower altitude and looking up. This meant that he could only pursue in a climb, which reduced his speed advantage. Over defended zones, the fighters were frequently dazzled by the searchlights and shot at by "friendly" flak. Finally, concentrations of searchlights often gave away the position of worthwhile targets to the bombers.

The next step was to shift the searchlights away from industrial areas and establish a continuous belt of lights and sound locators on the approaches to Germany. Night fighters then patrolled the edges of the belt, ready to pursue any bomber unfortunate enough to be caught in the beams. This was an improvement, but it was still not very productive. If there was more than five-tenths cloud cover the searchlights were ineffective, and clearer conditions than this were rare over northern Europe. Furthermore, when the bombers reached the beginning of the fourteen-mile-wide illuminated area, they opened the throttles and sped across it as fast as possible, reducing the time available for the night fighter to engage to a maximum of three minutes. Unless a fighter was ideally placed at the first sighting, this was insufficient.

There were, however, a few successes. Werner Streib of the newly formed *I/NJG 1* scored his first night victory on July 20, 1940, without the aid of searchlights. Quite by chance he spotted an indistinct shape about 900 feet ahead and off to starboard. It looked like another Bf 110. Fearing a tragedy, Streib crept up until he was almost wingtip to wingtip. Only at this range could he identify it as a Whitley bomber. He swung away, carefully so as not to lose contact, then made a quartering attack from astern. Two brief bursts of fire, ineffectually answered by the enemy gunner, set the starboard engine on fire. On the following night he did it again, as did four others, among them the budding *Experten* Walter Ehle (final score 38) and Siegfried Wandam (10). But this promising beginning proved illusory: it was a long time before five more victories were again claimed in a single night.

What was needed was a system that was not dependent on favorable weather conditions. This meant a comprehensive radar detection, tracking, and reporting system, allied to close ground control. This did not yet exist, and it would take time to set up and become operational.

Intruders

There was, however, an alternative. British bombers could always be found over their own bases, and intruder missions, if they caused enough casualties, could disrupt raids on the Third Reich. Ideally an intruder needed the endurance to loiter over Britain for extended periods while looking for trade, it needed a heavy gun armament for air-to-air encounters, and it should also carry a small bomb load with which to attack the airfields themselves. The Bf 110 lacked the necessary endurance, nor did it have provision for an internal bomb load.

A ready-made alternative was to hand. A bomber unit based in Norway rather unusually contained a single *Zerstörer Staffel*. It was equipped with the Junkers Ju 88C-2, which differed from the bomber variant in having a "solid" nose fitted with a single 20mm MG FF cannon and three 7.9mm machine guns. Redesignated *4/NJG 1*, this unit was transferred to Germany in July 1940, where it was joined by *5/NJG 1*, equipped with the solid-nosed Dornier Do 17Z-10, and the newly formed *6/NJG 1*, which also flew Ju 88C-2s, to become *II/NJG 1*. As the idea of a complete intruder *Geschwader* gained ground, it was redesignated *I/NJG 2*.

Intruder operations began in August 1940. A German airborne radar was still far in the future, although the Dorniers were fitted with an infrared searchlight. As the range of this device was a mere 650 feet, it was as good as useless. Consequently the German night fighters were reliant on visual contact. Over England this was not as hopeless as it was in the cloud-laden skies of Germany. Airfield flarepaths would act as a magnet for them; returning bomber crews would be tired and off guard, and on many occasions they burned their navigation lights as a guard against collision with friendly aircraft.

The first sorties were largely a test of the British defenses, but the *Nachtjagdflieger* soon gained confidence enough to prowl across East Anglia, the Midlands, and northern England. Eighteen victory claims were submitted during the remainder of 1940, although RAF records appear to indicate that some of these were a trifle optimistic. The price was high. One aircraft was shot down and another damaged by British night fighters, one fell to ground defenses, six were lost in crashes (some of them on training flights), and four simply went missing. Yet others sustained varying degrees of damage.

Things improved in 1941, when a total of 123 claims was made by mid-October, for losses of 28. Radar-equipped British night fighters accounted for seven of these, while another two are believed to have been "own goals," shot down by "friendly" intruders. Two collided with their targets, one was downed by return fire from a bomber, ten crashed for various reasons, and six went missing without trace.

One of the more successful intruder pilots was Heinz Sommer, who was credited with ten victories in the role. In the small hours of April 30, 1941, he was patrolling over East Anglia when

I saw an English aircraft fire recognition signals and flew toward it where I found an airfield, illuminated and very active. I joined the airfield's circuit at between 200 and 300 meters [altitude] at 00:15 hours and after several circuits an aircraft came within range. I closed to between 100 and 150 meters and fired. After a short burst the aircraft exploded in the air and fell to the ground. At 00:20 hours I saw another aircraft landing with its lights on which I attacked from behind and above at roughly 80 meters. The aircraft crashed after my burst of fire and caught fire on hitting the ground. In the light of the flames from the two wrecks, I could see fifteen to twenty aircraft parked on the airfield. I dropped my bombs on these. . . .

Sommer went on to attain a final score of 19 before his death in action on February 11, 1944. Victories were not always this easy: intruders in the vicinity were usually the signal for all lights to be switched off, while the radar-equipped Beaufighters of the RAF made life increasingly hazardous. Nor, it must be admitted, did intruder activity ever reach the stage where it reduced the level of intensity of British raids on Germany. British records show that, during 1941, 86 aircraft were known to have been attacked by intruders (many others were lost to unknown causes). Of these, slightly less than half were bombers from operational squadrons, two-fifths were trainers, and the rest were fighters. Given this proportion, it would have been strange indeed if RAF bombing had been affected.

A few pilots were outstandingly successful in the intruder role. When in November 1941 operations ceased, Wilhelm Beier had accounted for 14 aircraft and Hans Hahn and Alfons Köster 11 each. Beier's specialty was following returning bombers over the North Sea, and all his combats took place near the English coast. Two fighters, a Hurricane and a Defiant, were among his victims. He survived the war with a total of 36 victories. Hahn was killed on October 11, 1941, when he collided with his twelfth and final victim. Köster died when he crashed in fog on January 7, 1945, having accounted for 29 aircraft. Of the others, Heinz Strüning was shot down by an RAF night fighter on Christmas Eve 1944, his score 56, and Paul Semrau fell to Spitfires at Twente on February 8, 1945, with 46 victories to his credit.

Table 13. Reich Night Defense Fighter Units, 1942

Unit	Base	Aircraft Type	*Kommandeur*
I/NJG 1	St. Truiden	As *I/NJG 1*	As I/NJG 1
I/NJG 1	Venlo/Hangelar	Do 215B, Bf 110C/F	Werner Streib
II/NJG 1	Stade	Do 17Z, Do 217J, Bf 110C/F	Walter Ehle
III/NJG 1	Deelen/Twente	Bf 110C/F	Wolfgang Thimmig
5/NJG 2	Wittmundhaven	As *II/NJG 2*	As II/NJG 2
II/NJG 2	Leeuwarden	Do 17Z, Do 215B, Do 217J, Ju 88C, Bf 110C/F	Helmut Lent
I/NJG 3	Vechta	Do 217J, Bf 110C/F	Egmont zur Lippe-Weissenfeld
3/NJG 3	Werneuchen	As *I/NJG 3*	As I/NJG 3
II/NJG 3	Mainz-Finthen	Ju 88C, Bf 110C/F	Günther Radusch
5/NJG 3	Schleswig	As *II/NJG 3*	As II/NJG 3
7/NJG 3	Lüneberg	Ju 88C, Bf 110C/F	Heinz Nacke

The Defense of the Reich

It was always apparent that the night fighter needed outside assistance if it was to find its prey, and that radar, allied to close ground control, was the only feasible method. Speed being of the essence, the *Luftwaffe* used what was readily available. The result was three separate radars to cover a single small area, one for early warning, a second to track the bomber, and a third to track the night fighter. The latter had to be guided to within visual distance of the bomber within seven minutes, the time it took for the bomber to cross the radar zone. This was not too bad on a moonlit night with good visibility, but in poor conditions visual distance was reduced to perhaps 200 feet, making the task close to impossible. There were, however, a few fighter pilots who consistently beat the odds, among them Werner Streib and Ludwig Becker.

The next step was airborne interception radar, the first successful interception with which took place on August 9/10, 1941. It was obviously far easier to direct the fighter to within radar range of its target, perhaps two to three miles, than to the 200–300 meters needed for visual contact. Once in radar contact, the fighter could close to visual distance unaided.

The end of 1941 saw the night *Experten* building up respectable scores. In the lead with 22 was Werner Streib, closely followed by Paul Gildner with 21 and Helmut Lent

Table 14. Night Fighters, 1940–42

	Messerschmitt Bf 110G-4	Dornier Do 217J	Junkers Ju 88C-6c
Wingspan	53ft. 5in.	62ft. 4in.	65ft. 11in.
Length	41ft. 7in.	59ft. 0½in.	47ft. 1in.
Height	13ft. 1in.	16ft. 4in.	16ft. 8in.
Wing Area	413 sq. ft.	614 sq. ft.	587 sq. ft.
Engines	2 × Daimler-Benz DB 605B inlines rated at 1,475hp	2 × BMW 801ML radials rated at 1,580hp	2 × Junkers Jumo 211J radials rated at 1,340hp
Loaded weight	20,723lb.	29,057lb.	27,225lb.
Wing loading	50lb./sq. ft.	47lb./sq. ft.	46lb./sq. ft.
Maximum speed	297mph	264mph	307mph
Service ceiling	26,248ft.	29,530ft.	32,480ft.
Rate of climb	2,165ft./min.	c.1,350ft./min.	1,770ft./min.
Range	491 miles	1,133 miles	645 miles

with 20. In the main their victories had been gained solely with the aid of ground control, aided by the fact that in the summer months the German night sky is always fairly light to the north. An approach from the south of a bomber therefore gave a good chance of a visual sighting.

At this time the British bombers flew singly, with each crew responsible for its own courses and timings. This was the threat that the German night defense system had to counter. The number of radar-controlled night fighter zones was increased, while in February 1942 the first production airborne radar sets reached the operational units. Like their RAF counterparts, the German night fighter crews at first had little time for temperamental "black boxes," but, encouraged by Becker's successes of the previous year, they persevered. Gradually bomber losses rose.

In warfare nothing is ever certain. Just when it appeared that the *Nachtjagdflieger* had taken the measure of their opponent, a change of British tactics reversed the situation. Instead of dozens of bombers operating individually, they were concentrated in time and space. On the night of May 30, 1942, the first "Thousand Bomber Raid" was launched against Cologne. Penetrating on a narrow front, the bombers swamped the few radar zones that they crossed. Only about 25 night fighters could be brought into action, leaving dozens of others sitting helplessly on the ground with no targets. Bomber losses fell. The obvious counter to the bomber stream was a much looser form of fighter control which could feed fighters into it, there to hunt autonomously with their own radars. But this was not done for some time; instead, the defensive zones were deepened and two fighters rather than one were used in each.

By autumn that year all night fighters were equipped with radar. Bomber losses once more started to rise. Among the *Nachtjagdflieger*, Helmut Lent now led the field with 49, outstripping Reinhold Knacke and Ludwig Becker with 40 each. Knacke, a rising star of *I/NJG 1*, had set a record on September 16/17, 1942, with five victories in one night.

Paul Gildner of *II/NJG 1* and Prince Egmont zur Lippe-Weissenfeld of *5/NJG 2* were equal fourth with 38 apiece.

The Aircraft

At the start of the night offensive against Germany, the RAF deployed three main types of twin-engine bomber, the Hampden, the Whitley, and the Wellington. The first two were phased out during 1942 in favor of the new breed of four-engine bombers, the Stirling and the Halifax in the first half of 1941 and the Lancaster in March 1942. All except the Hampden were heavily armed against attack from the rear by a powered gun turret fitted with four 0.303in.-caliber Brownings, while the four-engine types also featured a twin-gun dorsal turret. While the hitting power of the Browning was not very great, it still made a stern attack hazardous for the *Nachtjagdflieger*.

As noted, the main *Luftwaffe* night fighter of this period was the Bf 110. The first variant produced specifically for night fighting was the F-4, which had a position for a third crew member to work the radar and was powered by two DB 601E engines rated at 1,300hp. The main night fighter variant was the Bf 110G, which was introduced late in 1942. It was armed with two 20mm MG 151 cannon and four MG 17 machine guns, plus a swiveling gun in the rear cockpit. Despite greater available power, increasing weight allied to the drag of the bristling radar aerials reduced performance considerably. The Junkers Ju 88 started life as a high-speed bomber but, as related, was quickly adapted for the night role. It was not as docile and was less maneuverable than the Bf 110, but its performance made it well suited to night fighting. The Dornier Do 17Z-10 was quickly replaced by the more potent Do 215B-5, but only a few of these were produced. The final Dornier variant was the Do 217J, which entered service in the early summer of 1942, but this was overweight and its performance was poor. It was phased out in 1943.

The *Experten*

The demands of night fighting were very different from those of the day battle. Patience and perseverance were the keynotes, allied to superior blind flying and navigational skills. In the early years, the weather was the main enemy. Ice and fog accounted for more night fighters than the RAF gunners, while frustration at the lack of results was undoubtedly a cause of many accidents.

Successful night interceptions were primarily the result of teamwork. Skillful ground control could position a fighter very close to a bomber on the darkest night, but only if the pilot displayed equal skill in following instructions. With the advent of airborne radar, it became a matter of teamwork between the pilot and his operator. The ability of the latter to interpret where the bomber was—and, even more important, what it was doing—from small blips of light on two or even three cathode ray tubes was vital. Mutual trust was essential. The radars of the day had a rather long minimum range, and often contact was lost before a visual sighting became possible. The pilot then had to keep closing, in the full knowledge that the target was somewhere close ahead, and the slightest misjudgment could result in a midair collision. Successful night fighting demanded not only a first-class pilot, but a first-class radar operator also.

HELMUT LENT Like many other *Nachtjagdflieger*, Helmut Lent commenced the war as a *Zerstörer* pilot. Flying with *I/ZG 76*, he shot down a Polish fighter on the second day of the war, two British Wellingtons over the German Bight in December 1939 and a Norwegian Gladiator over Oslo-Fornebu in April 1940. With a score of eight victories by day, he was posted as *Staffelkapitän* of *6/NJG 1* in January 1941.

By April several of his pilots had scored, but Lent had flown two dozen fruitless sorties. Disturbed by his failure to find the bombers at night, he requested a transfer back to day fighters. He was persuaded to give it another try, and on his 35th sortie on May 12/13, he accounted for two Wellingtons. Having discovered the secret, his score mounted swiftly. On January 8, 1943, he accounted for a Halifax, to become the first *Nachtjagdflieger* to reach 50. On April 20/21, 1943, he was the first night flyer to shoot down a Mosquito, and he topped the 100 mark by destroying three Lancasters on June 15/16, 1944. It was not without cost: he was wounded on three occasions. Helmut Lent was killed in a landing accident at Paderborn on October 5, 1944, his total score 110, of which 102 were at night.

LUDWIG BECKER A pioneer night fighter with *II/NJG 1*, Becker contributed a great deal to *Nachtjagdflieger* tactics in the early days. He it was who scored the first ground-assisted night victory on October 16, 1940. Flying a Dornier Do 17Z-10, he reported:

> I was well positioned at the correct altitude of 3,300m . . . and directed on to the enemy by means of continual corrections. Suddenly I saw an aircraft in the moonlight, about 100m above and to the left; on moving closer I made it out to be a Vickers Wellington. Slowly I closed in from behind, and aimed a burst of 5–6 seconds' duration at the fuselage and wing root. The right motor caught fire immediately, and I pulled my machine up. For a while the Englishman flew on, losing height rapidly. The fire died away but then I saw him spin toward the ground, and burst into flames on crashing.

Becker had been lucky. In bright moonlight he had closed to a range of about 50 meters before opening fire without being spotted. It would not always be so easy. Two hours later *Unteroffizier* Fick of the same unit was guided to another Wellington, only to open fire at too long a range. Thus warned, the bomber escaped.

Becker also carried out the first German interception using airborne radar. On the night of August 9/10, 1941, he eased his

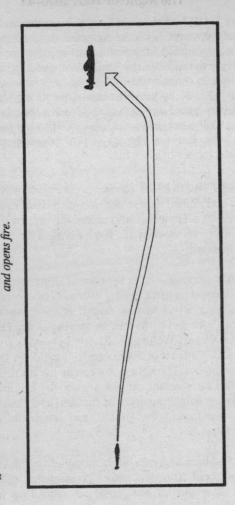

Fig. 19. Ludwig Becker's Night Stalk

Directed by ground radar, Becker closes in on the bomber, slightly lower to silhouette it against the sky. He then gains speed in a shallow dive to bring him within range quickly. Having leveled off and matched his speed to that of the bomber, he eases up into position, then pulls his nose up and opens fire.

Dornier Do 215 off the runway at Leeuwarden and climbed to his patrol position. Soon the controller directed him toward a contact. After a certain amount of jockeying for position, radar operator Josef Staub obtained a contact about 6,500ft. away and carefully steered his pilot toward it. Twice evasive action by the bomber broke the radar contact, which was only regained by a hard turn in the direction that the target had vanished. Finally Becker and Staub closed to visual range and opened fire. Between August 12 and September 30 Becker claimed a further five bombers.

During this time Becker developed a specific method of attack which he passed on to other *Nachtjagdflieger*. On gaining radar contact, he closed on his quarry from a slightly lower altitude until he gained visual contact. In this way his fighter was masked against the dark ground below, while the bomber was limned against the lighter sky. Provided nose-to-tail separation distance at visual contact range permitted, he then pushed his nose down and accelerated in a slight dive to close the horizontal separation quickly. This reduced the chance of being spotted by the enemy rear gunner. Having attained a suitable position behind and below, Becker then leveled off and decelerated to match his speed to that of the bomber. Easing up until he was barely 150 feet lower, he then pulled the nose up, on which his fighter mushed and lost speed, and, as he fired, the bomber was raked from nose to tail by a hail of shells. See Fig. 19.

Effective though this method was, it was not foolproof. On very dark nights visual contact could only be gained at ranges too close to use the "up and under" approach. In this case, all that could be done was to come in from astern and hope that the British rear gunner was not ready and waiting. But even the "up and under" method had its problems. It demanded a very high level of piloting skill to get into exactly the right attack position, and few *Nachtjagdflieger* were good enough to do it consistently—and even if they were, it was a hazardous procedure. If the bomb load was hit and detonated, the night fighter stood little chance of surviving the ensuing explosion. On the other hand, if the bomber suffered catastrophic damage from the first burst, the attacker was hard-pressed to stand from under as it fell from the sky. Many *Nachtjagdflieger* died when they collided with their stricken victim.

Ludwig Becker, not to be confused with the later *Experte* Martin Becker (58 victories from September 1943), was needlessly lost in daylight, intercepting a formation of USAAF heavy bombers over the North Sea on February 26, 1943. With him went Staub, who had shared in 40 of his 46 night victories.

7. THE YANK HE COMETH, 1943–45

From quite early in the war, RAF Bomber Command had found that daylight raids by unescorted bomber formations generally resulted in prohibitive casualties. Consequently, with one or two notable exceptions, deep penetration raids on German targets were made at night. The inherent inaccuracy of night bombing limited its effectiveness and was wasteful of resources, but, as it was the only means available of hindering German industrial output, these drawbacks were accepted.

By contrast, the USAAF pinned its faith on precision bombing, which could only be carried out in daylight. The American theory was that the cross fire from massed formations of heavily armed bombers would provide an effective defense against fighter attack. Their main heavy bomber type was the Boeing B-17 Flying Fortress, later variants of which carried up to ten 0.50in. machine guns, which packed a heavy weight of fire and were effective out to a range of over 2,000 feet.

The first American heavy bomber units arrived in England in 1942 determined to demonstrate that daylight bombing was a viable proposition. For all that, they were initially cautious, and the first targets selected were in Occupied France. The onus of finding the best method of tackling the four-engine giants thus fell upon the two resident units, *JG 2* and *JG 26*.

The great size of the B-17 (it had a wingspan of nearly 104ft.) caused problems in judging distance, both horizontally and vertically. On October 9, 1942, Josef "Pips" Priller led *III/JG 26* against a bomber formation. Three times he misjudged the aircraft's height and had to back off and climb once more until at last he pulled up level with them. Once there, he led his unit into a standard attack from astern, but his pilots had the greatest difficulty assessing range. Otto Stammberger of the same unit recalled the difficulties:

> We attacked the enemy bombers in pairs, going in with great bravado: closing in fast from behind with throttles wide open, then letting fly. But at first the attacks were all broken off much too early—as those great "barns" grew larger and larger our people were afraid of colliding with them. I wondered why I had scored no hits but then I considered the size of the things: 40 meters span! [A slight exaggeration.—Author.] The next time I went in I thought: get in much closer, keep going, keep going. Then I opened up, starting with his motors on the port wing. By the third such firing run the two port engines were burning well, and I had shot the starboard outer motor to smithereens. The enemy "kite" went down in wide spiraling left-hand turns, and crashed just east of Vendeville; four or five of the crew bailed out.

Stammberger was shot down by a Spitfire on May 13, 1943, his score at seven, all heavy bombers. He was quoted as saying, "I simply couldn't handle the Spitfires. It might be that I wasn't cut out for turning around, but I am built more for boring straight in!" His injuries were so severe that he never returned to a fighter cockpit.

Farther south, the great naval bases on the Brittany coast frequently received the attentions of the Fortresses. Air defense in this area was the responsibility of *JG 2 "Richthofen."* As many were to find later, the conventional attack from astern was hazardous. Overtaking from behind was a lengthy process during which the attackers were assailed by literally hundreds of heavy machine guns. While the standard of gunnery in the USAAF was not high, the sheer volume of fire was such that many fighters were hit even before they had come within effective firing range.

Egon Mayer, *Kommandeur* of *III/JG 2*, in conjunction with *Staffelkapitän* Georg-Peter Eder, sought a better method—one that would reduce the risks to the *Jagdflieger* but still allow them to bring down heavy bombers. Examination of shot-down aircraft showed that the weakest area of defensive fire was the front. Early models of the B-17 carried a single rifle-caliber machine gun in the nose, but this was rightly regarded as little more than a "scare" weapon. Therefore, Mayer and Eder concluded, the best solution was to attack from head-on (Fig. 20). This had added advantages. First, the high closing speed of a head-on attack reduced the time that the German fighters were under fire to a matter of a few seconds. Second, a head-on attack made the control cabin the main target. With no frontal armor or other protection, this was very vulnerable, and hits in this area were likely to bring success.

The head-on attack was tried for the first time on November 23, when the Fortresses raided St. Nazaire. Another innovation tried at this time, although not retained for long, was for the fighters to fly in *Ketten* of three aircraft to match the American Vics. It was a success: four bombers went down and others were badly damaged.

Mayer and Eder now began to refine their tactics. To be effective, the attack had to be made from exactly head-on. Even a few degrees' difference gave apparent movement to the target, making accurate shooting more difficult and increasing the risk of collision. When the Fortresses were still tiny dots in the distance, it was difficult to judge whether the attack was truly head-on or not; and by the time it became apparent that it was not, it was too late to do anything about it.

To eliminate this, *III/JG 2* met the bombers well forward, and followed them for a short while to determine their exact course and altitude. They then pulled off to one side and accelerated past out of range to a position about two miles ahead. Once there, the fighters turned through 180 degrees, lined up and ran in to attack. The closing speed of about 700 feet per

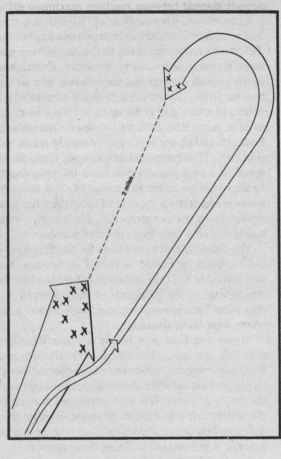

Fig. 20. Against the "Heavies"
Egon Mayer and Georg-Peter Eder of JG 2 developed this method of attacking American heavy bomber formations. Having tailed them to establish exact course, altitude, and speed, they then moved out to a safe distance on one flank and overtook them. Having gained a lead of about two miles, the German fighters turned in for a head-on pass.

2 miles

second meant that the firing pass was very brief: less than two seconds elapsed between reaching maximum effective firing range and having to break to avoid a collision.

Seen through the Revi gun sight, the B-17s at first looked like tiny dots with thin wings as each German pilot selected a victim. The wings slowly grew lumps, which turned into engines. Finally the entire bomber grew, first filling the sight, then spreading across the entire windshield at nightmarish speed (Fig. 21). Only the stoutest could hold on until the last split second before hauling clear. Even then the order of the day was "gently does it." Too hard a pull on the stick caused the fighter to mush off speed, making it an easier target for the air gunners. The technique was to go just over, making sure there was enough clearance to miss the huge fin, or just under. Once past, the fighters kept going flat out until clear of the defensive fire zone before pulling up to reposition.

Once proven, the head-on attack was adopted by the entire *Jagdwaffe* as the best means of tackling the American "heavies." On average it took twenty hits with 20mm shells to bring down a heavy bomber. Given the average standard of *Jagdflieger* marksmanship, this was rarely achieved in a single burst, even though the German fighters, Bf 109s and FW 190s, were later up-gunned. More often, bombers were damaged in the first pass and forced out of formation. Once away from the combined defensive fire of the box, stragglers could be hacked down relatively easily.

Air combat against enemy fighters was widely regarded as an exciting if lethal sport, in which the best pilot won. Attacking the massed daylight bomber formations was a different matter entirely. Shooting apart, there was little opportunity for the exercise of traditional combat skills. In fact, it had much in common with infantry going "over the top." The attacker was under fire all the way, and survival was very much a matter of chance. A fighter pilot could do everything by the book and still get shot down, for no other reason than an American gunner happened to fire in the

Fig. 21. Head-On Against the "Heavies"
Combined closing speeds made attacking heavy bombers from head-on a frightening experience. From top to bottom: Range two miles, time to collision 15 seconds; range one mile, time to collision seven seconds; range 3,000ft., time to collision four seconds; range 1,800ft., time to collision 2.5 seconds, open fire; range 750ft., time to collision one second, stop firing and break!

right direction at the right time. Carrying out what amounted
to a cavalry charge on the bombers was a supreme test of
nerve. Hans Philipp became *Kommodore* of *JG 1* on April
1943, after a very successful spell in the East. He described
it thus:

> To fight against twenty Russians that want to have a bite of
> one, or also against Spitfires, is a joy. And one doesn't know
> that life is not certain. But the curve into seventy Fortresses
> lets all the sins of one's life pass before one's eyes. And
> when one has convinced oneself, it is still more painful to
> force to it every pilot in the wing, down to the last young
> newcomer.

On October 8, 1943, Hans Philipp, victor of 206 combats, 177
of which were in Russia, was shot down and killed by Thunderbolt escort fighters near Nordhorn.

The Defense of the Reich

Emboldened by early success, the American heavy bombers
penetrated German airspace for the first time on January 27,
1943, with a raid on Wilhelmshaven. They were intercepted by
the FW 190As of *JG 1*. Lacking the experience of the Channel
coast *Geschwader*, *JG 1* attacked from astern, only to be dis-
mayed by the amount of return fire. Only three B-17s were shot
down, at the cost of seven fighters.

As American penetrations became ever deeper, Reich
home defense was strengthened, and the *Jagdflieger* gradually took the measure of this new threat. Bomber losses rose,
although not to the point where they became unacceptable.
One thing was quickly evident, however: the armament of
the German fighters was inadequate for the task. Various
expedients were tried to remedy this. Heinz Knoke,
Staffelkapitän of the recently formed *5/JG 11*, hit on the idea
of aerial bombing. A time-fused bomb, released about 3,000
feet above a tightly packed bomber formation, could have a
lethal effect. On March 22, 1943, he tried it for the first time:

I edge forward slowly until I am over the tip of the enemy formation, which consists entirely of Fortresses. For several minutes I am under fire from below, while I take a very rough sort of aim on my target, weaving and dipping each wingtip alternately in order to see the formation below. Two or three holes appear in my left wing.

I fuse the bomb, take final aim, and press the release button on my stick. My bomb goes hurtling down. I watch it fall, and bank steeply as I break away.

Then it explodes, exactly in the center of a row of Fortresses. A wing breaks off one of them, and two others break away in alarm.

The bombing experiment continued for a while, but with limited success. The problems of accurate aiming were simply too great. Aiming was also the Achilles' heel of the 21cm rocket mortar, which could be launched from astern, outside the defensive fire of the bombers. Time-fused, to be effective it had to detonate within 90ft. of a bomber. Not only did range estimation prove intractable, but low all-burnt velocity meant that the weapon needed to be aimed about 200ft. above its target. While some bombers were shot down with this weapon, its main value was as a means of breaking up a bomber formation, thus rendering individual aircraft more vulnerable to conventional attack.

Laden with bombs or rocket mortars, the *Jagdflieger* were extremely vulnerable to escort fighters. As the latter became more numerous and longer-ranged, the use of these weapons was finally abandoned. At first the only Allied escort fighters available were short-legged Spitfires. Then, in April 1943, the first P-47 Thunderbolts made their appearance, closely followed by P-38 Lightnings. The Thunderbolts could barely reach the German border and the usual *Jagdwaffe* ploy was to delay until they turned for home, when a series of conventional attacks could be made. An innovation at this time was the use of shadowing aircraft. These followed the bombers at a distance and radioed back information on force composition, heading, and speed. Ground control then used this to position the *Jagdgruppen* for attack.

On August 17, 1943, the USAAF launched a two-pronged attack on Regensburg and Schweinfurt with 363 heavy bombers in two waves. This was their deepest penetration yet, and it cost them dearly. The *Jagdflieger* flew more than 500 sorties, accounting for the lion's share of the 60 bombers downed and badly damaging many others, losing 25 of their own number in the process. This was a victory for the defenders, even though both targets were bombed. Deep penetration raids were few over the next seven weeks. Then, on October 14, the USAAF returned to Schweinfurt in strength. Once again the *Jagdwaffe* reacted with ferocity, broke up many bomber formations, and inflicted heavy losses. This was the last unescorted deep penetration raid of the war.

With the aid of long-range drop tanks, Thunderbolts were able to extend their operational radius well into Germany. The Lightnings could range even farther afield, while 1944 saw the operational debut of the P-51B Mustang, which could reach Berlin. From this point on the bombers would never fly alone: escort fighters would always be on hand to protect them.

The *Jagdwaffe* was caught on the horns of a dilemma. With the failure of less conventional weapons, it had resorted to adding extra guns to many of its fighters. Heavier calibers were also used, mainly 30mm cannon. Just three hits from this weapon were usually enough to knock down a four-engine bomber, as opposed to the twenty hits needed with 20mm shells. But the extra weight and drag of these cannon, which were often mounted in underwing gondolas, reduced maneuverability and rendered the fighters more vulnerable in combat against American fighters.

The casualty rate was horrific: over 1,000 German fighter pilots were lost in the first four months of 1944. While the vast majority were novices, all too many were irreplaceable veterans. To name but a few, Horst-Günther von Fassong

(136 victories) fell to Thunderbolts on January 1; head-on attack pioneer Egon Mayer (102, of which 24 were heavy bombers), the first to reach 100 victories entirely in Western Europe and known to his opponents as "the man in the white scarf," was shot down by Thunderbolts near the Luxembourg border on March 2; and Emil Bitsch (108) fell to Spitfires over Holland on March 15, Wolfe-Dietrich Wilcke (162) to Mustangs on the 23rd, Josef Zwernemann (126) to Mustangs on April 8, and Kurt Übben (110) to Thunderbolts on April 27. Nor were the bomber gunners idle, accounting for Gerhard Loos (92) and heavy bomber *Experte* Hugo Frey (32, of which 26 were four-engine), both on March 6. It was the shape of things to come.

Gefechtsverband

Raids at this time typically consisted of between 600 and 800 four-engine bombers and a similar number of escort fighters. However, for technical reasons the escorts had to operate in relays. In practice this meant that only a fraction of the escort fighter force was on station at any one time, to protect a bomber stream several miles wide and between 70 and 100 miles long. Consequently the American fighters could not be everywhere, let alone in strength.

General der Jagdflieger Adolf Galland sought to exploit this potential weakness. While the head-on attack gave a reasonable kill-to-loss ratio, it was obvious that far better results could be achieved by the traditional attack from astern, if only this could be done without incurring unacceptable losses. His solution was the *Gefechtsverband*—a large mixed fighter battle formation. The heart of this was the *Sturmgruppe*, which flew the FW 190A-8/R8 *"Sturmbock"* (Battering Ram). This carried two 30mm MK 108 cannon in the outboard wing positions, two 20mm MG 151s in the wing roots and two 12.7mm machine guns in the engine cowling, giving it a very heavy punch. For protection, extra armor was fitted to the engine, cockpit, and gun magazines, with bulletproof glass panels scabbed on to the quarterlights and canopy sides. The other two *Gruppen*, the function of which was to hold off the escort fighters, flew the Bf 109G-10, which was optimized for air combat.

In action the *Sturmgruppe* flew in *Staffeln*, each in arrow-head formation. They closed from astern to a range of 300ft. or less, braving the defensive fire. Walther Hagenah of *IV (Sturm)/JG 3* later recalled:

> During the advance each man picked a bomber and closed on it. As our formation moved forward the American bombers would, of course, let fly at us with everything they had. I can remember the sky being almost alive with tracer. With strict orders to hold our fire until the leader gave the order, we could only grit our teeth and press on ahead. In fact, however, with the extra armor, surprisingly few of our aircraft were knocked down by the bombers' return fire: like the armored knights of the Middle Ages, we were well protected. A *Staffel* might lose one or two aircraft during the advance, but the rest continued relentlessly on.

Meanwhile the function of the two *Begleitengruppen* was to ward off the Allied escorts and allow the *Sturmgruppe* to do its work without let or hindrance. But on the occasions when they failed, the slow and unmaneuverable *Sturmböcke* were, despite their added protection, easy prey for Allied fighters.

The greatest difficulty was getting the *Gefechtsverband* into position. Containing between 90 and 100 aircraft, it was unwieldy to maneuver. Operating under close ground control, with enough warning to allow the component units to take off, form up, and reach altitude, there was no real problem in clear skies. But clear skies were, as we have already noted, rare in Northern Europe, and maintaining formation integrity while climbing through cloud was nigh on impossible. The other imponderable was the American fighter force. Unlike the *Jagdflieger* in the Battle of Britain, it was not shackled to the bombers, but was free to range out in front and on the flanks of the bomber stream. Once discovered, a *Gefechtsverband* acted as a Mustang magnet, drawing in the escorts from far and wide. Walter Hagenah later recalled that he got into position behind an American bomber on only four occasions in the summer of 1944. While he claimed an American bomber on each, this was a poor return for the effort expended.

The fact was that, by the middle of 1944, the *Jagdwaffe* had lost control of the skies over the Fatherland. Outnumbered and technically matched, they fought for their very lives on four fronts—the East, the West, the Italian, and the Reich. Shortage of fuel curtailed flying training; bomber pilots were remustered to the *Jagdwaffe*, where their previous training proved a handicap. The "old heads" daily grew fewer in number and the replacement pilots were barely worthy of the name. The year 1944 was critical for the *Jagdwaffe*: it never recovered its former supremacy.

With the Third Reich fighting for its very life, it is easy to portray the German fighter pilots as merciless automata. This was far from the case, as many examples quoted later prove. One incident from this period took place on December 20, 1943. A B-17 of the 379th Bombardment Group flown by Lieutenant-Colonel Charles Brown was badly damaged by flak and fighters over Bremen. With the Plexiglas nose shattered, one engine out, and two others damaged, Brown recovered control at low level and set course for England. He was intercepted by Bf 109 pilot Franz Stiegler of *6/JG 27*, a North African veteran with 27 victories, who in 1992 recalled:

I came up behind him to see what kind of reaction I would get from the tail gunner. Nothing happened. I got closer; still nothing. By then I was flying in formation [with the B-17], on the right side. I looked across at the tail gunner and all I could see was blood running down his gun barrels. I could see into Brown's plane, see through the holes, see how they were all shot up. They were trying to help each other. To me, it was just like they were in a parachute. I saw them and I couldn't shoot them down!

Stiegler escorted the badly damaged B-17 out over the North Sea, saluted it, and returned to his base. He had committed a court-martial offense, but, as he said later, "I saw the men; I just couldn't do it!" In this he was not alone. Stiegler, who now lives in Canada, ended the war flying Me 262s with *JV 44*.

The Fighters

It may seem strange that the FW 190A, a much later design than the Bf 109, used the latter to protect it. The fact is that the performance of the FW 190A fell away above 24,000 feet, which was an average attack height for the B-17. Above this level the later variants of the Bf 109 were superior and it was better suited to the air combat mission. The Bf 110 was largely supplanted in the *Zerstörer* role by the Me 410, but in the presence of escort fighters this twin-engine fighter was far too vulnerable. Eduard Tratt of *II/ZG 26*, the top-scoring *Zerstörer* pilot of the war with 38 victories, was shot down and killed while flying an Me 410, by Mustang pilot Jack Oberhansley on February 22, 1944.

Of the USAAF escort fighters, the Republic P-47 Thunderbolt was the most widely used in the initial stages. Large and heavy, its great strengths were in the dive, its high rate of roll, and its heavy armament of eight 0.50in. machine guns. The Lockheed P-38 Lightning was a strange twin-engine, twin-boom design. Very fast at altitude, it was generally outmatched by the German single-seaters in one-versus-one combat. Fortunately for its pilots, one-versus-one combats rarely occurred, and teamwork compensated for many of its shortcomings. The most important type was the North American P-51 Mustang. Good at low altitude in its original form, it was re-engined with the Rolls-Royce Merlin, making it a match for the Bf 109 and FW 190. Its great strength was its long range, which allowed it to rove the length and breadth of the Third

Table 15. *Luftwaffe* **Piston-Engine Fighters, 1943–45**

	Messerschmitt Bf 109G-6	Focke-Wulf FW 190A-8	Messerschmitt Me 410a-2
Wingspan	32ft. 7in.	34ft. 5½in.	53ft. 8in.
Length	29ft. 7in.	29ft. 0in.	40ft. 9in.
Height	11ft. 2in.	13ft. 0in.	14ft. 0in.
Wing area	173 sq. ft.	197 sq. ft.	390 sq. ft.
Engine(s)	Daimler-Benz DB 605 inline rated at 1,800hp	BMW 801D radial rated at 2,100hp	2 × Daimler-Benz DB 603A inlines rated at 1,750hp
Loaded weight	6,945lb.	9,750lb.	23,483lb.
Wing loading	40lb./sq. ft.	49lb./sq. ft.	60lb./sq. ft.
Maximum speed	387mph	408mph	388mph
Service ceiling	38,550ft.	37,400ft.	32,810ft.
Rate of climb	4,560ft./min.	c.3,600ft./min.	c.2,800ft./min.
Range	450 miles	500 miles	1,447 miles
Armament	1 × 30mm MK 108, 2 × 20mm MG 151, 2 × 12.7mm MG 131	4 × 20mm MG 151, 2 × 12.7mm MG 131	2 × 30mm MK 108, 2 × 20mm MG 151

Note: For anti-bomber work a few Me 410s were armed with the 50mm BK 5 cannon. This carried only 21 rounds, had a slow rate of fire, and severely reduced the aircraft's maneuverability.

Reich. Once it entered service in numbers, no German fighter pilot could ever feel safe from attack.

The *Experten*

Steel nerves and marksmanship were the qualities needed to do well against the American heavy bombers, plus an element of luck to survive running the gauntlet of the defensive fire time after time. These were possessed to the full by Herbert Rollwage of *II/JG 53*, the leading heavy bomber *Experte*, who accounted for no fewer than 44 "heavies" in his total of 102.

Only eleven of his victories were scored on the Russian Front; the rest were all against the West, including twenty over Malta. He survived the war.

GEORG-PETER EDER Although his tally of 78 victories places him low (equal 155th) on the overall list of *Experten*, Eder had one of the most amazing records of the whole war. Shot down seventeen times, he was wounded, often severely, on twelve different occasions. His score might have been far higher if he had not on many occasions declined to finish off a damaged adversary. While this smacks of propaganda, it has since been confirmed from Allied sources. His aircraft became known as "Lucky 13" to those whom, their aircraft badly damaged, he allowed to escape. For this he was probably the most deserving of all the *Experten* who survived the war.

Eder joined *JG 51* on the Channel coast in December 1940 but failed to score. Transferred to the East for Barbarossa, he then accounted for ten Russian aircraft before being badly wounded on July 24, 1941. In 1942 he returned to operations with *7/JG 2*, and as related earlier, helped develop tactics against USAAF bomber formations in conjunction with Egon Mayer. Here he describes an action on July 14, 1943:

I pushed the black button on the right of the panel and the three yellow rings and cross flicked on in the sight glass. I was leading the first four of the *Gruppe*, with one on the left and one on the right, just back, and the fourth behind them in the center, higher—the same formation with our *Schwarm* in the *Gruppe* as was flown by the *Gruppen* in the *Geschwader*. We were doing about 450km/hr now and were coming down slightly, aiming for the noses of the B-17s. There were about 200 of us attacking the 200 bombers but there was also the fighter escort above them. We were going for the bombers. When we made our move, the P-47s began to dive on us and it was a race to get to the bombers before being intercepted. I was already close and about 600

Table 16. American Fighters, 1943–45

	P-47D Thunderbolt	P-38L Lightning	P-51D Mustang
Wingspan	40ft. 9in.	52ft. 0in.	37ft. 0in.
Length	36ft. 1in.	37ft. 10in.	32ft. 3in.
Height	14ft. 2in.	12ft. 10in.	13ft. 8in.
Wing Area	300 sq. ft.	328 sq. ft.	233 sq. ft.
Engine(s)	Pratt & Whitney radial rated at 2,300hp	2 × Allison V-1710 inlines rated at 1,600hp	Rolls-Royce Merlin inline rated at 1,695hp
Loaded weight	14,600lb.	17,500lb.	10,100lb.
Wing loading	49lb./sq. ft.	53lb./sq. ft.	43lb./sq. ft.
Maximum speed	429mph	390mph	437mph
Service ceiling	40,000ft.	40,000ft.	40,000ft.
Rate of climb	2,780ft./min.	3,800ft./min.	3,475ft./min.
Range	950 miles	900 miles	2,080 miles
Armament	8 × 0.50in. Brownings	1 × 20mm. Hispano, 4 × 0.50in. Brownings	6 × 0.50in. Brownings

feet above and coming straight on; I opened fire with the twenties at 500 yards. At 300 yards I opened fire with the thirties. It was a short burst, maybe ten shells from each cannon, but I saw the bomber explode and begin to burn. I flashed over him at about 50 feet and then did a chandelle. When I had turned around I was about a thousand feet above and behind them, and was suddenly mixed in with American fighters.

Straight in front was a Thunderbolt, as I completed the turn, and I opened fire on him immediately, and hit his propwash. My fire was so heavy his left wing came off almost at once and I watched him go down. By now I had only three fighters with me—my lead *Schwarm*—the others had split away in the attack. We flew south, ahead, for a few seconds, preparing for another strike at the bombers and then, coming from above, I saw them. I called a warning: *"Indianer über uns!,"* and as they came in behind us we banked hard left. There were ten P-47s and four of us and we were all turning as hard as we could, as in a Lufbery. I was able to turn tighter and was gaining. I pulled within 80 yards of the P-47 ahead of me and opened fire. I hit him quickly and two of the others got one each, so that in a minute and a half three of the P-47s went down. The pilot of the one I hit bailed out and I saw his 'chute open. But one of my men had been shot down and there were now three against seven and I called on the radio for an emergency dive to get away: *"Nacht unten vereisen!,"* and we all rolled over and did a Split-S and dived with full throttle.

The Split-S was a standard *Jagdwaffe* escape ploy. Emergency power caused a lot of smoke from the exhausts, and often caused Allied pilots to believe that a German fighter was badly hit and going down. In this case the Americans did not follow, possibly because the Thunderbolt was not at its best at low level.

Of Eder's 78 victories, 36 were four-engine bombers. Later in the war he claimed twelve victims while flying the Me 262 with *Kommando "Nowotny"* and *JG 7*. Characteristically, he ended the war in the hospital after being shot down by Mustangs.

WALTHER DAHL The operational careers of Eder and Walther Dahl have striking similarities. Both flew on the Channel coast in 1940 and 1941 without success; both claimed their first victories in the East on the first day of Barbarossa; both flew aircraft with the number 13; and both were credited with the destruction of 36 heavy bombers. Dahl's score of 128, amassed in some 600 sorties, included 77 on the Eastern Front. It was Dahl who pioneered the *Gefechtsverband* in 1944 and did much to ensure its success. On November 30 of that year he was placed under house arrest by Goering personally for refusing to take off in appalling weather. Within a matter of weeks he was appointed Inspector of Day Fighters, a position he held until the end of the war.

8. RED SKY AT NIGHT, 1943–45

By 1943 new blind bombing aids and developing techniques allowed the RAF to attack with a fair degree of accuracy, even on moonless nights and in cloudy conditions. This made life far more difficult for the defenders, who now had to get much closer to the bombers before they could obtain visual contact. Between the beginning of March and the end of June German night fighters accounted for roughly 700 bombers, but this apparently horrific loss represented only about four percent of the total sorties flown and was easily made good. At least ten percent was needed to make the British loss rate prohibitive.

The greatest shortcoming was the German *Himmelbett* system of close control. Operating on a narrow frontage, the bomber stream crossed only a handful of *Himmelbett* zones on its way to the target. The few night fighters allocated to these zones had more targets than they could possibly handle, while the rest of the force had nothing. Typically, only about 50 of the 300 or so night fighters available were brought into action against any one raid, and the majority of these were unsuccessful.

This was wasteful of resources. Better results could have been achieved by scrambling all fighters in areas not directly affected and allowing them to freelance in the bomber stream. A few *Experten* had already experimented in this manner, but it took many months and a major disaster before it became general practice. The major disaster was the week-long Battle of Hamburg, which commenced on the night of July 24/25, 1943.

Window on Hamburg

Shortly before midnight on July 24, early warning radars detected a force of RAF bombers far out to sea. As the plot neared the coast, night fighters were scrambled. So far it was a routine heavy raid by several hundred bombers. Then, without prior warning, the picture on the radar screens changed. Instead of hundreds of contacts, there were thousands! The screens were full of them—completely saturated. All semblance of tracking was lost. With this the ground control system was paralyzed. The chaos on the ground was only matched by that in the sky. Airborne that night was Wilhelm Johnen of *3/NJG 1*:

. . . my sparker [radar operator] announced the first enemy machine on his Li [radar]. I was delighted. I swung around on to the bearing in the direction of the Ruhr, for in this way I was bound to approach the [bomber] stream. Facius proceeded to report three or four pictures on his screens. I hoped that I should have enough ammunition to deal with them!

Then Facius suddenly shouted: "Tommy flying toward us at a great speed. Distance decreasing . . . 2,000 meters; 1,500 . . . 1,000 . . . 500 . . ."

I was speechless. Facius already had a new target. "Perhaps it was a German night fighter on a westerly course," I said to myself, and made for the next bomber.

It was not long before Facius shouted again: "Bomber coming for us at a hell of a speed. 2,000 . . . 1,000 . . . 500 . . . He's gone."

"You're crackers, Facius," I said jestingly.

But soon I lost my sense of humor, for this crazy performance was repeated a score of times and finally I gave Facius such a rocket that he was deeply offended.

This tense atmosphere on board was suddenly interrupted by a ground station calling: "Hamburg, Hamburg. A thousand enemy bombers over Hamburg."

This performance was repeated in fighter after fighter as their onboard radars showed contact after contact, all apparently moving at high speeds. The British were dropping Window— bundles of aluminum strips cut to length to match the characteristics of the German radars, which showed each bundle as though it were a bomber.

The *Nachtjagdflieger*, unable to differentiate between Window and bombers, fruitlessly chased spurious contacts around the sky. In fact, there was a difference, but in the confusion it mainly went unnoticed. Window clouds were virtually stationary, and on the radar screens the fighter appeared to close on them very rapidly; by contrast, the echo from a genuine bomber would have a much slower relative speed (fighter speed minus bomber speed).

Airborne that night was Bf 110 pilot Hans Meissner (final score 20 victories) of *2/NJG 3*. After several futile chases after Window clouds, his radar operator Josef Krinner noticed that whereas most contacts on his screen were fast-moving, one seemed to be almost stationary. As this was more like contacts obtained on previous nights, he directed his pilot toward it. Eventually Meissner gained visual contact with a Stirling and shot it down in flames. This was, however, exceptional. The *Nachtjagdflieger* gained few successes during that or the following nights. Shorn of its defenses, Hamburg was devastated.

The greatest weakness of the German air defense system was that too many of its detection systems used the same wavelengths, with the result that Window jammed the lot. The painstakingly built-up German night air defense system lay in ruins. New radars were desperately needed, but these were not immediately available. The *Luftwaffe* was forced to seek other means to redress the balance as a matter of desperate urgency.

Silk Purses from Sows' Ears

Fortunately for the Third Reich, other means were to hand. *Himmelbett* had long had its critics, mainly because it signally failed to employ more than a fraction of the available fighter strength at any one moment. Means to remedy this were already in the pipeline, under the names of *Wilde Sau* and *Zähme Sau* (Wild Boar and Tame Boar). The disaster at Hamburg was the catalyst which thrust them to the fore.

Wilde Sau was the brainchild of former bomber pilot Hans-Joachim ("Hajo") Herrmann. Interestingly, it exploited the very success of the bombers. Once a raid had begun, fires on the ground provided a backdrop against which bombers were visible from above. Combined with searchlights, this illuminated the area for fighters to intercept visually. When there was light cloud over the target, the searchlights playing evenly on the underside formed a *Mattscheibe* (literally, "shroud") against which bombers were clearly visible from above. *Wilde Sau* fighters, single-seat Bf 109s and FW 190As, could be used under these conditions given that the flak ceiling was limited, allowing them to operate freely above it.

The next problem was how best to get the short-range *Wilde Sau* fighters to the right place at the right time. Germany was networked with radio beacons for navigational purposes. When the likely target had been deduced, the *Wilde Sau* fighters were assembled at a nearby radio beacon, flying left-handed orbits at preset heights by *Staffeln*. Once the attack commenced they were ordered into the area, there to hunt visually. It was of course an expedient. The bombing could not be minimized: all that could be done was to inflict maximum casualties over the target area.

Zähme Sau, pioneered by Viktor von Lossberg, had many features in common with *Wilde Sau*. However, it differed primarily in that it was flown by longer-legged, twin-engine fighters and was intended to intercept before the target was reached. The fighters were scrambled early to orbit a radio beacon on the projected course of the bomber stream. Often they were moved from beacon to beacon as circumstances dictated.

Unlike *Himmelbett*, only a loose form of ground control was exercised in the form of a running commentary on bomber movements as a whole. The radars might be jammed, but the Window trail was a fair indicator of the track of the bombers.

But, just to make life interesting, the British became adept at making spoof raids, with a handful of aircraft laying Window while the main force made radical course changes to throw off its pursuers. To complicate matters still more, British communications jamming had by now reached a fine level of sophistication.

Once established among the bombers, the fighters operated as best they might. At least they knew that if Window jamming was present, the bombers could not be too far away. One technique was to fly to where the Window was thickest and search visually. Like the day fighters at this time, the night fighters followed the course of the bombers while fuel and ammunition lasted, then landed at the nearest available airfield. What was called the *Luftwaffe*'s "migratory period" commenced. *Zähme Sau* became the backbone of the *Nachtjagdflieger* for the rest of the war, made even more effective later with new electronics.

New Threats

The summer of 1943 saw two more hazards emerge. Unlike the *Luftwaffe*, the British had persevered with night intruders, and now Mosquitos took to loitering in the vicinity of known fighter airfields, waiting to catch the unwary. To counter them, patrols of Bf 110s were flown, but the heavily laden night fighter was too slow to be effective. During the whole of 1943 only four Mosquitos fell to night fighters, and at least some of these were bombers rather than intruders.

Theoretically it had long been possible for the British to send night fighter escorts with their bombers. That they had not done so earlier was due to the impossibility of telling friendly bombers from German fighters before visual range (and firing range for the bomber gunners) was reached. But by the summer of 1943 they had developed a passive detector that homed on German radar emissions.

On August 17, with a major bombing raid outbound over the North Sea, German ground radar detected a small group of aircraft off the Frisian Islands, flying at typical heavy bomber

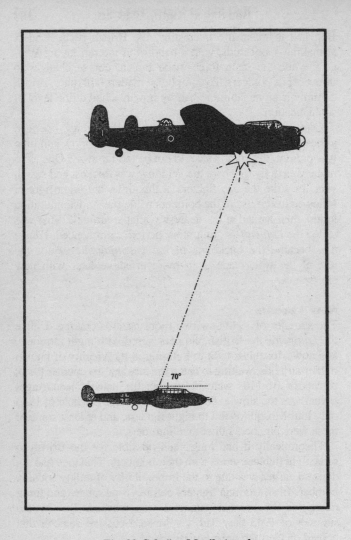

Fig. 22. Schräge Musik *Attack*
The Schräge Musik *installation allowed attacks to be made from
the blind spot almost directly underneath a bomber, and this could
be continued even if the bomber took mild evasive action.*

speeds. Five Bf 110s of *IV/NJG 1* were vectored to intercept. Of the five, one turned back with engine failure. Heinz-Wolfgang Schnaufer (121 victories) aborted after being damaged by "friendly" flak. The three remaining Messerschmitts bored on. Reaching the area, they switched on their radars and commenced to search.

Georg Kraft was in a gentle left turn when he was suddenly hit from astern by a fusillade of 20mm cannon shells from a Beaufighter. He nosed down, only to be hit again, set ablaze and sent plunging vertically into the sea. Kraft (15 victories) was never seen again. Close by was Heinz Vinke. *Unteroffizier* Gaa, his gunner, had a grandstand view of Kraft's demise. The Beaufighter was astern, off to the right, and slightly lower. Gaa warned Vinke, who at once broke hard into it. The British pilot gained visual contact just in time and turned inside the Messerschmitt, firing from very close range and barely avoiding a collision as he did so. Ripping through the German fighter, 20mm shells wounded Gaa and the radar operator and tore the control column from Vinke's hands. All three German crewmen bailed out of their stricken fighter, but only Vinke survived. He was rescued after eighteen hours in the sea, only to succumb to Spitfires in daylight six months later, his final score 54. Shortly afterward, the third Bf 110 fell to a second Beaufighter.

This was a significant defeat for the *Nachtjagdflieger*. All three aircraft were lost for no result, and two *Experten* were shot down. It was a triumph for British electronics expertise, and a harbinger of things to come. The double victor, Bob Braham, had not yet finished with the *Experten*. On September 29 he shot down August Geiger (53 victories) over the Ijsselmeer. Geiger bailed out successfully but was drowned.

The first *Wilde Sau* mission was actually flown before the Hamburg raids. The flak failed to limit its firing, but twelve single-seaters, led by Hajo Herrmann, attacked anyway, claiming twelve bombers. The original unit, *Kommando "Herrmann,"* was quickly expanded to full *Geschwader* strength, although two *Gruppen* had to "borrow" fighters from day units on the same bases. This led to friction between personnel: around-the-clock usage reduced serviceability to unacceptably low levels. But, as successes mounted, the *Geschwader, JG 300*, was given its own complement of aircraft, and two more *Wilde Sau Jagdgeschwader* were formed.

Wilde Sau suffered from many of those weaknesses that had been the downfall of illuminated night fighting. Although making visual contact with the enemy was far easier, instrument flying and navigation at night was just as difficult as it had ever been. This was particularly hard on the boys drafted in from training schools, and the accident rate was very high. Many *Wilde Sau Experten* came from bomber or transport units; they could navigate about Germany quite happily in darkness, and could consistently land at night without incident. They were the exception.

The most successful of all was Friedrich-Karl Muller, universally known as "Nasen" Muller, both on account of his truly aristocratic proboscis and to distinguish him from day fighter *Experte* Friedrich-Karl "Tutti" Muller (140 victories). Nasen was an old *Lufthansa* hand who had spent the early part of the war flying bombers and transports. A founder member of *Kommando "Herrmann,"* he claimed 30 victories in 52 night missions, 23 of them as a *Wilde Sau* pilot.

The high-water mark of the *Wilde Sau* units came in the late summer of 1943, but with the onset of autumn their star began to wane. No longer were they aided by light summer nights: the weather clamped in and accidents rose. The Bf 109 came to be preferred over the FW 190A for night work: a bad landing simply wiped off the undercarriage and left the aircraft right side up, whereas the more sturdy Focke-Wulf tended to go over on its back. In winter, less experienced pilots were unable to make their way down through heavy cloud and icing; instead, they abandoned undamaged fighters and took to their parachutes. *Wilde Sau* units remained in service well into 1944, but they were never again as effective and were often called upon to fly by day.

A number of new devices entered service at about this time. Among them was the SN-2 radar set, which used a longer wavelength and, for the moment at least, was not susceptible to Window, and electronic gadgetry which enabled the fighters to home on emissions produced by the bombers. These last were passive detectors, which, while they gave no indication of range, did not betray the presence of the fighters to the lurking Mosquitos. They also solved the problem of finding the bomber stream.

Schräge Musik

Whereas standard procedure with forward-firing armament was to dive below the bomber before swimming up from the depths like a shark, a new form of attack now emerged. This hinged on *Schräge Musik*, cannon set in the fuselage to fire upward at an angle of between 60 and 70 degrees. The idea was hardly new—it dated back at least to 1916—but its widespread application in 1943 was revolutionary. See Fig. 22.

The fighter now crept up behind and below the bomber, where it was least likely to be seen. It then formated about 200 feet below and matched speeds precisely, while the pilot took careful aim through a standard reflector sight mounted on the roof of his cabin. The preferred aiming point was the fuel tank in the wing between the fuselage and the engine of the bomber. Hits in this area were usually lethal, and as no tracer rounds were used the bomber crew often had no idea where the firing was coming from. The loss rate of the raiders rose.

The first quarter of 1944 saw both a bad reverse and a resounding victory for the *Nachtjagdflieger*. In fighter combat, the few run up big scores while the many blunder around the sky for little result. These few are an example and an inspiration to others and, as such, have an effect on the force as a whole out of all proportion to their numbers and achievements. Conversely, their loss is devastating. For the *Nachtjagdflieger*, the night of January 21/22, 1944, when not one but two leading *Experten* fell, was a major disaster.

The occasion was a heavy raid on Magdeburg. *Prinz* Heinrich zu Sayn-Wittgenstein had just shot down five bombers to bring his score to 83, making him briefly the top-ranking night *Experte*, when his Ju 88 was caught from behind by a Mosquito. He bailed out, but his parachute failed to open. A few miles away Manfred Meurer (65 victories) attacked a bomber from below with *Schräge Musik*. Stricken, the bomber plunged downward and collided with Meurer's He 219. Victim and victor fell interlocked in flames. The *Nachtjagdflieger* was devastated by this double loss.

Nuremberg

The resounding victory came on March 30/31 when the RAF struck in force at Nuremberg. It was one of the few times when almost everything favored the defenders. The spoof raids were all identified in good time and 246 night fighters were scrambled to deal with the main force, most being assembled over a radio beacon right on the bombers' course. Higher winds than forecast scattered the bomber stream over a wide front, while atmospheric conditions were such that condensation trails from the exhausts of the bombers' engines formed at a much lower height than usual.

A bright half moon in a clear sky shone on the ghostly white contrails, making the bomber stream visible from many miles away. The scene was set for slaughter: the *Nachtjagdflieger* could hardly fail to find targets on such a clear night. A running battle developed over the next 200 miles, its path marked by fires on the ground, each denoting a shot-down bomber. Helmut Schulte (25 victories), of *II/NJG 5*, takes up the story:

> Normally our biggest problem was to find the bomber stream but on this night we had no trouble. I found the enemy at a height of 6,000 meters. I sighted a Lancaster and got underneath it and opened fire with my slanting weapon. Unfortunately it jammed, so that only a few shots put out of action the starboard inner motor. The bomber dived violently and turned to the north, but because of good visibility we were able to keep him in sight. I now attempted a second attack after he had settled on his course, but because the Lancaster was now very slow we always came out too far in the front. I tried the *Schräge Musik* again and after another burst the bomber fell in flames. Our plane [a Bf 110] stalled but I was able to regain control 2,000 meters lower.

Schulte accounted for three more bombers that night, and other *Experten* also notched up multiple victories. The best performance of all was by Martin "Tino" Becker, a former reconnaissance pilot who joined *I/NJG 4* in 1943, opening his score in September of that year. In his first mission of the night, a *Zähme Sau*, he shot down three Lancasters and three Halifaxes. After refueling and rearming, he was sent to a *Himmelbett* box, where he accounted for a further Halifax, for a total of seven. What makes his performance even more creditable was that as his Bf 110 was not fitted with *Schräge Musik* he was forced to rely on his standard forward-firing armament. He survived the war with a total of 58 confirmed night victories.

The nervous strain of night fighting was tremendous: the stealthy approach, wondering if the rear gunner was already taking aim; the risk of collision in the dark; the lurking British intruders—all took their toll. Helmut Schulte, four victories already to his credit that night and his *Schräge Musik* jammed, encountered another Lancaster south of Nuremberg. His first attack came to naught because he had forgotten to arm his front guns; the bomber spotted him and began to corkscrew. He followed at a distance until it settled down, then closed in behind. He later recalled:

At first he didn't object to this formation flying and he must have been watching me as I got into position again. As soon as I opened fire he dived away and my shells passed over him. I thought that this chap must have nerves of steel: he had watched me formate on him and then had dived just at the right time. He had been through as much as I had—we had both been to Nuremberg that night—so I decided that was enough.

It was also enough for Bomber Command. Of the 795 bombers that set out for Nuremberg, 94, an unacceptable 12 percent, failed to return. Of these, 79 fell to the *Nachtjagdflieger*, who shared two more with the Flak.

However, not all the German fighters had seen action. A notable failure that night was Schnaufer, who was a little too

clever for his own good. Attempting to intercept as far forward
as possible, he headed for the coast, missed the bomber stream
completely, and never caught it up. Also unlucky were the Bf
110s of *II/NJG 6*. Initially sent too far north, they also failed to
get among the bombers.

The Beginning of the End

Nuremberg was the *Nachtjagdflieger*'s last great victory. The
Normandy invasion punched a great hole in the early warning
screen, through which the Allied bombers were directed. A
concerted attack on the German oil industry followed, reducing output to well below the minimum necessary. Pilot training
virtually ceased, and defensive operations were severely curtailed by lack of fuel. Efficiency suffered.

In December 1944 the *Nachtjagdflieger* claimed a mere 66
victories—0.7 percent of bomber sorties flown. In the process
they lost 114 fighters. The greatest hazard was the ubiquitous
Mosquito, which by now ranged the length and breadth of the
Third Reich to hunt down German fighters. So extreme did this
become that *Experten* took to returning to base at very low
level to escape the attentions of the British aircraft. At night
this was not without risk, and it became ironically known as
"*Ritterkreuz* height." Hans Krause (28 victories), of *I/NJG 4*,
developed his own unique method of returning home. Lining
up on the runway at 3,000 meters, he asked for the runway
lights to be switched on briefly. Having taken his bearings, he
dived steeply, pulled out hard to mush off excess speed, and
touched down on a darkened airfield. His only comment on
this amazing performance was that if a Mosquito shot him
down, at least he had plenty of time to bail out! He survived
the war.

Nachtjagdflieger resistance was at a very low level for the
final months of the war, but the *Experten* could and did hit back
hard. Of the 43 recorded occasions when five or more victories
were claimed in a single night, eight took place in Feb-
ruary/March 1945. But by then the night air war was lost.

Table 17. German Night Fighters, 1943–45

	Junkers Ju 88G-6	Heinkel He 219A-5
Wingspan	65ft. 11in.	60ft. 9in.
Length	51ft. 1in.	51ft. 0in.
Height	15ft. 11in.	13ft. 6in.
Wing area	587 sq. ft.	479 sq. ft.
Engines	2 × Junkers Jumo 213A inlines rated at 1,750hp	2 × Daimler-Benz DB603E inlines rated at 1,800hp
Loaded weight	28,900lb.	33,730lb.
Wing loading	49lb./sq. ft.	70lb./sq. ft.
Maximum speed	389mph	364mph
Service ceiling	32,800ft.	30,840ft.
Rate of climb	1,655ft./min.	c.1,750ft./min.
Range	1,398 miles	960 miles

The Aircraft

Galloping weight increases made the performance of the Bf 110 demonstrably inadequate, and production ceased in December 1944, although the aircraft remained in service to the end. The Ju 88C was replaced by the G series from 1944. This was an altogether more capable machine, and equipped almost all of the night fighter force in the closing months. Among the *Experten* who flew it were Helmut Lent of *NJG 3*, with 102 night victories before his death in a landing accident on October 5, 1944; Heinz Rokker of *2/NJG 2*, with 63 at night; Paul Zorner of *II/NJG 100*, with 59; Martin Becker of *IV/NJG 6*, with 58; Gerhard Raht of *I/NJG 2*, with 58; and Heinz Strüning of *9/NJG 1*, with 56. The last was shot down and killed by a Mosquito on Christmas Eve 1944.

The Heinkel He 219 was introduced during 1943, but for various reasons only 268 were built. Brochure performance figures were impressive, and for this reason the failure to get the aircraft into service in large numbers is often cited as an example of German mismanagement. The truth is more prosaic: the brochure figures could not be matched. In addition, its extremely high wing loading made the aircraft unmaneuverable at altitude. This inevitably raises the question: could Manfred Meurer have avoided colliding with his victim if he had been flying a more maneuverable aircraft? That we shall never know!

The *Experten*

As with the day fighters, competition between pilots was fierce. At the beginning of 1943 Helmut Lent led with 49. Trailing him were Reinhold Knacke and Ludwig Becker with 40 apiece. One year later Lent was still on top with 79, but the fast-scoring *Prinz* Heinrich zu Sayn-Wittgenstein now lay second with 68. Knacke was killed while trying to land his badly damaged fighter on February 3, 1943, while Ludwig Becker was shot down in daylight later in the month. Way back in 14th place lay Schnaufer with 42, but 1944/45 saw him surpass the others with 79 victories to bring his score to 121. To bring this feat into perspective, the next-highest scorers during this period were Heinz Rökker and Gustav Francsi with 56 each, followed by Martin Becker with 52.

PRINZ HEINRICH ZU SAYN-WITTGENSTEIN One of two aristocratic *Experten* in the *Nachtjagdflieger* (the other was *Prinz* Egmont zur Lippe-Weissenfeld with 51 night victories), Wittgenstein started the war as a bomber pilot but transferred to night fighters in August 1941. As *Kommandeur* of *I/NJG 100* he flew on the Russian Front, where he scored 29 victories. Transferred to Reich defense, he scored rapidly and reached second place by January 1, 1944, with 68 victories, just behind Lent.

The first three weeks of that month saw Wittgenstein add another 15 to his total, but Lent stayed just ahead. Then, on the night of the 21st/22nd, Wittgenstein took the lead for the first time. He was never to savor his triumph. Immediately after his fifth victory of the night he was caught from behind by a Mosquito. He bailed out, but apparently hit the tailplane of his doomed Ju 88. His parachute failed to open.

Wittgenstein was totally dedicated to his craft. He is reputed to have once made his radar operator stand to attention in the cockpit (quite how this was supposed to have been done is a mystery) and confined him to quarters for three days for losing a contact. And this in the middle of the bomber stream! Resuming the mission, they shot down three bombers, after which he pardoned the man and awarded him the Iron Cross First Class!

On the night before his death Wittgenstein shot down three bombers and had a very narrow escape. Radar operator Friedrich Ostheimer takes up the story:

> . . . I already had the next aircraft on my screen; almost as a matter of routine we flew up to the target. *Prinz* Wittgenstein came pretty close to the Lancaster, which was being flown very erratically. On this occasion, too, a burst from *Schräge Musik* blew a big hole in the wing and started a blazing fire. This time the British pilot reacted unusually: he remained at the controls of his burning machine and dived down on top of us. Our *Prinz*, too, whipped the Ju 88 into a dive, but the blazing monster came closer and closer and hung in visual contact over our cabin. I had only one thought: "We've had it!" A heavy blow staggered our aircraft, *Prinz* Wittgenstein lost control of the machine, and we went into a spin, plunging down into the night.

Wittgenstein recovered control 3,000 meters lower and headed for the nearest airfield. Damage was severe—six feet torn from the starboard wing and a large hole in the rear fuselage. A belly landing followed, which ripped the floor away, sending chopped-up pieces of turf hurtling through the cabin. Next morning, in a new machine, Wittgenstein flew back to base to meet his appointment with destiny.

HEINZ-WOLFGANG SCHNAUFER Unlike many of the top night *Experten*, Schnaufer joined the *Nachtjagdflieger* straight from training to fly *Himmelbett* sorties with *II/NJG 1*. His first victory came on June 2, 1942, and for the next year or so his scoring was steady if unspectacular. His combat report from May 29, 1943, reads:

> At about 00:35 hours I was directed on to an incoming enemy aircraft at an altitude of 3,500 meters. It was located on the [airborne radar] and after further instructions [from Dr. Baro, his operator] I made out a four-engined bomber at 00:45 hours, about 200 meters away above and to the right. I attacked the violently evading bomber from behind and below at a range of 80 meters, and my rounds started a bright fire in the left wing. The blazing enemy aircraft turned and dived away steeply, hitting the ground and exploding violently at 00:48 hours.

The timetable was ten minutes from ground control directive to visual contact, but only three minutes from visual contact to the target hitting the ground. The chase was slow and painstaking, the strike swift and deadly.

By August 1943 Schnaufer's score had reached 23 and he became *Staffelkapitän* of *12/NJG 1*. At about this time he teamed up with talented radar operator Fritz Rumpelhardt, with whom he developed an almost telepathic understanding and shared 100 victories. Prior to this Schnaufer had had two regular operators, Baro, with whom he shared twelve, and Erich Handke, eight. Handke later struck up a successful partnership with Martin Drewes. The other member of the most successful crew in the *Nachtjagdflieger* was Wilhelm Gänsler, a marksman with exceptional night vision. Gänsler shared in 115 victories, 17 with Ludwig Becker and 98 after joining Schnaufer.

With Rumpelhardt on the radar, Schnaufer's score rose rapidly. Four Lancasters fell to his guns on December 16/17 of that year, bringing his score to 40. The weather was atrocious that night, and he felt his way in to land beneath a cloud base at barely 100 feet—a further testament to his flying skill.

During 1944 he scored 64 victories—a record unequaled by anyone—many at a time when the *Nachtjagdflieger* was outnumbered and technically overmatched. His final fifteen victories came in 1945, nine of them in one 24-hour period on February 21, giving him a total of 121. His secret was superb aircraft handling combined with marksmanship (three victories were scored against violently corkscrewing bombers) and Rumpelhardt on the radar. Schnaufer flew only the Bf 110. He survived the war but died in a road accident in France in 1950.

9. OVERLORD TO GÖTTERDÄMMERUNG

Spring 1944: the German High Command knew full well that before long the Allies would launch a huge amphibious attack across the Channel, although they could only guess at where and when. Equally, they knew that their only chance was to halt it on the beaches. With the Reich under air attack by day and by night, they were unable to release *Luftwaffe* units to strengthen the area beforehand: they were forced to rely on contingency plans to rush reinforcements in once the invasion started.

In the preceding months the Allies had started to soften up the defenses of Fortress Europe. Road and rail systems, communication and command centers, radar stations—all were targeted, as well as the more obvious troop concentrations and supply depots. This was done over a wide area so as to give no clue as to where the landings were to take place. Tactical bombers and fighter-bombers roamed the skies of France and the Low Countries, their fighter escorts never far away.

A softening-up of the *Jagdwaffe* was also part of the plan, although the general level of Allied air activity was so high as to make it seem almost incidental. In the 61 days between April 6 and June 5, 1944, 98,400 Allied counter-air sorties were flown, against which the *Jagdwaffe* could pit only 34,500. Allied fighter losses to all causes were 1,012. This was high, but with both aircraft and pilots streaming off the production lines, it was affordable.

Jagdwaffe losses were even higher, at 1,246. The German aircraft industry was performing minor miracles at the time, and the fighters could be replaced. The flying schools still turned out pilots, but they were green and undertrained. Not only were they inadequate as replacements for the "old heads," but they were no match for the better-trained and aggressive Allied fighter pilots. Few survived their first half-dozen sorties. Worse still, many high-scoring *Experten* went down during this period, and these were irreplaceable.

In the face of overwhelming air superiority, *Luftwaffe* reconnaissance failed to detect not only the massing of the vast invasion fleet on the south coast of England, but its sailing. Not until the landings were under way did the German High Command realize the fact, and even then they were slow to react. Only about a hundred sorties were flown on the first day, against an Allied air umbrella of more than 3,000 fighters flying in relays. Nor did the reinforcement plans work as advertised. As Adolf Galland later commented,

> When the invasion finally came, the carefully made preparations immediately went awry. The transfer of the fighters into France was delayed for 24 hours because *Oberkommando West* would not give the order, expecting heavier landings to be attempted in the Pas-de-Calais area. The *Luftwaffe* finally issued the order on its own authority, and the transfer began.
>
> Most of the carefully prepared and provisioned airfields assigned to the fighter units had been bombed and the units had to land at other hastily chosen landing grounds. The poor signals network broke down, causing further confusion. Each unit's advance parties came by Junkers 52, but the main body of ground staff came by rail, and most arrived days or even weeks later.

Worse was to come. Over the next 90 days, the Allies put up the massive total of 203,357 fighter sorties, against which the *Jagdwaffe* could muster only 31,833, a more than 6:1 disparity which was reflected in the casualty list—516 Allied fighters lost to all causes against 3,527 German fighters. Many of the latter were destroyed on the ground by strafing, but the loss was still tremendous. Four high-scoring *Experten* were killed in the first three days of the invasion. Karl-Heinz Weber of *II/JG 1* (136 victories, all in the East), was shot down south of Rouen. The others were Zweigart (69 victories), Hüppertz (68), and Simsch (54), all of whom had flown extensively in the East.

Some units were decimated. About 40 FW 190As of *II/JG 6* surprised a dozen Lightnings in the act of strafing an airfield near St. Quentin and shot down six in short order. Then two more squadrons of Lightnings arrived on the scene. In the melee that followed, one more Lightning went down, but so did sixteen Focke-Wulfs, with others damaged. On paper, the German fighter was more than a match for its twin-engine opponent, but in practice German pilot quality was so poor as to reverse the situation. Shortly afterward, *II/JG 6* was withdrawn from the front. It was far from being the only one.

Three centurions had fallen by the first week in September, Josef "Sepp" Wurmheller of *III/JG 2* (102 victories, of which 93 were in the West) collided with his *Kacmarek* during a dogfight on June 22. Otto Fonnekold of *II/JG 52* (136 victories, mainly in the East) was caught during his landing approach by American fighters and shot down. Emil "Bully" Lang was the greatest loss. Widely regarded as the bravest man in the *Luftwaffe*, he scored 148 victories in the East, including a purple patch of 72 in less than three weeks at the end of 1943. This included eighteen in one day, making him the only man to surpass Marseille in the annals of mass destruction. Transferred to home defense, Lang continued scoring, and he became *Kommandeur* of *II/JG 26* in June 1944. By September 3 he had raised his score to 173, when he encountered Thunderbolts over Belgium. An unlucky hit on his hydraulic system caused his wheels to drop; thus handicapped, he was quickly shot down and killed.

As the Allied armies poured across Europe, the *Luftwaffe* was constantly forced to retreat through a succession of temporary landing grounds, harassed the while by Allied fighters which frequently moved into airfields just vacated. Confusion was high: on occasion the *Jagdflieger* were unable to locate their newest bases from the air and landed where they could.

Logistics and communications were chaotic and ground control virtually nonexistent, while from August operations were restricted by fuel shortages. The *Jagdwaffe* in the West was a spent force, its strength diminishing daily.

Help was at hand, and from an unexpected source. By early autumn the logistics problems of maintaining the huge Allied armies were outrunning their supplies. Gradually the offensive stalled, and with this the urgency of defensive air operations was reduced. The *Jagdwaffe* used the breathing space well. Bases were reorganized, fuel stocks were laboriously built up, and each *Jagdgruppe* was expanded to four *Staffeln*. New aircraft were in plentiful supply, and fifteen *Jagdgruppen* were completely reequipped. The main cloud on the horizon was the dearth of trained fighter pilots, and the numbers were made up with men drawn from disbanded bomber units.

By now one thing was clear. The American bombing raids had to be stopped. *General der Jagdflieger* Adolf Galland produced an ambitious scheme to achieve just this objective. He reasoned that if 400–500 bombers could be shot down in a single day, the USAAF would be forced to call a halt, giving the Reich a valuable breathing space. To do this, he assembled a force of eighteen *Jagdgruppen* with over 3,000 fighters. By November 12 all was ready. It was just a question of waiting for suitable weather.

It was not to be. Many fighters were frittered away in supporting the abortive Ardennes offensive. Even more were squandered in *Operation Bodenplatte,* the New Year's Day attack on Allied airfields by about 900 fighters. About 200 Allied aircraft were written off on their airfields, but German losses were nearer 300. The difference was that, whereas few Allied pilots were lost, the *Luftwaffe* pilot casualty list was 237 killed, missing, or taken prisoner and eighteen more wounded. To make matters worse, twenty of these were experienced leaders, among them Horst-Günther von Fassong of *III/JG 11* (about 135 victories, mainly in the East), who was shot down by Thunderbolts near Maastricht, Heinrich Hackler of *11/JG 77* (56 victories), missing near Antwerp, and the very experienced, one-eyed Günther Specht, *Kommodore* of *JG 11* (score unknown, but at least 32 in the West, including fifteen heavy bombers), who fell to flak near Brussels.

The *Jagdwaffe* never recovered. Opposition to the daylight incursions of the USAAF noticeably weakened. Great hopes were pinned on the new jet fighters (see Chapter 11). As these were too fast to be caught by propeller-driven fighters, the Allies took to lurking in the vicinity of known jet airfields in the hope of catching them at slow speeds shortly after takeoff or while preparing to land. Consequently the new wonder fighters needed protection at these times, and piston-engined *Jagdgruppen* were assigned to the task of patrolling the airfield approaches. Had the jets scored a series of dazzling victories, this would have been effort well spent. As it was, it is debatable whether or not this was a misuse of conventional fighters.

With British, American, Canadian, and French armies closing from the West, and the Russians from the East, the war, clearly, was lost. *Jagdflieger* morale slumped. Pilot quality, the ultimate arbiter in fighter combat, was reflected in the results of the engagements that took place, while many of the more successful pilots were transferred to the new jet formations. Those still flying conventional fighters in the West frequently came off worst, often because they were outnumbered, but not always. To quote but one example, on February 25 fifteen Bf 109Gs of *I/JG 27* were attacked by eight Tempests. In the ensuing melee they shot down one Tempest but lost four aircraft and four more damaged. In the final weeks, units sometimes avoided combat. When it was forced on them, they fought hard, but to little avail.

The Fighters

The conventional German fighters of this period were the Messerschmitt Bf 109G and Focke-Wulf FW 190A, both in their later variants. The latter was, however, developed into the "Dora"—the FW 190D-9—and its high-altitude counterpart, the Ta 152, although very few of the latter entered service before the end of the war.

The "Dora" entered large-scale service in the autumn of 1944. Outwardly it was still recognizable as an FW 190, but it

differed from them in having an extended nose which housed a
Junkers Jumo 213A inline engine, ahead of which was an
annular radiator which gave the impression of a radial. Water-
methanol injection was used to boost power for short periods.
To compensate for the extra nose length, the fuselage was
stretched and the tail surfaces enlarged. The standard armament was two 20mm MG 151 cannon in the wing roots and
two 12.7mm MG 131 machine guns above the engine.

At first its pilots were a little suspicious of their new mount.
The rate of roll was slower than the radial-engine variant, and
the extra length made it sluggish in pitch. However, it had its
virtues. It accelerated better, was faster, and had a better dive
and climb performance than its predecessor, which was really
saying something. Whereas its radius of turn was no better than
that of the A-8, it did not bleed off speed so quickly. To its
Allied opponents it was universally known as the "Long-
Nose," and treated with great respect.

The American fighters were primarily the Thunderbolt and
Mustang, described in Chapter 7, while the Spitfire IX was still
in widespread use with the RAF. British newcomers were the
Spitfire XIV, a very potent Griffon-engine variant which
entered service early in 1944, and the Hawker Tempest V,
which arrived at the front later that year. The latter was optimized for air superiority at low and medium altitude. A big
machine, it was nevertheless very fast and very agile.

The Dora was the most formidable piston-engine fighter to
enter *Luftwaffe* service in any numbers. In sheer performance it
outmatched the Thunderbolt and Lightning, and in some
respects even the Mustang. The accompanying table shows it
to be generally inferior to the Spitfire XIV and Tempest V. Its
wing loading was so much higher that, speed for speed, it
would have been out-turned with ease. Only in rate of roll did
it have any real advantage. This poses the question: why did it
not get cut to pieces every time by the British fighters?

The answer lies in the nature of air combat. A level playing
field is no part of the game. Surprise is the dominant factor:
flying the best fighter in the world is of little avail if its pilot is

Table 18. Tactical Fighters, Western Front, 1944–45

	Focke-Wulf FW 190D-9	Supermarine Spitfire XIV	Hawker Tempest V
Wingspan	34ft. 5¹/₂in.	36ft. 10in.	41ft. 0in.
Length	33ft. 5in.	32ft. 8in.	16ft. 1in.
Height	11ft. 0in.	12ft. 8in.	33ft. 8in.
Wing area	197 sq. ft.	242 sq. ft.	302 sq. ft.
Engine	Junkers Jumo 213A inline rated at 2,240hp	Rolls-Royce Griffon 65 inline rated at 2,050hp	Napier Sabre II inline rated at 2,420hp
Loaded weight	9,480lb.	8,500lb.	11,500lb.
Wing loading	48lb./sq. ft.	35lb./sq. ft.	38lb./sq. ft.
Maximum speed	426mph	448mph	435mph
Service ceiling	39,372ft.	44,500ft.	36,000ft.
Rate of climb	c.4,200ft./min.	4,580ft./min.	4,700ft./min.
Range	520 miles	460 miles	740 miles
Armament	2 × 20mm MG151, 2 × 12.7mm MG 131	2 x 20mm Hispano, 2 × 0.50in. Browning	4 × 20mm Hispano

caught napping. The tactical fighter battles over Western Europe usually started with a surprise bounce, with the attacker making full use of the sun, or of cloud cover. The "Dora" pilots knew this full well, and took advantage of it. Only when the engagement degenerated into a confused multibogey dogfight would pilot quality and aircraft quality begin to tell. As they had done since 1940, the *Jagdflieger* adopted the old saying: "he who fights and runs away . . . !" This policy maximized effectiveness and minimized casualties, as it had done throughout the war.

There was one other relevant factor which offset poor training. Thrown into the crucible, if the youngsters survived their first sorties they gained combat experience rapidly. This was in stark contrast to the better-trained Allied flyers, many of whom had little opportunity of meeting the enemy. To digress for a moment, between 1943 and the end of the war, over 5,000 fighter pilots flew operationally with the U.S. Eighth Air Force. Of these, just 2,156 (43 percent) claimed so much as a share in a victory! Like every other human activity, air combat demands practice. Raw Allied pilots got far less than their opponents, and were thus very much at risk if they happened upon an *Experte*.

The *Experten*

Heavily overmatched, at risk from the time they began their takeoff roll to the time they switched off their engines after a mission, there was little scope for raw, young pilots, with perhaps a dozen hours on type, to make their mark. Staying alive was difficult enough, let alone running up a score, although a handful did moderately well. By and large, *Experten* who succeeded against the Allied tactical fighters had gained experience in less demanding scenarios, and had developed that strange sixth sense known as situational awareness.

JOSEF "PIPS" PRILLER "Pips" was just five feet four inches tall, but a giant in a fighter cockpit, one of the few to register over 100 victories entirely against the West. He started the war with *II/JG 51* and flew with them throughout the French campaign and the Battle of Britain, during the latter stages of which the *Geschwader* was commanded by Werner Mölders. His style of leadership was marked by a quirky sense of humor, and he was reputed to be the only fighter leader to be able to make Goering laugh when things were going badly. The following comment on an incident during the Battle of Britain is typical:

> I remember one occasion when a lad who hadn't, as we used to say, tasted much English air, lost sight of our formation after some frenzied twisting and turning about the sky: he had dived steeply and was over the outskirts of London. He should have stayed with the *Staffel* instead of chasing off on

his own. When he grasped the situation he called for help: "Come quickly! I'm on my own over London."

He hadn't called in vain. By return post, as it were, his *Schwarm* leader, whom he couldn't see but who could see him clearly and had followed astern and above him, gave the comforting message: "Hang on a second and you'll have a couple of Spitfires behind, then you won't be alone any longer."

By October 19 Priller had scored his twentieth victory, and a month later he was transferred to *1/JG 26* as *Staffelkapitän*. The next few months were quiet, but when the RAF commenced Circus operations in the early summer of 1941 he began scoring rapidly, claiming 20 victories between June 11 and July 14, including eighteen Spitfires. The last of these was of particular interest as the attack was made from head-on at 33,000 feet against the middle Spitfire of a section of three flying in line astern. Priller seems not to have seen the leader. In the rarefied air at high altitude, engine power falls markedly, while, to obtain sufficient lift, the angle of attack of the wings has to be increased. At 33,000 feet an aircraft in level flight adopts a distinct nose-up attitude, which restricts still further the already limited view ahead. Priller took full advantage of this by attacking in a shallow climb, closing to 100 meters' range. The Spitfire pilot bailed out, but then "Pips" had to dive away to escape the attentions of the third fighter.

Further successes followed, and Priller became *Kommodore* of *JG 26* on January 11, 1943, at which time he was the leading *Experte* of the *Geschwader*. His standards were high, so much so that, when in February 1943 *III/JG 54* transferred from the East to come under his command, he refused to declare them operational for some considerable time.

Priller's score continued to mount, and twelve victories between April 5 and 13 took it to 96. During this year he also conducted a considerable amount of weapons and other testing, while increased responsibilities on the ground restricted his operational flying. His century was a long time in coming.

When, on June 6, 1944, the Allies landed in Normandy, *JG 26* was caught unprepared. Two *Gruppen* were in the process of moving to bases farther inland; the third was in southern France. Only the *Stab* was in a position to mount an immediate sortie, and this was flown by Priller himself, with his regular *Kacmarek*, Heinz Wodarczyk. Taking full advantage of low cloud, the two FW 190 pilots made a full-throttle strafing run over "Sword" Beach, then returned the way they came. They were the only *Luftwaffe* presence over the invading forces that morning.

Priller's 100th victory came on June 15 when leading a fighter sweep over Normandy. His mixed formation of *II* and *III/JG 26*, and *III/JG 54*, encountered a formation of American heavy bombers with a strong fighter escort. His combat report read:

> I made a front quarter attack on the first box from the same altitude, and obtained several strikes on one of the Boeings on the left of the formation. After a battle at close range with the very strong escort, I attacked a formation of about 20 Liberators from head-on. I fired at the Liberator flying in the left outboard position in the first Vic, and saw strikes on the cockpit and both port engines. After I dived away, I saw the Liberator fall away from its formation with bright flames coming from three engines. I did not see it hit the ground because of the continuing air battle.

A double command now came Priller's way, which restricted his flying still more. His 101st and final victory was a P-51 Mustang on October 12. Only eleven heavy bombers featured in his overall tally: as a general rule he preferred to take on the escorts. Priller's final mission was leading *JG 26* in *Operation Bodenplatte* on January 1, 1945. At the end of that month he was transferred to a staff job.

"Pips" Priller's greatest value in the post-invasion period was not the number of victories scored, but his leadership and example. Of the eight pilots who scored 100 or more against the Western powers, only Adolf Galland (103), Egon Mayer

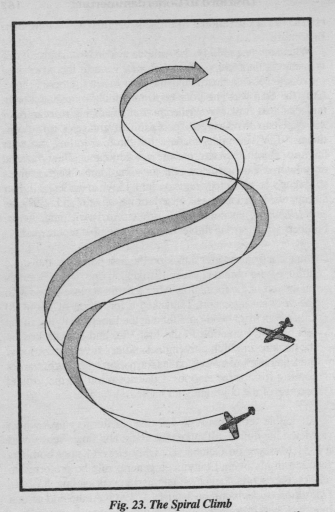

Fig. 23. The Spiral Climb
Heinz Knoke of JG 11 was one of many German fighter pilots to use the spiral climb as a means of evading American escorts. With the angle and distance constantly changing, it made his Messerschmitt an almost impossible target. The spiral dive was an alternative, for the same reasons.

(102), and Josef Priller (101) did so exclusively in Western Europe. It is also worthy of note that RAF top scorer Johnnie Johnson saw fit to record in his book *Full Circle* that most of Priller's claims could be confirmed from Allied records.

ADOLF GLUNZ The little-known "Addi" Glunz had a truly remarkable record. By *Jagdwaffe* standards his victory tally of 71, three of which were in the East, was good but not exceptional. What was unusual was that, in 574 sorties, the vast majority of which were over Western Europe, and in which he encountered the enemy on 238 occasions, he was never once shot down or wounded. The nearest he ever came to losing an aircraft was on October 13, 1944, when a broken oil pipe caused his motor to seize during a fight with two Thunderbolts. Engineless, he evaded the American fighters by hard turns, followed by a near-vertical dive into cloud. Having shaken off his pursuers, he made a good wheels-up landing in a field.

Glunz joined *4/JG 52* on the Channel coast in March 1941, but his first three victories came with this unit during the first three weeks of the Russian campaign. He was then sent back to the Channel, to *4/JG 26*. Having converted to the FW 190A, his score slowly mounted.

Addi Glunz was both determined and persistent. A confused multibogey battle on March 13, 1942, separated him from his unit. Alone but undaunted, he stalked a Spitfire formation out to sea, picked one off in a surprise attack, then damaged a second before making good his escape. The Schweinfurt raid of August 17, 1943, saw a further example of his coolness. As *II/JG 26* lined up to assault the bombers on their homeward journey, they were bounced by Thunderbolts and scattered. In the general confusion Glunz dodged the escorts and shot down a B-17. His was the only bomber success of the action.

Proficiency in instrument flying led to his 45th victory on November 14. Daylight nuisance raids by single Mosquitos did little actual damage but, by activating air raid warnings across the Reich, caused considerable disruption to industry. Addi took off alone and, directed by ground control, climbed through heavy cloud to 28,000 feet. Soon he saw the Mosquito skimming along below, a few hundred feet above the dazzling white cloud tops. His FW 190A was above its best height here, but a gentle dive brought him below and behind. Slowly he closed on his prey, then with it firmly in his sights he pressed the firing buttons. This was the first of three Mosquitos that fell to his guns.

Glunz's greatest day in combat came on February 22, 1944. By now a *Staffelführer* (a probationary *Staffelkapitän*), he led *5/JG 26* into action against the American heavy bombers. In the first mission of the day he shot down two B-17s and forced a third out of formation. That afternoon he claimed another two B-17s and a Thunderbolt. Only three B-17s and the P-47 were confirmed, but these brought his score to 58.

The invasion and its aftermath saw Allied fighters fill the skies, yet Glunz continued to fly, to survive, and to score. The weather was often on the side of the *Luftwaffe*: heavy cloud provided a useful means of escape when things got tough. This was the case on June 10. Hurtling around the cloud banks, he got behind an American fighter and sent it down in flames before seeking the foggy interior of a cumulus to avoid retribution. Inside, he almost collided with the tail of another American. As they hurtled out of the cloud he pressed the firing buttons and his shells tore into the doomed fighter. But as he fired, he saw the American's wingman barely 30 feet away! Without ceasing to fire, Addi kicked the rudder to skid his Focke-Wulf sideways, liberally spraying the other aircraft at close range. It fell away. All three victories were confirmed, bringing his total to 64.

Addi Glunz survived *Operation Bodenplatte,* during which he was credited with the destruction of five aircraft on the ground. In February 1945 he was assigned to *JG 7* to convert to the Me 262, but, so far as is known, he never flew the jet operationally. Of his 68 victories in the West, 20 were four-engine bombers.

To what did Glunz attribute his success? He was an expert aircraft handler, owing to his having been an aerobatic pilot from an early age. His exceptional distance vision gave him a tactical advantage; in this he is similar to American ace Charles

Yeager. He was a natural shot, and there were all too few of them in any service. Finally, when he first joined *JG 26*, he came under the influence of Adolf Galland, whose principle was: "Never abandon the possibility of attack. Attack even from a position of inferiority, to disrupt the enemy's plans. This often results in improving one's own position."

10. RETREAT IN THE EAST

The German defeat at Kursk in July–August 1943 marked the beginning of a series of retreats which ended twenty months later when the Russians entered Berlin. In fact, this period has been aptly described as the *Blitzkreig* in reverse. The *Luftwaffe* had long suffered from numerical inferiority, aggravated from the autumn of 1943 by the withdrawal of fighter units for Reich air defense. To this was now added Soviet strategic initiative. Russian pressure along the whole vast front made it necessary to deploy *Jagdflieger* in small groups in order to provide cover everywhere. In doing so, the principle of concentration of force, which might have ensured local air superiority at critical points, was abandoned. No attempt was made to strengthen the German fighter force: virtually all spare capacity went to the Western and Mediterranean fronts.

By June 1944 the *Jagdwaffe* deployed a mere 395 single-engine fighters in the East, on a front which, despite extensive Russian gains, was still more than 1,500 miles long. Against them were ranged a massive 13,500 aircraft, of which just under half were fighters. The odds were great; they would get still greater. To make matters worse, the vital Romanian oil fields were not only threatened by the Russian advance; they were now within range of American heavy bombers based in Italy.

So thinly was the German Army stretched that on occasion Russian armor broke through and overran *Luftwaffe* forward airfields. Emergency evacuations were frequent, and often the "black men" (ground crews, so called because of the color of their overalls) had to be left to fend for themselves as best they might. Added to the inevitable loss of spares, this did nothing to aid serviceability. By autumn of that year the Axis allies Finland and Romania were out of the war, while shortly afterward *Luftflotte 1* was cut off and isolated in Courland. From this time on, fuel shortages bit deep, as they did on all other fronts.

In a last desperate attempt to stem the Red tide, the *Luftwaffe* switched about 650 fighters from the West in late January and early February 1945. While this brought the numbers up to between 850 and 900, it was too little, too late. The Soviet Air Force had expanded at a still greater rate and by now deployed approximately 16,000 combat aircraft. One *Jagdgeschwader*, with about 80 brand-new FW 190As on strength, was so limited for fuel that it could only put up four fighters at a time!

As in the first years of the Russian campaign, the use of airpower was almost entirely tactical and engagements took place at medium and low levels. The *Jagdflieger* had two main tasks for most of this period: to protect their own infantry from enemy attack aircraft, and to protect their own tank-busting aircraft from enemy fighters. In either case they were usually heavily outnumbered, and when they encountered the elite Russian Guards Fighter Regiments they were sometimes outfought.

The Russian fighter pilots had come a long way since 1941. Apart from adopting pairs and fours as standard fighting units, they tended to fly everywhere at full throttle to keep their speed high. Offensively, this reduced the time between sighting and attacking, thus improving their chances of gaining surprise; defensively, it reduced the chance of their being surprised from astern by increasing the time taken by an opponent to close to firing range, while making greater demands on his time/distance judgment. Another Russian measure against surprise attack was the habit of flying in large and apparently undisciplined gaggles, with sections twisting and turning at random. As they rarely operated over long distances, they were able to afford a relatively low formation speed over the ground.

The Fighters

Several thousand British and American fighters were supplied to the Soviet Union during the war, of which the P-39 Airacobra was numerically the most important. At home, the Lavochkin and Yakovlev design bureaus produced some truly outstanding fighters. This was done by developing existing machines, which had the further advantage of causing the least disruption to production when switching from one model to the next.

Table 19. Russian Fighters, 1943–45

	Lavochkin La-5FN	Yakovlev Yak-9	Yakovlev Yak-3
Wingspan	31ft. 9in.	32ft. 10in.	30ft. 3in.
Length	28ft. 7in.	28ft. 1in.	27ft. 11in.
Height	11ft. 9in.	9ft. 10in.	9ft. 10in.
Wing area	188 sq. ft.	185 sq. ft.	160 sq. ft.
Engine	Shvetsov ASh-82FN radial rated at 1,850hp	Klimov VK-105PF inline rated at 1,240hp	Klimov VK-105PF-2 inline rated at 1,290hp
Loaded weight	7,407lb.	6,746lb.	5,864lb.
Wing loading	39lb./sq. ft.	36lb./sq. ft.	37lb./sq. ft.
Maximum speed	403mph	367mph	407mph
Service ceiling	31,150ft.	36,100ft.	35,430ft.
Rate of climb	4.7 min. to 16,400ft.	4.5 min. to 16,400ft.	4.5 min. to 16,400ft.
Range	475 miles	565 miles	415 miles
Armament	2 × 20mm ShVAK	1 × 20mm ShVAK, 2 × 12.7mm UBS	1 × 20mm ShVAK 2 × 12.7mm UBS

The Lavochkin La-5 was initially the LaGG-3 adapted to take the more powerful Shvetsov ASh-82A radial engine. As the engine of the latter aircraft was a liquid-cooled inline, considerable modification was needed to the forward fuselage. The next step was to cut down the rear fuselage and fit an all-around-vision canopy. To protect the back of the pilot's head, armored glass was used. The La-5 was then subjected to considerable redesign. The engine was the new ASh-82FN, with fuel injection. Weight was saved by replacing wooden wing spars with metal ones, and boundary-layer leading-edge slats were fitted. The new model became the La-5FN, which entered service in 1943. Light, well-harmonized controls gave it excellent qualities in the rolling plane while moderate wing loading allowed it to turn tightly.

The final Lavochkin design to enter service in any numbers (from 1944) was the La-7. Although powered by the same engine, it showed marked improvements over the La-5FN, thanks to various small aerodynamic refinements. Although a later model, it did not replace the La-5FN, but is believed to have been introduced as an interceptor to counter the FW 190A-8. Top Soviet ace Ivan Kozhedub gained all his 62 victories while flying Lavochkin fighters.

Alexsandr Yakovlev's Yak-1 spawned a whole family of new and agile fighters. Numerically the most important of these were the Yak-9, optimized for low-level work, and the Yak-3, a slightly smaller and lighter machine which performed well at the higher altitudes. Externally they were very similar, which made life difficult for a *Jagdflieger* who was trying to decide what he was up against, and both bore a marked resemblance to the Yak-1, except for a cut-down rear fuselage and an all-around-vision canopy. The Yak-9 made its combat debut at Stalingrad in December 1942, while the Yak-3 entered service late in 1943. French pilots in the Normandie-Niemen Regiment claimed that the Yak-3 was even smoother to fly than the early Spitfires. It was certainly faster and had a better rate of climb, and whereas the ailerons on the British fighter stiffened up at high speeds, those of the Yak-3 remained light.

The German fighter types on the Eastern Front between 1943 and 1945 were the later variants of the Bf 109G and FW 190A, which have been dealt with in previous chapters. Given that the fighting on the Russian Front took place almost entirely at medium and low levels, it seems surprising that the FW 190A, a dogfighter par excellence, was not used by all fighter units. In fact, the demands for this machine were such that there were never enough to go around. Reconnaissance, close air support (the *Schlachtgruppen*), and even antishipping units all clamored for the Focke-Wulf.

The shortage of *Jagdgruppen* meant that close air support units had frequently to provide their own fighter escort, and, as a result, a few *Schlachtflieger* ran up respectable scores in air combat. The most outstanding was August Lambert. Previously an instructor, he arrived at the front in April 1943. At first Lambert scored slowly, but in the Crimea in spring 1944 he had an incredible run of 70 victories in three weeks, 46 of which were scored in the course of three separate days! Shortly afterward he returned to instructing. He was killed on April 17, 1945, when Mustangs caught him shortly after takeoff, his final score 116.

Although the FW 190A was the better machine in the dogfight, many leading Russian Front *Experten* preferred the Bf 109G, despite its nasty qualities during takeoff and landing and its inferior rearward vision during combat.

Flying the Bf 109G

Start by climbing onto the port wing, then walk forward to the cockpit. Grab the framing, then stretch your right leg in past the control column, ducking under the canopy as you do so. Shuffle down, pulling your left leg after you, and seat yourself on the parachute which is submerged in the metal bucket seat. Now for the straps. Parachute harness first, then restraining straps. For heaven's sake don't mix them up—a mistake could be fatal. And strap in tight. If you have to make a wheels-up landing this trip, it will probably hurt anyway, but tight straps help. And if you have to bail out and your parachute harness is at all loose, it'll make your eyes sparkle!

It's a tight fit inside. The cockpit sills almost brush your shoulders, so keep your elbows tucked in. Your mechanic lowers the canopy and locks it. If you need to bail out during this sortie you can jettison it. The roof almost brushes the top of your leather flying helmet, while the side transparencies are only inches away. How confined it all is! The seat is very low to the floor and your legs are almost horizontal. This is an advantage in hard maneuvering, as it retards the onset of gray-out caused by blood draining from the head.

Time to start up. Select one-third flap, trim for takeoff, propeller to fine pitch, radiator flaps open, mixture to full rich, pump the yellow priming handle, then open the throttle. A mechanic on the starboard wing inserts a crank and begins to wind the inertia starter, slowly at first, then with ever-increasing speed. When it is turning fast enough, he removes the crank and you can now pull the small black starter handle. A few bangs, and puffs of black smoke from the exhausts, then the engine roars into life.

Time to taxi. The ground angle is steep, and the long nose blocks forward vision. You don't want to hit anything, so swing the aircraft from side to side while looking forward through the quarterlights. The ride is harsh, and you feel every bump. If you ran over a *pfennig* you could tell if it was heads or tails.

Takeoff! Throttle lever smoothly back (back to accelerate was standard continental practice) and the Daimler-Benz gives out its distinctive clattering "Thor's Anvil" song as it winds up. Brakes off, and the acceleration presses you back in the seat. A bootful of right rudder to hold you straight against the torque. Edge the stick forward: the nose rises and at last you can see ahead. Hold it down: if you let it rise too soon it will roll straight over onto its back—not nice! Speed builds up—185kph—that's enough; ease back on the stick and let the aircraft fly itself off.

Gear up, flaps up, radiator flaps closed, and back on the

stick. The 109G climbs like a bird at about 900 meters a minute, indicated speed something over 250kph. The controls are positive if a little heavy, but there is plenty of feel. Level out and ready for action! Flip the safety lid on the control column which covers the gun buttons. Switch on the gun sight, and a yellow circle and bars appear in the sighting glass which is offset to the right, in front of your "shooting eye." You are now ready for anything.

Keep a sharp lookout, especially toward the sun. That's where they'll come from. Don't get too low over the undercast: they'll see you from miles away against the white background. Actually the view "out of the window" is not so good. The heavy framing of the windshield and canopy could conceal a whole gaggle of Russians, so keep your head moving to peer into the blind spots, especially astern. Weave so that you can check under your tail, and cover your wingman.

Time to go home. Down again, circle the field and line up for landing. Don't let the speed drop too much. Gear down and full flap. You are very busy, and this is where many 109 pilots come to grief. Nose high and plenty of power as the angle of attack increases and the drag builds. As speed decays through 160kph, the port wing becomes heavy. Ease the stick to the right to counter it, but gently. If speed bleeds off too quickly, drop the nose a tad. Whatever you do, don't bang the throttle open now: if you do, the torque will roll you uncontrollably to port and you've no height left in which to recover. Ease onto the ground at about 135kph. The tires shriek, throttle forward, and suddenly your once graceful bird is jolting and bumping across the grass. Don't brake hard or you will ground-loop. That's it. You're down! You've done it!

The *Experten*

As Russian strength grew, the *Jagdflieger* operated in an increasingly target-rich environment. This had its drawbacks. While opportunities to score were plentiful, so were the chances of finding a Russian fighter on one's tail, and in the final two years of the war there were plenty of competent

Russian pilots. The secret of success was to survive, but this was far from easy. When shooting, the fighter pilot had to concentrate every ounce of his being on his target, oblivious to danger from behind, which, in a multibogey dogfight, was never far away. There were two ways of doing this. The first was teamwork, flying with three top-notch pilots making up the *Schwarm* to give cover; the second was keeping the situation controllable.

WALTER NOWOTNY Perhaps the greatest exponent of the first method was Walter Nowotny of *JG 54*, whose *Schwarm* became famous on the Eastern Front. It consisted of his regular *Kacmarek* Karl "Quax" Schnorrer (35 victories in Russia, 46 total), Anton Döbele (94, all in Russia), and Rudolf Rademacher (90 in Russia, 126 total). In his early days Schnorrer was involved in a series of landing mishaps which earned him the nickname "Quax." The original Quax was an accident-prone cartoon character in training films—the *Luftwaffe* version of Pilot Officer Prune. This notwithstanding, Schnorrer not only did a great job in covering Nowotny's tail, but later scored eleven victories while flying the Me 262 before being shot down and losing a leg. Of the others, Döbele was killed in a collision with a friendly fighter in November 1943 while Rademacher died in a glider crash a few years after the war.

Nowotny was an Austrian, and his first victories were scored in July 1941, but he was a relatively slow starter and he took more than a year over his first 50. His fast-scoring days began in June 1943, in which month he reached 100. The next 100 took a mere 72 days, by which time he was the fourth-highest scorer, while on October 14 he became the first pilot to reach 250. Five more followed before he was posted to a training wing. In July 1944 he returned to action with *Kommando "Nowotny,"* to fly the Me 262. He added only three more to his score before he was killed in action on November 8, 1944.

ERICH HARTMANN The highest-scoring *Experte* of all, with 352 victories, Hartmann survived the war without a scratch, even though downed many times. He was that rare bird, an unmilitaristic warrior, and spent virtually the entire war in the lower echelons. This allowed him to concentrate on the day-to-day business of air fighting and survival, without getting ensnared in the problems of higher command. His career has been documented in considerable detail, which allows us to gain a remarkably clear picture, not only of his tactics and methods, but how they were formed.

One consistent thread runs through Erich Hartmann's early years. He was fortunate in his formative influences. His mother was an early aviatrix, who introduced him to gliding when he was 14 years old. When, in early 1942, he learned to fly the Bf 109, one of his instructors was *Experte* and former aerobatic champion Erich Hohagen (55 total victories), who encouraged him to explore the maneuver capabilities of the type. In October 1942 he joined *9/JG 52*, and he was lucky again in his commanders. *Kommodore* Dietrich Hräbak (125 victories) and his *Kommandeur* Hubertus von Bonin (77) took a relaxed view of discipline at the front. This was just as well for the less-than-Prussian Hartmann. Under a more rigid commander, such as Karl Borris (43 victories) of *II/JG 26*, his career might have taken a very different course.

Hartmann was equally lucky in his first section leaders. Edmund "Paule" Rossmann (93 victories) was an excellent mentor for the novice. Unable to haul his Messerschmitt around in hard maneuvers due to an injured arm, Rossmann had been forced to develop standoff tactics. These consisted of standing back to weigh up the situation, attacking only with the advantage of surprise to make sure of a nonmaneuvering target, then opening fire from long range. This demanded a high degree of marksmanship, which fortunately Hartmann possessed.

Ace fighter pilots are often described as fearless. This is far from the truth. On his first encounter with an enemy aircraft Ernst Udet froze with fear and was unable to fight. Yet he went on to become the highest-scoring surviving German ace of the Great War, with 62 victories. As with Udet, so with Hartmann. On his first mission with Rossmann he lost his leader, panicked, and ended up belly-landing out of fuel far from his base. This humbling experience taught him to control his fear.

Three other section leaders helped shape the tactics of the budding *Experte*. The difficulties of downing the heavily armored I1-2 have been mentioned. Alfred Grislawski (133 victories) taught Hartmann to aim for the oil cooler. Not only did this call for marksmanship of a high order, it required close-range shooting. Hartmann's first victory, on November 9, 1942, was an I1-2, but he paid a high price. Pieces torn off the stricken Russian damaged his aircraft, forcing him to belly-land. The other two were Hans Dammers (113) and Josef Zwernemann (126). Like Grislawski, they taught the novice to get in close before firing.

It was February 27, 1943, before Hartmann, flying as *Kacmarek* to these three, scored his second victory. Shortly after this two new mentors appeared. These were Günther Rall, who replaced von Bonin as *Kommandeur*, and Walter Krupinski (197 victories, 177 in the East). Generally known as "*Graf* Punski" owing to his propensity for living life to the full, Krupinski would have been an outstanding character in any air force. In the air, he was a barroom brawler type of flyer with a habit of getting himself into impossible situations which he somehow survived. Hartmann was coerced into becoming his *Kacmarek* and under his tuition was encouraged to get in close before firing. Krupinski it was who gave Hartmann the nickname "Bubi" (Boy), and it stuck.

Toward the end of April 1943, Hartmann had acquired eight victories and become a *Rottenführer* (section leader). He was now free to develop his own ideas, which emerged as an amalgam of Rossmann's carefully considered attacks coupled with the "stick your nose in the enemy cockpit" approach of the others. Many years after the war he described it thus:

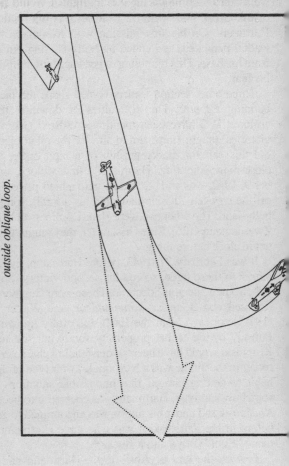

Fig. 24. Hartmann's "Last Ditch" Evasion Maneuver
As the enemy fighter approached, Hartmann used rudder to point his fighter in a slightly different direction from the way it was going, to mislead the attacker into misjudging the amount of deflection required. When his opponent opened fire, Hartmann slammed the stick into the far corner of the cockpit, putting his Messerschmitt into the first half of an outside oblique loop.

I never cared much for the dogfight. I would never dog-fight with the Russians. Surprise was my tactic. Get the highest altitude and, if possible, come out of the sun . . . ninety percent of my attacks were surprise attacks. If I had one success, I took a coffee break, and watched the area again.

Finding [the enemy] depended purely on being where the action was concentrated on the ground and on visual look-out. Ground stations called us by radio the position of the enemy after a coordinate system on our maps. So we could search in the right direction and choose our best attack alti-tude. If I covered the sky, I preferred a full-power, sun attack from below, because you could spot the enemy very far away against a white cloudy sky. The pilot who sees the other pilot first already has half the victory.

The second step of my tactic was the point of decision. That is, you see the enemy and decide whether to attack immediately, or wait for a better situation, or maneuver to make it more favorable, or not attack at all. For example, if you have to attack the enemy against the sun, if you don't have enough altitude, if the enemy is flying in broken clouds, you keep your enemy in sight far enough so you can change your attack position in the sun or above the clouds, diving to sell your altitude for high speed.

Then attack. It doesn't matter if you pick on the straggler or the guy out of formation. The most important thing is to destroy an enemy aircraft. Maneuver quickly and aggres-sively and shoot in close, as near as possible to ensure the hit and save rounds. I told my men, "Only if the windshield is filled up, then pull the trigger."

Finally break or reverse. If you hit and run, think about survival. Immediately check six [o'clock] and reverse. Clear the area for potential attackers or pick a new point of re-entry and do it again, if you have the advantage.

Hartmann encountered the enemy in the air on more than 800 occasions, and it was inevitable that sometimes he became a target. To counter this he had his own particular method:

Fly quickly straight ahead, and push the rudder so you fly a slight straight-ahead skid that will not be recognized by the attacker. If he opens fire, you push for negative Gs down left or right, not forgetting through the whole maneuver to push the rudder. Your attacker will hang with negative Gs in his belt, unable to pull the trigger. With that maneuver I saved my life several times.

Not until the middle of 1943 did Hartmann really get into his stride. At dawn on July 7 he had 21 victories. By dusk on September 20 that had risen to 100. The legends started. Hartmann is popularly supposed always to have flown a Bf 109G with a bleeding heart insigne below the cockpit inscribed with the name "Usch" (his fiancée), but at least one of his machines carried the legend "Dicker Max" in the heart! His personal aircraft is often depicted with a black tulip pattern painted on the engine cowling. In fact he flew a machine marked in this way on five or six occasions only, in the Ukraine. Success eluded him on these missions, so he abandoned it. Finally, he was widely supposed to be known to the Russians as "The Black Devil," a name widely at variance with his unmilitary call sign of "Karaya [Sweetheart] One," which of course was well known to his opponents.

Over the next months Russian after Russian fell before Hartmann's guns, and on July 1, 1944, he reached 250, the fifth and last pilot to do so. Still his tried and proven methods served him well, while less cautious *Experten* fell by the wayside. In March 1945, his score at 336, he was transferred to *JG 7* to fly the Me 262 jet fighter. But, with the airfield under constant attack, flying was limited, and shortly afterward he returned to *JG 52*, to finish the war in Romania. It was there that he encountered American Mustangs. He accounted for seven in all, but on one occasion he was trapped by eight American fighters and forced to bail out through fuel shortage, even though he had not been hit.

Shortly after this, the war ended. Erich Hartmann's final score was 352, of which 260 were fighters. He flew only the Bf 109G, of which he said:

It was very maneuverable, and it was easy to handle. It speeded up very fast, if you dived a little. And in the acrobatics maneuver, you could spin with the 109, and go very easy out of the spin. The only problems occurred during takeoff. It had a strong engine, and a small, narrow-tread undercarriage. If you took off too fast it would turn [roll] ninety degrees away. We lost a lot of pilots in takeoffs.

Erich Hartmann's score will never be matched. Few air forces have as many as 352 aircraft to lose, let alone to one man!

11. THE JET ACES

By 1944, piston-engine fighters were nearing the limits of what was technically possible, and tremendous increases in power were needed to make quite minor gains in performance. Further progress depended on a new form of propulsion. This was available in the form of the reaction motor, either the gas turbine or the rocket. Germany was well advanced in both, but the desperate war situation demanded that they be rushed into service before the technology was really mature. Nevertheless, the *Luftwaffe* had no fewer than three new types of jet or rocket fighter in service at the war's end. While this was a remarkable achievement, it was, again, too little, too late. The Allies dominated the sky over the Third Reich, and quality was ground down and defeated by quantity.

The Jets and Their Opponents

Two of the new fighter types achieved little, produced no *Experten*, and can therefore be dismissed after a cursory examination. These were the Heinkel He 162 *Volksjäger* and the Messerschmitt Me 163 *Komet*.

The *Volksjäger* or People's Fighter was a last desperate attempt to build up the numerical strength of the *Jagdwaffe* very quickly. The keynote was "quick and cheap," with mass production by semiskilled labor using readily available materials, and with the aircraft mass-flown by semiskilled pilots who, at least initially, were to convert onto type direct from glider training.

Unusually, the BMW turbojet was mounted dorsally, where it largely obscured the rear view from the cockpit. The aircraft

Table 20. German Jets, 1944–45

	Heinkel He 162A-2 *Volksjäger*	Messerschmitt Me 163 *Komet*	Messerschmitt Me 262 *Schwalbe*
Wingspan	23ft. 8 in.	30ft. 7in.	40ft. 11^1/$_2$in.
Length	29ft. 8^1/$_2$in.	18ft. 8in.	34ft. 9^1/$_2$in.
Height	8ft. 4^1/$_2$in.	9ft. 0in.	12ft. 7in.
Wing area	120 sq. ft.	211 sq. ft.	234 sq. ft.
Engine(s)	BMW 109-003E turbojet,1,760lb. static thrust	Walter HWK 109-509A rocket, 3,750lb. static thrust	2 × Junkers Jumo 109-004B turbojets, 1,980lb. static thrust
Loaded weight	5,490lb.	9,042lb.	14,101lb.
Wing loading	46lb./sq. ft.	43lb.–21lb./ sq. ft.	60lb./sq. ft.
Maximum speed	522mph	596mph	540mph
Service ceiling	36,000ft.	54,000ft.	37,565ft.
Rate of climb	4,230ft./min.	11,810ft./min.	3,937ft./min.
Range	620 miles	50 miles	526 miles
Armament	2 × 20mm MG 151	2 × 30mm MK 108	4 × 30mm MK 108

itself suffered from instability, and only a handful were ever encountered in action. *Experten* known to have flown it, although not necessarily in action, include Heinz Baer, of whom more later; Herbert Ihlefeld (130 victories); and Paul-Heinrich Dahne (98 at least), killed on a training flight in an He 162 on April 24, 1945.

The *Komet* was a point-defense interceptor powered by a liquid-fueled rocket motor. While this gave a maximum speed far in excess of any piston-engine fighter, and a rate of climb more than twice as great, it used fuel at a fantastic rate. Even though the fuel load carried exceeded the empty weight of the aircraft, it gave a maximum of only eight minutes' endurance, and rather less if full throttle was used throughout the flight.

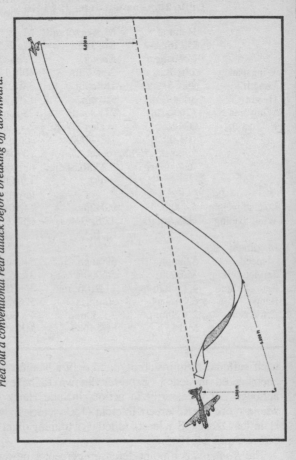

Fig. 25. The Roller-Coaster Attack

To attack American bombers, Me 262 pilots started from a position high astern. A shallow high-speed dive took them through the escorts to a point about one mile astern of the bombers and 1,500ft. below them. At this point they pulled up to dump speed and carried out a conventional rear attack before breaking off downward.

6,000 ft.

6,000 ft.

1,500 ft.

To minimize weight and thus maximize performance, the *Komet* did not have conventional landing gear: it took off from a wheeled dolly and landed back on a retractable skid. On a bumpy surface this was often hard, and back injuries to pilots were commonplace.

Two fuels were used, one of which was extremely corrosive, and pilots wore special resistant overalls. When in contact with one another, they ignited hypergolically. The mixture was very unstable, and the slightest leakage could result in an explosion. Accidents of this nature were frequent: the *Komet* killed more of its pilots than ever did the enemy.

In the air the *Komet* handled well, despite its unorthodox tailless configuration. Operationally it had to be held on the ground until the last minute, but when it was finally launched, its sparkling rate of climb took it to the altitude of the bombers in only two or three minutes. The smoke plume from its efflux meant that its approach could not be concealed, but it was too fast to be intercepted by conventional fighters. Once the fuel ran out, it became a glider. This was not quite as suicidal as it sounds. Even with power off, the *Komet* could be dived at speeds exceeding 500mph, while above 250mph it was remarkably agile. The real problem was getting it back to the airfield—and having to land at the first attempt.

Experten known to have flown the *Komet* were Wolfgang Späte (99 victories, mainly Eastern Front, plus five later with the Me 262) and Robert Olejnik (41 victories). The latter developed tactics for the *Komet* which involved roller-coastering through a bomber formation, going first over, then under each target in succession. On one occasion he accounted for three B-17s in a single sortie by this means, but shortly afterward was badly injured in a landing accident.

If the *Komet* could have been made reliable, it could have been an effective point defense interceptor. But, while it entered service with *JG 400*, it achieved little.

The only really effective German jet to see service was the Me 262, and this was limited by the short life and unreliability of its engines. Given the low thrust of the early turbojets, the choice was to go for a light and simple single-engine fighter such as the He 162 or produce a twin-engine design. In the case of the *Schwalbe*, the latter course was chosen. Two Junkers Jumo axial-flow turbojets were mounted underslung on the wings. With hindsight, that invaluable aid to decision-making, if the engines had been mounted side by side beneath the fuselage, the Me 262 might have been a better fighter. This configuration would have minimized problems of asymmetric handling, always a factor with unreliable engines, and have improved performance in the rolling plane. But this is with hindsight, and it didn't happen. One of the myths that have grown up around the Me 262 was that, had Hitler not seen it as a bomb-carrier, it could have been in service as a fighter much earlier. In fact, the *Führer*'s intervention cost a mere three weeks.

The great strength of the Me 262 was its overwhelming speed, which allowed it to penetrate the American escort screen with relative impunity. Its weaknesses were legion, even when the engines worked as they should. If an Me 262 could be forced to turn hard to evade, it bled off speed and became vulnerable. After takeoff, only slowly did it reach fighting speed, during which time it was vulnerable to enemy fighters. The basic armament consisted of four 30mm cannon. While these gave tremendous hitting power, the relatively low muzzle velocity meant that accurate shooting depended on getting to close range. Inevitably this brought the jet well inside the lethal range of return fire from the American bombers.

> Our "ground school" lasted one afternoon. We were told of the peculiarities of the jet engine, the dangers of flaming out at high altitude, and their poor acceleration at low speeds. The vital importance of handling the throttles carefully was impressed upon us, lest the engines catch fire. But we were not permitted to look inside the cowling of the jet engine—we were told it was very secret and we did not need to know about it!
> —Walther Hagenah, *III/JG 7*

Like all early jet engines, the Jumos were thirsty, and an average sortie lasted less than an hour. Nor was the Me 262 able to slow down quickly. To land it needed a long, straight approach, bleeding off speed as it went. During this time it was vulnerable and Allied fighters took to patrolling the approaches of known Me 262 airfields. Many Me 262s were lost in this way.

Schwalbe in Action

The first Me 262 unit was *Kommando "Nowotny,"* which commenced operations in July 1944. This was very much an operational trials unit, and problems with the underdeveloped engines ensured that rarely were more than four aircraft serviceable at any one time. Not until September was the Jumo 109-004 sufficiently advanced to enter mass production, and even then its life was short. Pilots had to fly the engines at least as much as the aircraft in order to keep temperatures within limits. The takeoff sequence was as follows:

Line up and apply both brakes. Set trim for 3 degrees nose-down, and flaps at 20 degrees. Start stopwatch. Open throttles to 7,000rpm, then release brakes and open throttles fully. Lift off between 175 and 200kph, with a gentle pull on the stick. Too hard a pull resulted in a high angle of attack, with a consequent increase in drag which the slow buildup of thrust might not be able to overcome. Brake wheels and retract undercarriage, avoiding exceeding 260kph while doing so. Retract flaps before speed reaches 360kph, then trim for normal flight. Engine revs for cruising: 8,000–8,300.

Once the 262 was in the air, the engine instruments and fuel gauges had to be monitored constantly. If the throttles were handled injudiciously, compressor stalls and flameout followed, while if the turbine temperatures rose too high fire was the normal result. To quote Adolf Galland on the subject, "The best thing was to go to a certain point and leave it, and then fly, and throttle back only when you are going to land." In combat, hard maneuvering with high angles of attack was avoided. Not only could this cause compressor stalling, but the increase in induced drag bled off speed at an alarming rate, which could only slowly be recovered. Once the speed advantage was lost, the *Schwalbe* was vulnerable to conventional fighters.

Landing was an equally delicate operation. First the engines were throttled back to 6,500rpm. Speed was then reduced to between 360 and 320kph. This was done by raising the nose to increase drag; at reduced power the aircraft continued to sink. Lowering the undercarriage made the Me 262 tail-heavy; this had to be trimmed out, and speed reduced to 300kph. Twenty degrees of flap was then selected. To turn, speed could not be allowed to fall below 280kph without risking loss of control.

According to the instruction manual, single-engine flight was quite possible, and turns could be made both into and against the dead engine. If the first landing approach was botched, an overshoot was theoretically possible, but, given the need to advance the throttles slowly, coupled with poor acceleration at low speed, this was obviously a marginal undertaking.

Me 262 in Service

The Me 262 equipped reconnaissance and bomber units during the war and several small specialist units such as *Kommando "Nowotny,"* but only a handful of fighter units. These were all three *Gruppen* of *JG 7*, and *I/KG(J) 54*, which employed bomber pilots because they were well used to instrument flying and could thus operate in adverse weather conditions. The argument was that it was quicker to train bomber pilots to fly fighters than to give instrument training to fighter pilots. *10/NJG 11* was the sole jet night fighter *Staffel*. Finally there was the famous *JV (Jagdverband) 44*, composed entirely of *Experten*.

Although the Allies had encountered the Me 262 in action from the late summer of 1944, the fact was that by the second week in January 1945 not one day fighter unit was operational. Not until February 9 did the new jet operate in force, and even then the day ended in disaster. Ten ex–bomber pilots of *I/KG(J) 54* intercepted a massive American bomber raid, only to lose six jets to Mustangs. Just one B-17 was damaged.

Rudolf Rademacher of *III/JG 7*, lately of the *"Nowotny*

Schwarm," scored all his eight jet victories during February. They consisted of a reconnaissance Spitfire, a Mustang, five B-17s, and a B-24. But few were so lucky. Then, toward the end of the month, *JV 44* was formed under the command of Adolf Galland. This was an elite unit in the truest sense of the term. Members included Gerd Barkhorn (301 victories), Heinz Baer (220), *"Graf* Punski" Krupinski (197), "Macky" Steinhoff (176), Günther Lützow (108 victories), and Heinz "Wimmersol" Sachsenberg (104). A galaxy of stars also gravitated to the much larger *JG 7*, among them Erich Rudorffer (222), Heinrich Ehrler (209), Theodor Weissenberger (208), and Walter Schuck (206). It was this unit which delivered the first large-scale Me 262 attack on March 3, 1945, when 29 jet sorties were flown against the American "heavies." Claims were six bombers and two fighters, for a single Me 262 lost.

On several occasions that month, between 20 and 40 jets tackled heavily escorted formations of over 1,000 bombers. The results showed what several hundred jet fighters might have achieved. Two notable *Experten* from *JG 7* paid the ultimate price during this period. They were Hans "Dackel" Waldemann (134 victories), who collided with another Me 262 in fog on March 18, and Heinrich Ehrler, who fell to return fire from the bombers on April 4.

Not until April 5 did *JV 44* fly its first sorties, and by that time the situation was so desperate that only a handful of aircraft could be scrambled at any one time. Galland's elite band could do no more than nibble at the fringes.

The *Experten*

The Me 262 came late into action, and virtually all its missions were flown against incredible odds. Only a handful of *Experten* scored double figures in the jet. But, bearing in mind the military situation at that time, this was a remarkable achievement. To digress for a moment, the German jet top score of 16 has only once been exceeded (by one), by an Israeli pilot almost thirty years later.

JOHANNES "MACKY" STEINHOFF Only six of "Macky" Steinhoff's 176 victories were with the Me 262, but as *Kommodore* of *JG 7*, the first ever jet fighter *Geschwader*, charged with evolving tactics suitable for the new type, he is arguably the *Experte* who had the greatest influence on its subsequent operations.

Steinhoff commenced the war as *Staffelkapitän* of the night-flying *10/JG 26*, equipped with Messerschmitt Bf 109Ds. This notwithstanding, his first victory occurred in daylight, a Wellington bomber on December 18, 1939. As related earlier, he then transferred to day fighters. He led *4/JG 52* throughout the Battle of Britain, then took part in the invasion of Russia with this unit. Steinhoff's 150th victory came in February 1943, then in the following month he was posted to *JG 77* in Tunisia as *Kommodore*. With this unit he had the unenviable task of supervising two evacuations in quick succession, first from North Africa and then from Sicily. In December 1944 he was appointed to command *JG 7*.

Steinhoff's first task was to prepare his new unit for operations. An early innovation was to drop the four-aircraft *Schwarm* in favor of the three-ship *Kette*. This was a matter of convenience. The Me 262 could not operate from grass fields, only from long, hard-surfaced runways. At a pinch, three Me 262s could line up abreast on a standard runway for a formation takeoff. Whereas the *Schwarm* had been adopted for mutual cover, sheer speed could protect the Me 262 against attack from astern. As we saw earlier, Egon Mayer of *JG 2* used the *Kette* against the "heavies," ceasing only when escort fighters made it impractical.

The next problem addressed was the attack. Sheer speed

Me 262 Aces

Heinz Baer 16	Hermann Buchner 12	Erich Rudorffer 12
Franz Schall 14	Georg-Peter Eder 12	Karl Schnorrer 11

was wonderful for evading (or surprising) escort fighters, but it could be embarrassing when attacking the much slower bombers. To quote Steinhoff,

> Swinging into the target's wake from above was out because of the danger of exceeding the maximum safe speed, the aircraft having no dive brakes with which to check the acceleration involved in such a maneuver. Frontal attack on a collision course with the bombers—a favorite with the *Experten* because the target was then virtually defenseless and the crews of the Flying Fortresses were exposed to the hail of bullets—was also out because the combined approach speeds (about 700mph) made a considered attack impossible.

> Even from astern the closing speed was still too high. The truth was that there was no ideal solution to the problem while the aircraft was restricted to attacking with guns. A compromise solution was to take position about three miles astern of the bombers and about a mile higher, then launch into a high-speed, shallow dive, aiming at a point about a mile astern and about 500 meters below. On reaching this the jets pulled up to bleed off speed, after which they were well placed to attack with a more reasonable rate of overtake. But they still had to run the gauntlet of the bombers' defensive fire, and losses to this cause were still high.

Politics then intervened, and Steinhoff left *JG 7* under a cloud. Shortly afterward he became a founder member of *JV 44*. In April he encountered USAAF Lightnings. Automatically he dived to the attack:

> . . . the Lightnings loomed up terrifying fast in front of me, and it was only for the space of seconds that I was able to get into firing position behind one of the machines on the outside of the formation. And as if they had received prior warning they swung around smartly as soon as I opened fire. *Pop, pop, pop* went my cannon in furious succession. I tried to follow a Lightning's tight turn but the gravity pressed me

down on my parachute with such force that I had trouble keeping my head in position to line the sight up with him . . . Then a shudder went through my aircraft as my leading-edge flaps sprang out: I had exceeded the permissible gravity load.

The highly wing-loaded Me 262 was no dogfighter. The Lightnings spiraled away downward and Steinhoff was unable to follow. His jet had no speed brakes, and it was impossible to dive the Me 262 steeply without reaching its limiting Mach number. A few days later Macky Steinhoff crashed on takeoff and was badly burned. He survived the war to command the new *Luftwaffe*.

KURT WELTER A flying instructor during the first years of the war, Welter joined the *Wilde Sau* unit *10/JG 300* in the summer of 1943, flying the FW 190A-8. In only 40 sorties he scored 33 victories, four of them by day. In the summer of 1944 his unit was absorbed by *2/NJG 11*. In December 1944 he started to fly the Me 262 at night, leading a small detachment called *Kommando "Welter."* Against heavy bombers at night, the great speed of the Me 262 was even more of an embarrassment than it was by day, but it was an excellent Mosquito hunter—the only night fighter handily to outperform the British aircraft. Welter also evaluated a night fighter variant of the Arado 234, but rejected this on the grounds that the paneled glazing of the cockpit caused too many distracting reflections.

While some of his jet victories were with a standard Me 262, flying under close ground control and using the searchlight illumination system, he also flew a single-seater fitted with the FuG 218 radar. He was credited with two heavy bombers and three Mosquitos with this aircraft. A handful of radar-equipped two-seaters were introduced into service in February 1945, and flown by *10/NJG 11* under Welter's command, the only jet night fighter unit in the *Luftwaffe*. In all, this unit, between its formation in January and the end of the war, was credited with destroying 43 Mosquitos at night and another five high-altitude reconnaissance aircraft by day. This was achieved in only 70 sorties.

Welter's exact score is unknown, but is generally agreed to exceed 50 victories, although some sources put it higher. About 35 of these were stated to be Mosquitos, one of which he rammed, although whether this was deliberate or accidental is unclear. He survived the war but is believed to have died in an accident in 1947.

✠ EPILOGUE

Whatever one's feelings about the regime for which they fought, the courage and ability of the *Jagdflieger* were beyond question, while their achievements in air combat surpassed those of any other nation by a wide margin. At first their scores were greeted with incredulity in the West, but extensive post-war research has led to widespread acceptance.

The ace fighter pilot is a modern phenomenon, a throwback to the days of the single-combat champion. He was born of the slaughter of the First World War, where tens of thousands of faceless ones died in the mud, slain by men like themselves, but by men whom they rarely if ever saw. At a time like this, heroes were desperately needed.

Air combat effectively commenced in 1915. The early flyers fought in the clean blue sky high above the trenches, man to man. Their achievements could not only be seen but measured by the number of enemy airplanes shot down. Inevitably they became the knights of the air, an illusion fostered by the adoption of their own unique forms of often irreverent heraldry.

Although the average artilleryman was responsible for the lives of far more enemy than the average fighter pilot, it was the latter who attracted the most attention. The fighter aces returned lost qualities to warfare—chivalry and glamour. In fact there was precious little chivalry in air combat, but the aura of glamour, and with it the inspiration to others, remained. The *Jagdwaffe* simply continued the tradition.

In any analysis of the *Experten*, three questions must be addressed. The first is the perennial vexed question of over-claiming, which has bedeviled researchers for many years. The second is, why did the *Experten* outscore their opponents by such a wide margin? The third is, who was the greatest German fighter pilot of all?

Overclaiming
Jagdflieger claims were often inflated to double or treble the true enemy losses. This trend was not of course confined to Germany; it was exhibited by all other nations without exception. There were several ways in which it could happen. The first and most obvious was that more than one fighter attacked the same target in quick succession and all claimed it in good faith. The second was that, while the target was hit and appeared to go down out of control, its pilot recovered at a lower altitude. The third, which applied more to inexperienced pilots, was that they opened fire, felt sure that they scored hits, then took their eyes off the target to clear their tails. Then, when they looked back, they saw an aircraft going down, and optimistically assumed it was their doing. In this connection, playing dead was a widely used ploy to shake off an attacker; if done convincingly this normally led to a mistaken claim.

The *Luftwaffe* checked claims as carefully as circumstances would permit, and a significant proportion were disallowed for various reasons. In some cases, if an enemy aircraft went down into the sea and there were no witnesses, pilots might not even bother to make a claim. The conclusion must be that claims were generally made and upheld in good faith.

The real problem is, what constitutes a victory? An enemy aircraft destroyed qualifies perfectly, but proving that this is the case is another matter. A badly damaged aircraft that had to force-land away from base could easily be repairable. At the other extreme, an enemy aircraft claimed only as damaged might crash unseen, or be struck off charge on its return to base.

If a nonsense on the subject of scores is to be avoided, we must eschew the controversial and emotive word "kill" and work on the principle that an aerial victory occurs when an enemy is defeated in combat in circumstances where the victor believes that it will be a total loss.

Relative Scores

A point that puzzles many is, how were the leading *Experten* able to outscore their opponents by such a wide margin? Many factors were involved in this. A superior tactical system in the first years of the war, which frequently put formation leaders in a prime shooting position, was undoubtedly one. Operational circumstance was another. For example, during the Battle of Britain, not only did the *Jagdflieger* usually have altitude and positional advantages, but their opponents were more concerned to get among the bombers than to tackle the fighters.

A principle whereby the highest scorer led the formation regardless of rank aided many to add to their totals quickly, and whereas Allied pilots were rested at frequent intervals, the German practice was to keep them in action for as long as possible. This had the advantage of building up unparalleled experience levels, although there can be no doubt that in the final twelve months of the war many high scorers were "flown out."

The main factor was opportunity. By and large the *Experten* flew more sorties than their Allied opponents, and encountered the enemy in the air far more times. In *Full Circle*, British top scorer Johnnie Johnson compared his record to that of "Pips" Priller:

> . . . with 38 victories, which may be compared with Priller's 101, for we both fought over the same territory for about the same time, but he saw many more hostile airplanes than I did . . .

At the other extreme, Hartmann entered combat on no fewer than 825 occasions, so, given that he survived and shot straight, his enormous score is hardly surprising. By comparison with some, his sortie-to-victory ratio was relatively modest. Some Allied pilots did much better: to quote but one example, American ace Bob Johnson took only 91 sorties to accumulate his 28 victories. And he flew the supposedly inferior Thunderbolt!

Mirror, Mirror, on the Wall . . .

Who was the greatest ace of all? There are many contenders. Galland as a great fighter leader, Hartmann as the absolute top scorer, and Marseille as top scorer against the Western allies—all have their backers. Much depends on what values are assigned to each theater. The record suggests that victories in the West were much harder to come by than those in the East, with North Africa, with its accent on purely tactical operations, somewhere in the middle. Fighter combat called for great flying skills and marksmanship; tackling the American "heavies" needed nerves of steel, with a fair helping of luck to aid survival. And what of the night defense of the Reich, facing not only the guns of the bombers and the technically superior Mosquito intruders, but the weather as a third, unrelenting foe?

Regardless of the relative difficulties of each front, the record shows quite clearly that *Experten* who were successful on one front frequently failed when switched to another. Only two top scorers did really well wherever they were sent. They were Heinz Baer and Erich Rudorffer.

HEINZ BAER Heinz "Pritzl" Baer began the war as a humble *Unteroffizier* (Corporal) with *JG 51* and ended it an *Oberstleutnant* (Lieutenant-Colonel) with *JV 44*. He opened his account, downing a French Curtiss Hawk 75, on September 25, 1939, and added three more victories by the end of the French campaign. The Battle of Britain almost proved his undoing. Always aggressive, he learned the hard way not to enter a turning fight with Spitfires or Hurricanes. On several occasions he force-landed his badly damaged Bf 109E back in France. Then, on September 2, once again returning damaged, he was shot down into the Channel by a marauding Spitfire.

Legend has it that Hermann Goering himself watched this rather uninspiring performance. He had the still-dripping pilot hauled in front of him and asked him what he thought about while in the water. Baer reportedly replied, "Your speech, *Herr Reichsmarschall*, that England is no longer an island!" This notwithstanding, at the end of 1940 Baer was the top-scoring

NCO pilot. Four more victories followed on the Channel front, bringing his total to 17 before *JG 51* was transferred east for Barbarossa.

Baer shot down 96 Russians over the next year, despite a spell in the hospital with spinal injuries. Then, as *Kommandeur*, he led *I/JG 77* from Sicily against Malta, and went on to North Africa. After the fall of Tunisia in the spring of 1943 he was withdrawn from operations with malaria and a stomach ulcer, his score 158.

He returned to combat late that year as *Kommandeur* of *II/JG 1*, on home defense, flying the FW 190 for the first time against the American heavy bombers. With at least 21 claimed, he ranks high among the heavy bomber specialists. His final assignments were as *Kommodore* of *JG 3*, with whom he scored his 200th victory on April 22, 1944; as commander of the jet fighter school at Lechfeld from January 1945, where he flew the He 162; and finally with *JV 44*, which he commanded after Galland was wounded and Günther Lützow (108 victories) was killed.

Baer's 220 confirmed victories place him eighth on the overall list of *Experten*. On the other hand, he accounted for more Western-flown aircraft (124) than any other German pilot except Marseille, and whereas almost all Marseille's victories were scored in Africa, Baer scored at least 75 of his against British and American-flown aircraft in Europe—a much tougher proposition. Of these, sixteen were scored with the Me 262, making him the leading jet ace of all nations until about 1973, a handful being scored with a special aircraft fitted with a rocket motor, so adapted to intercept high-flying Mosquitos.

It was not done without cost. Baer was a victim eighteen times in all, bailing out four times and force-landing the rest. Spitfires were responsible on seven of these occasions. Pritzl Baer survived the war, but he died in a light aircraft accident in 1957.

ERICH RUDORFFER The only record remotely comparable with Heinz Baer's is that of Erich Rudorffer, a natural marksman with a flair for high-angle-off attacks, who was reckoned to be one of the four best shots in the *Luftwaffe*.

Rudorffer's career parallels that of Baer in many ways. He began the war as an *Oberfeldwebel* (Flight Sergeant) with *I/JG 2* in 1940 and ended it as a *Major*. His first victory, like that of Baer, was over a Curtiss Hawk 75, on May 14, 1940. He scored eight more before the capitulation. He flew throughout the Battle of Britain, and legend has him being pursued down Croydon High Street below rooftop level by a Hurricane! His nineteenth victory was achieved on May 1, 1941, which put him slightly ahead of Baer at the time; he was appointed *Staffelkapitän* of *6/JG 2* the following month. With this *Geschwader* he stayed on the Channel coast, flying with such worthies as Mayer and Eder. Like Eder, he could be chivalrous. He recalled:

Once—I think it was August 31, 1940—I was in a fight with four Hurricanes over Dover. I was back over the Channel when I saw another Hurricane coming from Calais, trailing white smoke, obviously in a bad way. I flew up alongside him and escorted him all the way to England and then waved good-bye. A few weeks later the same thing happened to me.

In November 1942, by now equipped with FW 190As, Rudorffer's unit was sent to Tunisia. Like Werner Schroer, Rudorffer adopted Marseille's technique:

When we started for the bombers the Curtiss fighters came down on us and that's when the dogfight began. After a time the P-40s, which were not as fast as us, went into a Lufbery circle and I began to slip in from low and high and shoot them down. I managed to shoot down six in seven minutes. As I recall the combat report, I got one at 13:59; another at 14:00; a third within the minute; another at 14:02; one at 14:05; and the last at 14:06. By that time the fight had broken up and everyone had scattered.

After Tunisia fell, Rudorffer returned to the Channel, but in June 1943 he was transferred to the Russian Front as *Kommandeur* of *II/JG 54*. On November 6 he had his biggest-ever day, with thirteen victories. His score advanced rapidly against the Russians, but in January he was recalled to command *II/JG 7*. He scored twelve victories with the Me 262, to bring his final total to 222, of which 136 were on the Eastern Front and ten were American heavy bombers. The cost was high: he was shot down sixteen times, and he outclassed Baer in parachute jumps with no fewer than nine.

Although ranked in seventh place overall, one ahead of Baer, Rudorffer did less well against the Western powers. Of his 86 in the West, nine were in the French campaign and 26 in Tunisia.

There is little to choose between Baer and Rudorffer. But, having said that, contenders such as Schnaufer and Schroer should not be lightly dismissed.

Appendix I.
Luftwaffe Fighter Unit Organization

The organization and command structure of *Luftwaffe* units bore very little resemblance to British or American practice, and for this reason the author has not attempted to use English or American terminology, even as approximations.

The largest tactical formation was the *Jagdgeschwader*, usually abbreviated to *JG*, or in the case of night fighters, *NJG*, for *Nachtjagdgeschwader*. This varied in size, consisting of three, occasionally four, and rarely (toward the end of the war) five *Gruppen*, plus a *Stab* (staff) flight, typically of four aircraft. Its strength was normally between 90 and 120 fighters, and it was commanded by an officer whose rank could be anything from a *Major* to a full *Oberst*, who received the honorific title of *Kommodore*. (This is broadly comparable with the RAF practice of using acting ranks for unit commanders on some occasions.)

The basic fighting unit was the *Gruppe*, which generally consisted of three *Staffeln* plus a *Stab*. *Gruppe* numbering within the *Geschwader* was given in Roman numerals; for example, the third *Gruppe* of JG 26 was written as *III/JG 26*. *Gruppen* could be, and often were, detached from the *Geschwader* to operate autonomously, even to a different theater of operations. On other occasions, *Gruppen* were formed as independent units, usually prior to the formation of a new *Geschwader*. These were abbreviated as, for example, *JGr 101*. A *Gruppe* was commanded by an officer ranking from *Hauptmann* to *Oberstleutnant*, with the title of *Kommandeur*. Although often of comparable size, the *Gruppe* bore little relationship to the British Wing.

The *Staffel* was a subunit of the *Gruppe*, with a nominal strength of 10–12 aircraft. *Staffeln* were numbered within the *Geschwader* rather than the *Gruppe*, in arabic numerals; for example, the fifth *Staffel* of JG 2 is written as 5/JG 2 (and this also indicates that it is part of II/JG 2). A *Staffel* was commanded by anyone from a *Leutnant* to a *Hauptmann*, with the honorific of *Staffelkapitän*. In effect, the *Staffel* was, in British or American terms, more or less an overgrown Flight.

Other fighter units were *Zerstörergeschwader*, which were equipped with twin-engine heavy fighters, or destroyers (typically the Bf 110), and *Lehrgeschwader*, which were originally operational evaluation units but which on the outbreak of war retained their names. These are abbreviated as, for example, ZG 26 and LG 1 respectively. A final one-off fighter unit was the *Jagdverband*, formed in the closing months of the war; this was JV 44.

As mentioned in the Prologue, the basic fighting unit was the element of two, or *Rotte* (literally, "gang"), consisting of a leader, or *Rottenführer*, and his wingman, or *Rottenflieger*. Two *Rotten* made up a four-aircraft *Schwarm*, led by a *Schwarmführer*, and in action a *Staffel* consisted of two or three *Schwarme*, depending on aircraft availability. On rare occasions a three-aircraft *Kette* was used, but this was dictated by operational practicalities rather than actual *Luftwaffe* fighter doctrine.

Promotion to command in *Jagdflieger* units was largely based on combat success, with top scorers rising rapidly. In a few cases this meant that young men were promoted beyond their organizational or administrative capabilities, but by and large the system worked well. If for any reason the designated unit commanders were not available to lead in action, the next-best-qualified pilot took over. In practice this meant that a *Geschwader* might be led by the most successful *Gruppe Kommandeur*, a *Gruppe* might be led by the most successful *Staffelkapitän*, while, at *Staffel* level, the lead was often taken by an experienced NCO, with inexperienced officers in his formation.

While the fighter *Geschwader* were normally all equipped

with the same type of aircraft, this was not necessarily the case. It was not unknown for the *Gruppen* within the *Geschwader* to operate different types from each other, and sometimes the *Stab* was also differently equipped. In the later stages of the war, when it was inexpedient to withdraw units to reequip with a different type, this took place in situ, with the *Gruppen* using both the outgoing and incoming aircraft simultaneously. In particular the *Lehrgeschwader* varied, as these were responsible for the evaluation of both fighters and bombers. A *Lehrgeschwader* fighter subunit was designated as such, for example, *3 (Jagd)/LG 2* or *II(Z)/LG 1*.

Appendix 2.
Day Fighter *Experten*

As the *Luftwaffe* did not subscribe to the Western convention that five victories make an ace but used the term *Experte* to denote a pilot with a high level of achievement over a protracted period, this list has necessarily to be selective. Entries are therefore restricted to those with at least 60 victories, and are in numerical order of victories.

The following abbreviations/symbols have been used:

****	Knight's Cross with Oak Leaves, Swords, and Diamonds
***	Knight's Cross with Oak Leaves and Swords
**	Knight's Cross with Oak Leaves
*	Knight's Cross
KIA	Killed in action
MIA	Missing in action
POW	Prisoner of war
KAS	Killed on active service
S	Spain
P	Poland
F	France 1939–40
BoB	Battle of Britain
WF	Western Front
4/e	four-engine bombers
EF	Eastern Front
NA	North Africa
M	Mediterranean
TV	total victories
TS	total sorties

SR   strike rate (sorties per victory where known)
CD   combat debut
c.   circa

Where combat debut is uncertain—often the case prior to the opening of hostilities with the Soviet Union—the abbreviation WF 40 or WF 40/41 is used.

Erich Hartmann****JG 52. TV 352 (all EF but inc. 7 USAAF P-51s over Romania). CD EF Oct. 42. TS 1,425. SR 4.05.

Gerhard Barkhorn*** *JG 52, JG 6, JV 44*. TV 301 (all EF). CD BoB Aug. 40. TS 1,104. SR 3.67.

Günther Rall*** *JG 52, JG 11, JG 300*. TV 275 (272 EF, 3 WF). CD F 40. TS 621. SR 2.26.

Otto Kittel*** *JG 54*. TV 267 (all EF). CD EF autumn 41. TS 583. SR 2.18. KIA Courland 2/14/45.

Walter Nowotny**** *JG 54, Kdo "Nowotny."* TV 258 (255 EF, 3 WF inc. one 4/e). CD WF Feb. 41. TS unknown. KIA Achmer flying Me 262, 11/8/44.

Wilhelm Batz*** *JG 52*. TV 237 (232 EF, 5 WF inc. 2 4/e). CD EF Dec. 42. TS 445. SR 1.88.

Erich Rudorffer*** *JG 2, JG 54, JG 7*. TV 222 (136 EF, 26 NA, 60 F, BoB and WF inc. 10 4/e, 12 with Me 262). CD F spring 40. TS 1,000+. SR c.4.50.

Heinz Bär*** *JG 51, JG 71, JG 1, JG 3, JV 44*. TV 220 (4F, 13 BoB, 79 EF, 45 NA and M, 83 WF inc. 21 4/e, 16 with Me 262). CD F Sept. 39. TS c.1,000. SR c.4.54.

Hermann Graf**** *JG 51, JG 52, JG 50, JG 11*. TV 212 (202 EF, 12 WF inc. 10 4/e). CD EF July 41. TS c.830. SR c.3.92.

Heinrich Ehrler** *JG 5, JG 7*. TV c.209 (199 EF, 10 WF inc. 5 with Me 262). CD Norway 41. TS not known. KIA Stendal 4/4/45.

Theodor Weissenberger** *Zerstörerstaffel JG 77, JG 5, JG 7*. TV 208 (23 as Bf 110 pilot, 175 EF, 33 WF inc. 8 with Me 262). CD Norway Oct. 41. TS 500+. SR c.2.40.

Hans Philipp*** *JG 76, JG 54.* TV 206 (178 EF, 1 P, 29 WF, F and BoB inc. 1 4/e). CD P Sept. 39. TS not known. KIA Nordhorn 10/8/43.

Walter Schuck** *JG 5, JG 7.* TV 206 (198 EF, 8 WF all with Me 262, inc. 4 4/e). CD Norway 41. TS not known.

Anton Hafner** *JG 51, JG 3.* TV 204 (184 EF, 20 NA inc. 5 4/e). CD EF June 41. TS 794. SR 3.90. KIA EF 10/17/44.

Helmut Lipfert** *JG 52, JG 53.* TV 203 (all EF inc. 2 USAAF 4/e over Romania). CD EF Dec. 42. TS 700. SR 3.45.

Walter Krupinski** *JG 52, JG 5, JG 11, JV 44.* TV 197 (177 EF, 20 WF inc. 1 4/e). CD EF Jan. 42. TS c.1,100. SR c.5.58.

Anton Hackl*** *JG 77, JG 11, JG 300.* TV 192 (105 EF, 87 F, BoB and WF, inc. 32 4/e). CD F 39. TS 1,000+. SR c.5.21.

Joachim Brendel** *JG 51.* TV 189 (all EF). CD EF June 41. TS 950. SR 5.03.

Max Stotz** *JG 54.* TV 189 (173 EF, 16 F and BoB). CD F spring 40. TS 500+. SR c2.65. MIA Vitebsk 8/19/43.

Joachim Kirschner** *JG 3, JG 27.* TV 188 (167 EF, 21 M inc. 2 4/e). CD EF late 41. TS c.600. SR c.3.19. KIA Croatia 12/17/43.

Kurt Brändle** *JG 53, JG 3.* TV 180 (160 EF, 14 F/BoB, 6 WF). CD F 39. TS c.700. SR c.3.89. KIA North Sea 11/3/43.

Günther Josten** *Jagdgruppe "Trondheim," JG 51.* TV 178 (all EF inc. 1 4/e). CD Norway Nov. 41. TS 420. SR 2.36.

Johannes Steinhoff*** *JG 26, JG 52, JG 77, JG 7, JV 44.* TV 176 (148 EF, 28 BoB, NA, M and WF inc. 4 4/e, 6 with Me 262). CD German Bight Dec. 39. TS 993. SR 5.64.

Ernst-Wilhelm Reinert*** *JG 77, JG 27.* TV 174 (103 EF, 51 NA, 20 M and WF, inc. 2 4/e). CD EF June 41. TS 700+.SR c.4.02.

Günther Schack** *JG 51, JG 3.* TV 174 (all EF). CD EF June 41. TS 780. SR 4.48.

Heinz Schmidt** *JG 52.* TV 173 (all EF). CD BoB Aug. 40, TS c.700. SR c.4.05. MIA Russia 9/5/43.

Emil Lang** *JG 54, JG 26.* TV 173 (148 EF, 25 WF). CD EF 42. TS 403. SR 2.33. KIA Belgium 9/3/44.

Horst Ademeit** *JG 54.* TV 166 (165 EF, 1 BoB). CD F 1940. TS c.600. SR c.3.61. MIA EF 8/8/44.

Wolf-Dietrich Wilcke*** *JG 53, JG 3*. TV 162 (13 F and BoB, at least 4 M, 137 EF, 12 WF inc. 4 4/e). CD F 1940. TS 732. SR 4.52. KIA Germany 3/23/44.

Hans-Joachim Marseille**** *LG 2, JG 52, JG 27*. TV 158 (7 BoB, 151 NA). CD BoB 40. TS 382. SR 2.42. KAS 9/30/42.

Heinrich Sturm* *JG 52*. TV c.157 (all EF). CD EF July 41. TS not known. KAS Hungary 12/22/44.

Gerhard Thyben** *JG 3, JG 54*. TV 157 (152 EF, 5 WF). CD EF Dec. 42. TS 385. SR 2.45.

Hans Beisswenger** *JG 54*. TV 152 (all EF). CD BoB autumn 40. TS 500+. SR c3.29.

Gordon Gollob**** *ZG 76, JG 3, JG 77*. TV 150 (1 P, 5 F and BoB, 144 EF). CD P 39. TS 340. SR 2.27.

Peter Düttmann* *JG 52*. TV 150 (all EF). CD EF May 43. TS 398. SR 2.65.

Fritz Tegtmeier* *JG 54, JG 7*. TV 146 (all EF). CD BoB Oct. 40. TS 700. SR 4.79.

Albin Wolf** *JG 54*. TV 144 (all EF). CD EF May 42. TS not known. KIA Russia 4/2/44.

Kurt Tanzer* *JG 51*. TV 143 (126 EF, 17 WF inc. 4 4/e). CD EF Mar. 42. TS 723 inc. 187 *Jabo*. SR 5.06.

Friedrich-Karl Müller** *JG 53, JG 3*. TV 140 (100 EF, 8 BoB, 32 WF inc. 2 4/e). CD F 1940. TS c.600. SR c.4.29. KIA Salzwedel 5/29/44. ("Tutti" Muller should not be confused with *Wilde Sau Experte* "Nasen" Muller).

Karl Gratz* *JG 52, JG 2*. TV 138 (121 EF, 17 WF). CD EF autumn 42. TS 900+. SR c.6.52.

Heinrich Setz** *JG 77, JG 27*. TV 138 (132 EF, 6 WF). CD July 40 Norway. TS 274. SR 1.99.

Rudolf Trenkel* *JG 77, JG 52*. TV 138 (1 EF but inc. 1 4/e). CD EF Feb. 42. TS 500+. SR c.3.62.

Franz Schall* *JG 52, JG 7*. TV 137 (123 EF, 14 WF with Me 262). CD EF Feb. 43. TS c.550. SR c.4.01. KIA Parchim 4/10/45.

Walter Wolfrum* *JG 52*. TV 137 (all EF). CD EF Jan. 43. TS 423. SR 3.09.

Adolf Dickfeld** *JG 52, JG 2, JG 11*. TV 136 (115 EF, 18 NA and WF inc. 11 4/e). CD F 40. TS not known.

Horst-Günther von Fassong* *JG 51, JG 11.* TV c.136 (90 EF, 46 WF inc. 4 4/e). CD EF July 41. TS not known. KIA near Maastricht 1/1/45.

Otto Fonnekold* *JG 52.* TV 136 (mainly EF). CD EF late 42. TS c.600. SR c.4.41. KIA Siebenburgen 8/31/44.

Karl-Heinz Weber** *JG 51, JG 1.* TV 136 (all EF). CD EF spring 42. TS 500+. SR c.3.68. MIA 6/7/44 near Rouen.

Joachim Müncheberg*** *JG 26, JG 51, JG 77.* TV 135 (23 F and BoB, 33 EF, 18 M, 61 NA). CD F autumn 39. TS 500. SR 3.70. KIA 3/23/43 Tunisia.

Hans Waldmann** *JG 52, JG 3, JG 7.* TV 134 (121 EF, 13 WF inc. 2 with Me 262). CD EF Aug. 42. TS 527. SR 3.93. KIA 3/18/45 near Kaltenkirchen.

Alfred Grislawski** *JG 52, JG 50, JG 1, JG 53.* TV 133 (109 EF, 24 WF inc. 18 4/e). CD BoB summer 40. TS c.800. SR c.6.02.

Johannes Weise** *JG 52, JG 77.* TV 133 (all EF). CD EF summer 41. TS c.480. SR c.3.61.

Adolf Borchers* *JG 51, JG 52.* TV 132 (127 EF, 5 F and BoB). CD S 37. TS c.800. SR c.6.06.

Erwin Clausen** *LG 2, JG 77, JG 11.* TV 132 (114 EF, 1 P, 17 WF inc. 14 4/e). CD P Sept. 39. TS 561. SR 4.25.

Wilhelm Lemke** *JG 3.* TV 131 (125 EF, 6 WF). CD EF Nov. 41. TS c.700. SR c.5.34. KIA 12/4/43 Nijmegen.

Herbert Ihlefeld*** *LG 2, JG 52, JG 103, JG 25, JG 11, JG 1.* TV 130 (7 S, 25 F and BoB, 67 EF, 31 WF inc. 15 4/e). CD S 37. TS 1,000+. SR c.7.69.

Heinrich Sterr* *JG 54.* TV 130 (127 EF, 3 WF). CD EF 1942. TS not known, KIA 11/26/44 Vorden.

Franz Eisenach* *ZG 76, JG 1, JG 54.* TV 129 (all EF). CD F 40. TS 319. SR 2.47.

Walther Dahl** *JG 3, JG 300.* TV 128 (77 EF, 51 WF inc. 36 4/e). CD BoB 40. TS c.600. SR c.4.69.

Franz Dörr* *EJGr 3, JG 5.* TV 128 (122 EF, 6 WF). CD WF spring 41. TS 437. SR 3.41.

Rudolf Rademacher* *JG 54, JG 7.* TV 126 (90 EF, 36 WF inc. 10 4/e, 8 with Me 262). CD EF Dec. 41. TS 500+. SR c.3.97.

Josef Zwernemann** *JG 52, JG 77, JG 11*. TV 126 (106 EF, 20 WF and M). CD F 1940. TS c.600. SR c.4.76. KIA 4/8/44 near Gardelegen, Italy.

Gerhard Hoffmann* *JG 52*. TV 125 (all EF). CD WF 40. TS not known. MIA 4/17/45 near Gorlitz.

Dietrich Hräbak** *JG 54, JG 52*. TV 125 (16 F, BoB and WF, 109 EF). CD P Sept. 39. TS 820. SR 6.56.

Walter Oesau*** *JG 51, JG 3, JG 2, JG 1*. TV 125 (8 S, 32 F and BoB, 44 EF, 41 WF inc. 10 4/e). CD S 37. TS c.300 exc. S. SR c.2.40. KIA Eifel 5/11/44.

Wolf Ettel*** *JG3, JG 27*. TV 124 (120 EF, 4 M inc. 2 4/e). CD EF summer 42. TS 250+. SR c.2.02. KIA 7/17/43 Sicily.

Wolfgang Tonne** *JG 53*. TV 122 (5 F and BoB, 96 EF, 21 NA). CD F 40. TS 641. SR 5.25. KAS Tunis 4/20/43.

Heinz Marquardt* *JG 51*. TV 121 (120 EF, 1 WF). CD EF Aug. 43. TS 320. SR 2.64.

Robert Weiss** *JG 26, JG 54*. TV 121 (c.90 EF, c.31 WF). CD WF 41. TS not known. KIA nr Lingen 12/29/44.

Friedrich Obleser* *JG 52*. TV 120 (all EF but inc. 9 U.S. inc. 2 4/e). CD EF Jan. 43. TS c.500. SR c.4.17.

Erich Leie* *JG 2, JG 51, JG 77*. TV 118 (75 EF, 43 WF inc. 1 4/e). CD WF 40/41. TS c.500. SR c.4.24. KIA eastern Germany 3/7/45.

Franz-Josef Beerenbrock** *JG 51*. TV 117 (all EF). CD EF June 41. TS c.400. SR c.3.41. POW Russia 11/9/42.

Hans-Joachim Birkner* *JG 52*. TV 117 (EF inc. 1 P-51). CD EF 43. TS 284. SR 2.43. KAS 12/14/44 Krakow.

Jakob Norz* *JG 5*. TV 117 (probably all EF). KIA 9/16/44 near Kirkenes.

Heinz Wernicke* *JG 54*. TV 117 (all EF). CD EF spring 42. KIA Courland 12/27/44.

August Lambert* *SG 2, SG 151, SG 77*. TV 116 (all EF). KIA 4/17/45 over Saxony. Top-scoring attack pilot.

Werner Mölders**** *JG 53, JG 51*. TV 115 (14 S, 15 F, 31 BoB, 22 WF, 33 EF). CD S 37. TS 300+. SR c.2.61. KAS 11/22/41.

Wilhelm Crinius** *JG 53*. TV 114 (100 EF, 14 NA inc. 1 4/e). CD Feb. 42 EF. TS 400. SR 3.51. POW Tunisia 1/13/43.

Werner Schroer*** *JG 27, JG 54, JG 3*. TV 114 (61 NA, 12 EF, 41 M and WF inc. 26 4/e). CD BoB Aug. 40. TS 197. SR 1.73.

Hans Dammers* *JG 52*. TV 113 (probably all EF). CD WF 40. TS not known. KIA EF 3/17/44.

Berthold Korts* *JG 52*. TV 113 (all EF). CD EF July 42. TS not known. MIA Russia 8/29/43.

Kurt Bühligen*** *JG 2*. TV 112 (40 NA, 72 WF inc. BoB and inc. 24 4/e). CD BoB July 40. TS 700+. SR c.6.25.

Kurt Übben** *JG 77, JG 2*. TV 110 (90 EF, 20 WF, NA and M). CD 1939. TS not known. KIA France 4/27/44.

Franz Woidich* *JG 27, JG 52, JG 400* (with Me 163). TV 110 (2 NA, remainder believed EF). CD M July 41. TS c.1,000. SR c.9.09.

Reinhard Seiler** *JG 54, JG 104*. TV 109 (9 S, 4 F and BoB, 96 EF inc. 1 4/e and 16 at night). CD S 38. TS not known.

Emil Bitsch* *JG 3*. TV 108 (104 EF, 4 WF). CD EF July 41. TS not known. KIA Volkel 3/15/44.

Hans Hahn** *JG 2, JG 54*. TV 108 (20 F and BoB, 40 EF, 48 WF inc. 4 4/e). CD F 40. TS 560. SR 5.19. POW Russia 2/21/43.

Günther Lützow*** *JG 3, JV 44*. TV 108 (5 S, 15+ F and BoB. 3 WF, 84 EF). CD S 37. TS c.300. SR c.2.78. MIA Donauworth 4/24/45 in Me 262.

Bernard Vechtel* *JG 51*. TV 108 (all EF). CD EF May 42. TS 860. SR 7.96.

Viktor Bauer** *JG 2, JG 3, EJG 1*. TV 106 (102 EF, 4 WF). CD WF 40. TS c.400. SR c.3.77.

Werner Lucas* *JG 3*. TV 106 (100 EF, 4 WF inc. 1 4/e). CD BoB summer 40. TS not known. KIA Holland 10/24/43.

Adolf Galland**** *JG 27, JG 26, JV 44*. TV 104 (58 F and BoB, 46 WF inc. 4 4/e and 7 with Me 262). CD S 37. TS 425. SR 4.09.

Heinz Sachsenberg* *JG 52, JG 44*. TV 104 (103 EF, 1 WF). CD EF late 42. TS 520. SR 5.00.

Hartmann Grasser** *ZG 52, ZG 2, JG 51, JG 1, JG 210*. TV 103 (4 F and BoB, 86 EF, 11 NA inc. 2 4/e). CD F 40. TS c.700. SR c.6.80.

Siegfried Freytag* *JG 77, JG 7.* TV 102 (c.70 EF, c.12 NA, 25 M). CD EF 41. TS not known.

Friedrich Geisshardt** *LG 2, JG 77, JG 26.* TV 102 (1 P, 14 F and BoB, 75 EF, 9 M, 3 NA). CD P 39. TS 642, SR 6.29. KIA Genth 4/5/43.

Egon Mayer*** *JG 2.* TV 102 (all F, BoB and WF inc. 25 4/e). CD F 40. TS 353. SR 3.46. KIA Montmedy 3/2/44.

Max-Hellmuth Ostermann*** *ZG 1, JG 54.* TV 102 (93 EF, 9 F, BoB and Yugoslavia). CD F 40. TS 300+. SR c.2.94. KIA Russia 8/9/42.

Herbert Rollwage** *JG 53.* TV 102 (11 EF, 20 M, 71 WF inc. 44 4/e). CD EF 41. TS 500+. SR c.4.90.

Josef Wurmheller*** *JG 53, JG 2.* TV 102 (93 BoB and WF inc. 14 4/e, 9 EF). CD F 40. TS not known. KIA France 6/22/44.

Rudolf Miethig* *JG 52.* TV 101 (probably all EF). CD EF 41. TS not known. KIA Kuban 6/10/43.

Josef Priller* *JG 51, JG 26.* TV 101 (all WF inc. 20+ F and BoB). CD WF 39/40. TS 307, SR 3.04.

Ulrich Wernitz* *JG 54.* TV 101 (all EF). CD EF May 43. TS c.240. SR c.2.38.

Paul-Heinrich Dahne *JG 52, JG 1, JG 11.* TV c.100 (80 EF, 20 WF). CD EF 42. TS c.600. SR c.6.00. KIA 4/24/45 Warnemünde in He 162.

Leopold Steinbatz*** *JG 52.* TV 99 (all EF). CD BoB Nov 40. TS not known. MIA Russia 6/15/42.

Wolfgang Späte** *JG 54, JG 400, JG 7.* TV 99 (90 EF, 9 WF inc. 5 4/e with Me 262). CD EF June 41. TS 600+, SR c.6.06.

Heinrich Bartels* *JG 5, JG 27.* TV 99 (57 EF, 42 WF, M and NA inc. 2 4/e). CD WF Aug. 41. TS c.500. SR c.5.05. KIA nr Bonn 12/23/44.

Gustav Rödel** *JG 27.* TV 98 (1 at least F, 14 BoB, 1 EF, 52 NA and M, remainder WF inc. 12 4/e). CD F 40. TS 980. SR 10.00.

Horst Hannig** *JG 54, JG 2.* TV 98 (90 EF, 8 WF inc. 1 4/e). CD EF summer 41. TS not known. KIA Caen 5/15/43.

Helmut Ruffler* *JG 3, JG 51.* TV 98 (86 EF, 12 WF inc. 8 4/e). CD WF Feb. 41. TS c.690. SR c.7.04.

Hans Schleef* *JG 3, JG 5, JG 4.* TV 98 (92 EF, 6 WF inc. 1 4/e). CD WF 40. TS 500+. SR c.5.10. KIA Bergzabern 12/31/44.

Helmut Mertens* *LG 2, JG 3, EJG 1.* TV 97 (60 EF. remainder F, BoB and WF). CD F 40. TS 750. SR 7.73.

Diethelm von Eichel-Streiber* *JG 52, JG 77, JG 1, JG 26, JG 51, JG 27, JV 44.* TV 96 (94 EF, 2 WF). CD F 40. TS not known.

Heinrich Hofemeier* *JG 51.* TV 96 (all EF). CD WF Mar. 41. TS 490. SR 5.10. KIA Karatchev 8/7/43.

Siegfried Lemke* *JG 2.* TV 96 (95 WF inc. 21 4/e, 1 EF). CD WF autumn 42. TS c.325.SR c.3.39.

Hermann Schleinhege* *JG 3, JG 54.* TV 96 (probably all EF). CD and TS not known.

Leopold Munster** *JG 3,* TV 95 (70 EF, 25 WF inc. 8 4/e). CD and TS not known. KIA Hildesheim 5/8/44.

Rudolf Müller* *JG 5.* TV 94 (all EF). CD EF c.42. TS not known. POW Murmansk 4/19/43.

Anton Dobele* *JG 54.* TV 94 (all EF). CD EF 41. TS 458. SR 4.87. KIA near Smolensk 11/11/43.

Heinrich Klopper* *JG 51, JG 1.* TV 94 (86 EF, 8 WF inc. 4 4/e). CD EF 41. TS 500+. SR c.5.32. MIA Holland 11/29/43.

Rudolf Resch* *JG 52, JG 51.* TV 94 (1 S, remainder probably all EF). CD S 38. TS not known. KIA Orel 7/11/43.

Siegfried Schnell** *JG 2, JG 54.* TV 93 (23 F and BoB, 64 WF inc. 3 4/e, 6 EF). CD F 39/40. TS not known. KIA EF 2/25/44.

Edmund Rossmann* *JG 52.* TV 93 (6 F and BoB, 87 EF). CD BoB 40. TS 640. SR 6.88. POW Orel 7/9/43.

Helmut Bennemann* *JG 52, JG 53.* TV 92 (70 EF, 22 WF possibly inc. F, BoB and M, inc. 1 4/e). CD F 40. TS 400 plus. SR c.4.35.

Gerhard Loos* *JG 54.* TV 92 (78 EF, 14 WF inc. 2 4/e). CD EF late 42. TS not known. KIA Oldenburg 3/6/44.

Oskar Romm* *JG 52, JG 3.* TV 92 (82 EF, 10 WF inc. 8 4/e). TS 229. SR 2.49.

Anton Resch* *JG 52.* TV 91 (all EF). CD EF summer 43. TS 210. SR 2.31.

Eberhard von Boremski* *JG 77, JG 3, EJG 1.* TV 90 (mainly EF but possibly some F and BoB). CD F 39/40. TS 630. SR 7.00.

Heinz Kemethmüller* *JG 3, JG 26.* TV 89 (70 EF, 19 WF inc. 3 4/e). CD WF Dec. 40. TS 463. SR 5.20.

Georg Schentke* *JG 3.* TV 87 (4 F and BoB, 83 EF). CD F 40. TS not known. MIA near Stalingrad 12/25/42.

Josef Jennewein* *JG 26, JG 51.* TV 86 (5 BoB, 81 EF). CD BoB 40. TS 271. SR 3.15. MIA Orel 7/26/43.

Anton Mader* *JG 76, JG 2, JG 77, JG 11, JG 54.* TV 86 (61 EF, 25 WF inc. BoB). CD F 40. TS not known.

Friedrich Wachowiak* *JG 52, JG 3.* TV 86 at least (all EF). CD M May 41. TS not known. KIA Normandy 7/16/44.

Ulrich Wohnert* *JG 54.* TV 86 (all EF). CD EF spring 42. TS not known.

Gerhard Koppen** *JG 52.* TV 85 (probably all EF). CD and TS not known. MIA Russia 5/5/42.

Walter Zellot* *JG 53.* TV 85 (all EF). CD EF 41. TS 296. SR 3.48.KIA Stalingrad 9/10/42.

Heinz Ewald* *JG 52.* TV 84 (all EF). CD EF summer 43. TS 396. SR 4.71.

Peter Kalden* *JG 51.* TV 84 (all EF). CD EF 43. TS 538. SR 6.40. POW Danzig 3/11/45.

Werner Quast* *JG 52.* TV 84 (all EF). CD EF June 41. TS not known. POW Russia 8/7/43.

Otto Wessling** *JG 3.* TV 83 (70 EF, 13 WF inc. several 4/e). CD EF early 43. TS not known. KIA Eschwege 4/19/44.

Walter Ohlrogge* *JG 3, JG 7.* TV 83 (80 EF, 3 WF). CD F May 40. SR c.400. SR c.4.82.

Emil Pusch* Only details available TV 83 (inc. 17 4/e).

Hans Goetz* *JG 54,* TV 82 (probably all EF). CD F Jan. 40. TS 600+. SR c.7.32. KIA Russia 8/4/43.

Hans Grünberg* *JG 3, JG 7, JV 44.* TV 82 (61 EF, 21 WF inc. 14 4/e and 5 with Me 262). CD WF May 41. TS c.550. SR c.6.71.

Helmut Missner* *JG 54, EJG Ost.* TV 82 (all EF). CD and TS not known. KAS Sagan 9/12/44.

Franz Beyer* *JG 3.* TV 81 (70 EF, 21 M and WF, possibly inc. BoB). CD WF 40. TS not known. KIA Venlo 2/11/44.

Hugo Broch* *JG 54.* TV 81 (all EF). CD EF Jan. 43. TS 324. SR 4.00

Hermann Lucke* *JG 51.* TV 81 (probably all EF). CD EF 42. TS not known. KAS Russia 11/8/43.

Willi Nemitz* *JG 52.* TV 81 (believed all EF). CD WF 40. TS 500+. SR c.6.17. KIA Caucasus 4/11/43.

Wilhelm Philipp* *JG 26, JG 54.* TV 81 (22 F, BoB, early WF, 55 EF, 4 WF). CD F Oct. 39. TS 500+. SR c.6.17.

Rudolf Wagner* *JG 51.* TV 81 (all EF). CD EF 42. TS not known. MIA Shitomir 12/11/43.

Herbert Bachnick* *JG 52.* TV 80 (all EF, inc. 1 4/e). CD EF Dec. 42. TS 373. SR 4.66. KIA Silesia 8/7/44.

Otto Wurfel* *JG 51.* TV 79 (all EF). CD EF 42. TS not known. MIA Rogatchev 2/23/44.

Karl-Gottfried Nordmann** *JG 77, JG 51.* TV 78 (1 P, 8 BoB and WF, 69 EF). CD P 39. TS 800+. SR c.10.26.

Georg-Peter Eder** *JG 51, JG 2, JG 1, JG 26, Kdo "Nowotny," JG 7.* TV 78 (10 EF, 68 WF inc. 36 4/e, 12 with Me 262). CD EF June 41. TS not known.

Wolfgang Ewald* *JG 52, JG 3.* TV 78 (1 S, 2 F/BoB, 75 EF). CD S 37. TS not known. POW Russia 7/14/43.

Heinrich Krafft* *JG 51.* TV 78 (4 F and BoB, 74 EF). CD WF 40. TS not known. KIA Russia 12/14/42.

Alexander Preinfalk* *JG 51, JG 77, JG 53.* TV 78 (c.50 EF, remainder M and WF). TS not known. KIA WF 12/12/44.

Hubertus von Bonin* *JG 26, JG 54, JG 52.* TV 77 (4 S, 9 F and BoB, 64 EF). CD S 37. TS not known. KIA Vitebsk 12/15/43.

Josef Haibock* *JG 26, JG 52, JG 53.* TV 77 (16 F, BoB and early WF, 60 EF, 1 WF). CD F Dec. 39. TS 604. SR 7.84.

Johann-Hermann Meier* *JG 52, JG 26.* TV 77 (76 EF, 1 WF). CD EF 42. TS 305. SR 3.96. KAS WF 3/15/44.

Hans-Joachim Kroschinski* *JG 54.* TV 76 (all EF inc. 1 U.S. 4/e). CD EF June 42. TS 360. SR 4.74.

Maximilian Mayerl* *JG 51, EJG 1.* TV 76 (4 BoB and early WF, 72 EF). CD WF 40. TS 647. SR 8.51.

Alfred Teumer* *JG 54, Kdo "Nowotny."* TV 76 (66 EF, 10 WF). CD EF Dec. 41. TS 300+. SR c.3.95. KIA Hesepe 10/4/44.

Edwin Thiel* *JG 52, JG 51.* TV 76 (probably all EF). CD WF 40. TS not known. KIA EF 7/14/44.

Johann Bunzek* *JG 52.* TV 75 (all EF). CD EF 42. TS not known. KIA EF 12/11/43.

Helmut Grollmus* *JG 54.* TV 75 (all EF). CD EF 41/42. TS not known. KIA Finland 6/19/44.

Johann Pichler* *JG 77.* TV 75 (29 EF, 46 M, NA, WF, inc. 16 4/e). CD BoB Aug. 40. TS c.700. SR c.9.33. POW EF 8/30/44.

Joachim Wandel* *JG 76, JG 54.* TV 75 (mainly EF, at least 16 at night with Bf 109). CD S 38. TS not known. KIA Ostashkov 10/7/42.

Hans Roehrig* *JG 53.* TV 75 (c.50 EF, remainder M). CD and TS not known. MIA Catania 7/7/43.

Gustav Frielinghaus* *JG 3, EJG 1.* TV 74 (66 EF, 8 WF). CD EF June 41. TS c.500. SR c.6.76.

Otto Gaiser* *JG 51.* TV 74 (all EF). CD and TS not known. MIA Russia 1/22/44.

Friedrich Haas* *JG 52.* TV 74 (probably all EF). CD EF late 43. TS 385. SR 5.20. KIA Vienna 4/9/45.

Gerhard Michalski** *JG 53, JG 4.* TV 73 (9 F and BoB, 14 EF, 26 M, 24 WF inc. 13 4/e). CD WF 40. TS 652. SR 8.93.

Anton Lindner* *JG 51, EJG 1.* TV 73 (72 EF). CD F 39. TS 650. SR 8.90.

Otto Schultz* *JG 51.* TV 73 (40 EF, 20 NA, 13 M and WF inc. 8 4/e). CD BoB 40. TS 800+. SR c.10.96.

Klaus Mietusch** *JG 26.* TV 72 (57 F, BoB, NA and WF inc. 10 4/e, 15 EF). CD F 40. TS 452. SR 6.28. KIA Germany 9/17/44.

Wilhelm Mink** *JG 51, EJG 1.* TV 72 (70 EF, 2 WF). CD WF 40. TS not known. KIA Denmark 3/12/45.

Karl-Heinz Schnell* *JG 51, JG 102, JV 44.* TV 72 (61 EF, 11 WF). CD F 39. TS 500+. SR c.6.94.

Adolf Glunz** *JG 52, JG 26, JG 7.* TV 71 (3 EF, 68 WF inc.

20 4/e). CD WF Mar. 41. TS 574. SR 8.08. never shot down/wounded.

Hans Füss* *JG 3*. TV 71 (probably all EF). CD EF 41. TS not known. KIA EF Oct. 42.

Günther Scheel* *JG 54*. TV 71 (all EF). CD EF spring 43. TS 70. SR 0.99. KIA Orel 7/16/43.

Alfred Heckmann* *JG 3, JG 26, JV 44*. TV 71 (54 EF, 17 F, BoB and WF inc. 3 4/e). CD WF 40. TS c.600. SR c.8.45.

Hermann-Friedrich Joppien** *JG 51*. TV 70 (25 BoB, 17 WF, 28 EF). CD WF 40. TS not known. KIA Bryansk 8/25/41.

Heinz Lange* *JG 21, JG 54, JG 51*. TV 70 (69 EF, 1 WF). CD P 39. TS 638. SR 9.11.

Rudi Linz* *JG 5*. TV 70 (mainly EF). CD and TS not known. KIA Norway 2/9/45.

Emil Omert* *JG 3, JG 2, JG 77*. TV 70 (50 EF, 3 M, 17 WF). CD WF 40. TS c.700. SR c.10.00. KIA Ploesti 4/24/44.

Armin Köhler* *JG 77*. TV 69 (14 EF, 55 NA, M and WF inc. 13 4/e). CD EF Mar. 42. TS 515. SR 7.46.

Ernst Weismann* *JG 51*. TV 69 (all EF). CD EF autumn 41. TS 258. SR 3.74. MIA Rshev 8/13/42.

Eugen-Ludwig Zweigart* *JG 54*. TV 69 (54 EF, 15 WF inc. 1 4/e). CD EF 41. TS not known. KIA Normandy 6/8/44.

Günther *Freiherr* **von Maltzahn**** *JG 53*. TV 68 (35 WF inc. F, BoB and M, 33 EF). CD F 39. TS 500+. SR c.7.35.

Hans Strelow** *JG 51*. TV 68 (all EF). CD probably EF June 41. TS 200+. SR c.2.94. MIA EF 5/22/42.

Herbert Hüppertz** *JG 51, JG 5, JG 2*. c.68 (35 BoB and WF, 33 EF). CD WF 40. TS not known. KIA Caen 6/8/44.

Konrad Bauer* *JG 51, JG 3, JG 300*. TV 68 (18 EF, 50 WF inc. 32 4/e). CD EF Sept. 42. TS 416. SR 6.12.

Kurt Dombacher* *JGr "Trondheim," JG 51*. TV 68 (all EF). CD EF May 43. TS (exc. coastal patrols) c.300. SR 4.41.

Walter Hoeckner* *JG 52, JG 77, JG 26, JG 1, JG 4*. TV 68 (56 EF, 12 WF inc. 5 4/e). CD WF 40. TS 500+. SR c.7.35. KAS 8/25/44.

Heinrich Jung* *JG 54*. TV 68 (all EF). CD WF Nov. 40. TS not known. KIA EF 7/30/43.

Herbert Kaiser* *JG 77, JG 1, JV 44.* TV 68 (42 EF, remainder F, BoB, M, NA and WF). CD P 39. TS c.1,000. SR c.14.71.

Richard Leppla* *JG 51, JG 105, JG 6.* TV 68 (12 F and BoB, 55 EF, 1 WF). CD WF 40. TS 500+. SR c.7.35.

Fritz Losigkeit* *JG 26, JG 1, JG 51, JG 77.* TV 68 (57 EF, 11 WF inc. 1 4/e). CD S 38, TS c.750. SR c.11.03.

Ernst Süss* *JG 52, JG 50, JG 11.* TV 68 (60 EF, remainder F, BoB and WF). CD F 40. TS not known. KIA Oldenburg 12/20/43.

Otto Tange* *JG 51.* TV 68 (3 early WF, 65 EF). CD WF 40. TS 426. SR 6.26. KIA Russia 7/30/43.

Hubert Strassl* *JG 51.* TV 67 (all EF;). CD EF late 41. TS 221. SR 3.30. KIA Orel 7/8/43.

Hermann Staiger* *JG 51, JG 26, JG 1, JG 7.* TV 63 (50 WF, few possibly F and BoB and inc. 26 4/e later, 13 EF). CD F 40. TS 400+. SR c.6.35.

Erbo *Graf* von Kageneck** *JG 27.* TV 67 (13 F and BoB, 4 WF, 48 EF and 2 NA). CD F 39. TS not known. KIA NA 12/24/41.

Gustav Denk* *JG 52.* TV 67 (mainly EF but at least 2 BoB). CD F 39. TS 500+. SR c.7.46. KIA Krasnodar 2/13/43.

Fritz Dinger* *JG 53.* TV 67 (c.50 EF, 17 WF and M). CD WF 39/40. TS not known. KAS Sicily 7/27/43.

Herbert Findeisen* *JG 54.* TV 67 (all EF). Scored 42 victories as a reconnaissance pilot.

Franz Schiess* *JG 53.* TV 67 (14 EF, 13 NA, 40 M inc. 10 over Malta). CD WF spring 41. TS 540. SR 8.06. MIA off Capri 9/2/43.

Franz Schwaiger* *JG 3.* TV 67 (55 EF, 12 WF inc. 2 4/e). CD EF 41. TS not known. KIA Germany 4/24/44.

Erwin Flieg* *JG 51.* TV 66 (9 RAF 40/41, 57 EF). CD WF June 40. TS 506. SR 7.67. POW Russia 5/29/42.

Reinhold Hoffmann* *JG 54.* TV 66 (60 EF, 6 WF, all 4/e). CD EF 42. TS not known. KIA Brandenberg 5/24/44.

Hans Döbrich* *JG 5.* TV 65 (all EF). CD EF Feb. 42. TS 248. SR 3.82. No front-line service after injuries 7/16/43.

Heinrich Fullgräbe* *JG 52, JG 50.* TV 65 (probably all EF). CD and TS not known. KIA EF 1/30/45.

Berthold Grassmuck* *JG 52.* TV 65 (probably all EF). CD probably EF 41. TS not known. KIA Pitomnik 10/28/42.

Karl Kempf *JG 54, JG 26.* TV 65 (5 F and BoB, 49 EF, 11 WF inc. 2 4/e). CD F spring 40. TS 445. SR 6.85. KIA Belgium 9/3/44.

Waldemar Semelka* *JG 52.* TV 65 (probably all EF). CD EF 41. TS 240+. SR c.3.69. MIA Stalingrad 8/21/42.

Jurgen Harder** *JG 53, JG 11.* TV 64 (17 EF, 16 NA, 31 WF inc. 9 4/e). CD probably EF June 41. TS not known. KAS nr Berlin 2/17/45.

Rolf Hermichen** *ZG 1, JG 26, JG 11, JG 104.* TV 64 (11 F, BoB and early WF, 8 EF, 45 WF inc. 26 4/e). CD F 39/40. TS 629. SR 9.83.

Bernd Gallowitsch* *JG 51, I/JG 1* (with He 162). TV 64 (59 EF, 5 WF inc. BoB). CD WF June 40. TS 840. SR 13.13.

Viktor Petermann* *JG 52, JG 7.* TV 64 (probably all EF). CD and TS not known.

Heinrich Hoffmann** *JG 51.* TV 63 (1 BoB, 62 EF). CD WF 40. TS 258. SR 4.10. KIA Russia 10/3/41.

Franz Goetz* *JG 53, JG 26.* TV 63 (30 F, BoB and early WF, 17 EF, remainder NA, M and WF). CD F 40. TS 766. SR 12.16.

Karl Hammerl* *JG 52.* TV 63 (probably all EF). CD F 39. TS not known. MIA Russia 3/2/43.

Gerhard Homuth* *JG 27, JG 54.* TV 63 (15 F and BoB, 46 NA and M, 2 EF). CD F 40. TS c.450. SR c.7.14. MIA Orel 8/3/43.

Wilhelm Hübner* *JG 51.* TV 62 (all EF). CD EF 43. TS not known. KIA East Prussia 4/7/45.

Helmut Neumann* *JG 5.* TV 62 (all EF). CD EF Aug. 42. TS 162. SR 2.61.

Horst Carganico* *JG 5.* TV 60 (mainly EF). CD EF 41. TS c.600. SR c.10.00. KIA France 5/27/44.

August Mors* *JG 5.* TV 60 (48 EF, 12 WF inc. 1 4/e). CD EF June 41. TS not known. KIA France 8/6/44.

Karl Munz* *JG 52, JG 7*. TV 60 (57 EF, 3 WF inc. 1 4/e). CD WF 40. TS 600+. SR c.10.00.

Alfred Rauch* *JG 51*. TV 60 (56 EF, 6 WF and NA, at least 1 BoB and inc. 1 4/e). CD WF June 40. TS 647. SR 10.78.

Appendix 3.
Night Fighter *Experten*

The criteria adopted for night fighter *Experten* is the award of the *Ritterkreuz* for fighter combat with at least 25 victories. The same abbreviations as in Appendix 2 have been used throughout, plus RO (Radar Operator) and AG (gunner). Victories on fronts other than the West, or by day, are stated where known.

Heinz-Wolfgang Schnaufer**** *NJG 1, NJG 4*. TV 121. CD Spring 42. TS 164. SR 1.36. RO **Fritz Rumpelhardt*** shared in 100 victories and AG **Wilhelm Gänsler*** in 98.

Helmut Lent**** *ZG 76, NJG 1, NJG 2, NJG 3*. TV 110 (8 by day of which 1 P, 2 German Bight and 5 Norway). CD P 39. TS c.300. SR c.2.73. KAS 10/5/44. 80 night, 8 day victories with RO **Walter Kubisch***.

Heinrich *Prinz* zu Sayn-Wittgenstein*** *NJG 2, NJG 100, NJG 3*. TV 83 (29 EF). CD WF Aug 41. TS not known. KIA 1/21/44. Former bomber pilot.

Wilhelm Herget** *ZG 76, NJG 3, NJG 1, NJG 4, JV 44*. TV 72 (15 by day: 14 F and BoB, 1 WF with Me 262). CD P 39. TS 700+. SR c.9.72 57 night and 11 day victories with RO **Hans Liebherr***.

Werner Streib*** *ZG 1, NJG 1*. TV 66 (1 by day). CD F 40. TS not known. 14 shared with RO **Kurt Bundrock***.

Manfred Meurer** *NJG 1, NJG 5*. TV 65. CD probably F 40. TS not known. KIA Magdeburg 1/21/44. 60 victories with RO **Gerhard Scheibe***.

Günther Radusch** *ZG 1, NJG 1, NJG 3, NJG 2*. TV 65 (1

by day in Spain flying He 112). CD S 38. TS (WW2 only) c. 140. SR (WW2 only) 2.19.

Rudolf Schönert** *NJG 1, NJG 2, NJG 3, NJG 100, NJG 10, NJG 5.* TV 64 (35 EF). CD WF June 41. TS not known. Regular RO **Hannes Richter***.

Heinz Rökker** *NJG 2.* TV 64 (inc. 1 by day, several M). CD M spring 42. TS 170. SR 2.66. 61 night and 1 day victory with RO **Carlos Nugent***.

Paul Zorner** *NJG 2, NJG 3, NJG 100, NJG 5.* TV 59. CD WF July 42. TS 108. SR 1.83. 58 victories with RO **Heinrich Wilke***. Former transport pilot.

Martin Becker** *NJG 4, NJG 6.* TV 58. CD WF 43. TS c.83. SR c.1.43. Former reconnaissance pilot. All with RO **Karl-Ludwig Johanssen***.

Gerhard Raht** *NJG 3, NJG 2.* TV 58. CD WF 42. TS 171. SR 2.95. 56 with RO **Anton Heinemann***.

Heinz Strüning** *ZG 26, NJG 2, NJG 1.* TV 56. CD F 40. TS 250. SR 4.46. KIA Werl 12/24/44.

Josef Kraft** *NJG 4, NJG 5, NJG 6, NJG 1.* TV 56 (20 EF). CD probably 43. TS 145. SR 2.59.

Gustav Francsi* *NJG 100.* TV 56 (52 EF, 4 WF). CD and TS not known.

Hans-Dieter Frank** *ZG 1, NJG 1.* TV 55. CD WF 40. TS not known. KIA 9/27/43.

Heinz Vinke** *NJG 1.* TV 54. CD late 42. TS not known. KIA 2/26/44.

August Geiger** *NJG 1.* TV 53. CD spring 41. TS not known. KIA Ijsselmeer 9/29/43

Herbert Lütje** *NJG 1, NJG 6.* TV 53 (inc. 2 by day: 1 4/e). CD July 40. TS c.150. SR c.2.83.

Martin Drewes** *ZG 76, NJG 1.* TV 52 (9 by day inc. 7 4/e). CD WF 40. TS 235. SR 4.52. 37 victories with RO **Erich Handke***.

Werner Hoffmann* *ZG 52, ZG 2, NJG 3, NJG 5.* TV 52 (1 by day). CD WF 40. TS 190. SR 3.65.

Egmont *Prinz* zur Lippe-Weissenfeld** *ZG 76, NJG 1, NJG 2, NJG 5.* TV 51. CD WF 40. TS not known. KAS Ardennes 3/12/44.

Hans-Joachim Jabs** *ZG 76, NJG 1*. TV 50 (22 by day: 8F, 12 BoB, 2 WF). CD F 40. TS 710. SR 14.20. Most victories shared with RO **Erich Weissflog***.

Kurt Welter** *JG 301, NJG 11*. TV 50+ (at least 4 by day). Believed to have scored several night victories with Me 262. Leading *Wilde Sau* pilot. CD 43. TS not known.

Hermann Greiner** *NJG 1*. TV 50 (4 4/e by day). CD WF 42. TS 126. SR 2.52.

Reinhard Kollak* *NJG 1, NJG 4*. TV 49. CD Oct. 40. TS c.250. SR c.5.10.

Paul Gildner** *ZG 1, NJG 1*. TV 48 (4 by day, WF 40). CD WF 40. TS not known. KIA 2/24/43.

Walter Borchers* *ZG 76, NJG 3, NJG 5*. TV c.48 (12 by day F and BoB, 3 4/e by day WF). CD F 40. TS not known. KIA Leipzig 3/5/45.

Johannes Häger* *NJG 1*. TV 48 (1 4/e by day). CD WF 42/43. TS 99. SR 2.06.

Ludwig Becker** *NJG 1*. TV 46. CD WF 40. TS not known. KIA North Sea 2/26/43. RO **Staub** shared in 40 victories, AG **Wilhelm Gänsler*** in 17.

Paul Semrau** *NJG 2*. TV 46 (inc. 9 intruder over England 40/41). CD F 40. TS not known. KIA Holland 2/8/45.

Hans-Heinz Augenstein* *NJG 1*. TV 46. CD late 42. TS not known. KIA nr Münster 12/6/44.

Rudolf Frank** *NJG 3*. TV 45. CD summer 41. TS 183. SR 4.07. KIA Eindhoven 4/26-27/44. Most if not all victories with RO **Hans-Georg Schierholz***.

Ernst Drunkler* *ZG 2, NJG 1, NJG 5*. TV 45 (5 EF, 2 4/e by day). CD EF May 42. TS (night only) 87. SR (night only) 2.02.

Reinhold Knacke** *ZG 1, NJG 1*. TV 44. CD F 40. TS not known. KIA Holland 2/3/43. 35 shared with RO **Kurt Bundrock***.

Alois Lechner* *NJG 2, NJG 100*. TV 43 (all EF). CD c.42. Ts not known. MIA Mogilev 2/23/44. Former bomber pilot.

Werner Baake* *NJG 1*. TV 41. CD 42. TS 195. SR 4.76. All victories with RO **Bettaque**.

Leopold Fellerer* *NJG 1, NJG 5, NJG 6*. TV 41 (2 day). CD WF 40. TS not known.

Ludwig Meister* *NJG 1, NJG 4*. TV 41. CD WF Sept. 41. TS 120. SR 2.93.

Eckart-Wilhelm von Bonin* *NJG 1, NJG 102*. TV 39 (2 4/c by day). CD Oct. 40. TS c.150. SR c.3.85.

Dietrich Schmidt* *NJG 1*. TV 39. CD Sept. 41. TS 171. SR 4.38.

Günther Bahr* *SKG 210, NJG 4, NJG 6*. TV 37 (36 4/e at night WF and 1 day EF). CD EF June 41. TS (night only) c.90. SR (night only) c.2.50.

Wilhelm Beier* *NJG 2, NJG 1, NJG 3*. TV 36 (all WF, 14 intruder England 40/41). CD WF 40. TS c.250. SR c.6.94.

Helmut Bergmann* *NJG 4, NJG 1*. TV 36. CD July 41. TS c.135. SR c.3.75. MIA Avranches 8/6/44.

Walter Ehle* *ZG 1, NJG 1*. TV 36 (3 day, 2 of which P). CD P 39. TS not known. KIA St. Truiden 11/17/43.

Heinz-Horst Hissbach* *NJG 2*. TV 34. CD M 41. TS 200+. SR c.5.88. KIA Gelnhausen 4/14/45.

Wilhelm Johnen* *NJG 1, NJG 5, NJG 6*. TV 34. CD early 42. TS 200+. SR c.5.88.

Heinz-Martin Hadeball* *NJG 1, NJG 4, NJG 6, NJG 10*. TV 33. CD WF June 41. TS c.350. SR c.10.61.

Josef Kociok* *ZG 76, SKG 210, 10(NJ)/ZG 1*. TV 33 (all EF, 21 night). CD WF 40. TS c.200. SR c.6.06. KIA Kertsch 9/26/43.

Ernst-Wilhelm Modrow* *NJG 1,* TV 33. CD Nov. 43. TS 109. SR 3/30. Former transport pilot.

Werner Husemann* *NJG 1, NJG 3*. TV c.32. CD WF 42. TS 250+. SR c.7.81. Previously a weather reconnaissance pilot. Most later victories with RO **Hans-Georg Schierholz***.

Klaus Bretschneider* *JG 300*. TV at least 31 (17 by day inc. at least 3 4/e, and 14 *Wilde Sau* victories in 20 sorties). CD not known. SR *Wilde Sau* only 1.43. KIA Kassel 12/24/44.

Hubert Rauh* *NJG 1, NJG 4*. TV 31. CD Jan. 42. TS 150. SR 4.84.

Karl-Heinz Scherfling* *NJG 1*. TV 31 at least. CD WF summer 42. TS not known. KIA Belgium 7/21/44.

Gerhard Friedrich* *NJG 4, NJG 6*. TV 30. CD 42. TS not known. KIA 3/16/45. Previously transport pilot.

Friedrich-Karl Müller* *JG 300, NJG 10.* TV 30 (23 as *Wilde Sau* pilot). CD July 43. TS (night) 52. SR 1.73. Previously bomber and transport pilot.

Paul Szameitat* *NJG 1, NJG 5, NJG 3.* TV 29 (inc. 1 4/e by day). CD 43. TS not known. KIA Bückeburg 1/2/44.

Heinrich Wohlers* *NJG 1, NJG 4, NJG 6.* TV 29. CD 41. TS not known. KIA Echterdingen 3/15/44. Former reconnaissance pilot.

Anton Benning* *JG 106, JG 301.* TV 28 (inc. 18 4/e, about 15 at night as *Wilde Sau* pilot). CD June 43. TS c.100. SR c.3.57. Former transport pilot.

Hans Krause* *NJG 3, NJG 101.* TV 28. CD and TS not known.

Fritz Lau* *NJG 1.* TV 28. CD autumn 43. TS 76. SR 2.71. Former transport pilot.

Lothar Linke* *ZG 76, NJG 1, NJG 2.* TV 28 (3 by day). CD WF 39. TS 100+. SR c.3.57. KIA Holland 5/14/43.

Rudolf Sigmund* *NJG 1, NJG 3.* TV 28 (inc. 2 by day). CD spring 42. TS not known. KIA Kassel 10/3/43.

Hermann Wischnewski* *JG 300.* TV 28 (16 *Wilde Sau*, 12 by day, all WF). CD July 43. TS not known. Former transport pilot.

Heinz Grimm* *NJG 1.* TV 27 (1 4/e by day). CD WF 41. TS not known. KIA 10/9/43.

Alfons Köster* *NJG 2, NJG 3.* TV 25 at least (inc. 11 over England 40/41 and 5 NA). CD WF 40. TS 200+. SR c.8.00. KIA Oldenburg 1/7/45.

Helmuth Schulte* *NJG 5.* TV 25. CD Sept. 43. TS c.180. SR c.7.20. Former army observation pilot.

Appendix 4.
Strike Rates

The most usual way of assessing the performance of the aces is by victory totals. Using this method, Erich Hartmann is preeminent by a considerable margin. There are, however, other factors to consider, the major one of which is opportunity. Ideally, the best alternative would be to divide the number of sorties on which contact was made with the enemy by the number of victories to give a strike rate. Unfortunately this information is available only in rare cases, and the data obtained would be insufficient to give even a moderately accurate picture. On the other hand, the total number of sorties flown is known in the majority of cases. The author has adopted this method in the following table as a useful alternative. With one exception, only those pilots with a strike rate equal to or better than that of Hartmann are shown.

Abbreviations are as follows: SR—Strike Rate; TV—Total Victories; KIA—Killed in Action or on Active Service. "Front" refers to the theater of operations in which the majority of victories were scored.

		SR	TV	Front	
1	Günther Scheel	0.99	71	E	KIA
2	Werner Schroer	1.73	114	NA/M	
3	Walter Loos	1.74	38	W	
4	Wilhelm Batz	1.88	237	E	
5	Heinrich Setz	1.99	138	E	KIA
6	Wolf Ettel	2.02	124	E	KIA
7	Otto Kittel	2.18	267	E	KIA

8	Günther Rall	2.26	275	E	
9	Gordon Gollob	2.27	150	E	
10	Anton Resch	2.31	91	E	
11	Emil Lang	2.33	173	E	KIA
12	Günther Josten	2.36	178	E	
13	Ulrich Wernitz	2.38	101	E	
14	Theodor Weissenberger	2.40	208	E	
14	Walter Oesau	2.40	123	E/W	KIA
16	Hans-Joachim Marseille	2.42	158	NA	KIA
17	Hans-Joachim Birkner	2.42	117	E	KIA
18	Gerhard Thyben	2.45	157	E	
19	Franz Eisenach	2.47	129	E	
20	Oskar Romm	2.49	92	E	
21	Albert Brunner	2.55	53	E	KIA
22	Helmut Neumann	2.61	62	E	
22	Werner Mölders	2.61	115	W	KIA
24	Kurt Ebener	2.63	57	E	POW
25	Heinz Marquardt	2.64	121	E	
26	Max Stotz	2.65	189	E	MIA
26	Peter Düttmann	2.65	150	E	
28	Günther Lützow	2.78	108	E	KIA
28	Hans Weik	2.78	36	W	
30	Walter Adolph	2.82	29	W	KIA
31	Hans Strelow	2.94	68	E	MIA
32	Josef Priller	3.04	101	W	
33	Walter Wolfrum	3.09	137	E	
34	Josef Jennewein	3.15	86	E	MIA
35	Joachim Kirschner	3.19	188	E	KIA
35	Heinz Golinski	3.19	47	E	KIA
37	Hans Beisswenger	3.29	152	E	MIA
38	Hubert Strassl	3.30	67	E	KIA
39	Johann Schmid	3.34	41	W	KIA
40	Alfred Gross	3.36	52	E	
41	Wilhelm Galland	3.38	55	W	KIA

42	Siegfried Lemke	3.39	96	W	
43	Franz Dörr	3.41	128	E	
43	Franz Beerenbrock	3.41	117	E	POW
45	Helmut Lipfert	3.45	203	E	
46	Egon Mayer	3.46	102	W	KIA
47	Walter Zellot	3.48	85	E	KIA
48	Jürgen Brocke	3.57	42	E	KIA
49	Horst Ademeit	3.61	166	E	MIA
49	Johannes Weise	3.61	133	E	
51	Rudolf Trenkel	3.62	138	E	
52	Gerhard Vogt	3.63	48	W	KIA
53	Gerhard Barkhorn	3.67	301	E	
54	Karl-Heinz Weber	3.68	136	E	MIA
55	Waldemar Semelka	3.69	65	E	MIA
56	Joachim Müncheberg	3.70	135	W/NA/ M	KIA
57	Ernst Weismann	3.74	69	E	MIA
58	Viktor Bauer	3.77	106	E	
59	Hans Döbrich	3.82	65	E	
60	Kurt Brändle	3.89	180	E	KIA
61	Ludwig Hafner	3.90	52	E	MIA
62	Hermann Graf	3.92	212	E	
63	Hans Waldmann	3.93	134	E	KIA
64	Alfred Teumer	3.95	76	E	KIA
64	Hans Dortenmann	3.95	38	E/W	
66	Rudolf Rademacher	3.97	126	E	
67	Hugo Broch	4.00	81	E	
68	Franz Schall	4.01	137	E	KIA
69	Ernst-Wilhelm Reinert	4.02	174	E/NA/ M	
70	Erich Hartmann	4.05	352	E	
70	Heinz Schmidt	4.05	173	E	
72	Adolf Galland	4.09	104	W	

Interestingly, strike rates for night fighters where known match the best of those of the day fighters. Heinz-Wolfgang Schnaufer scored at the rate of one victory for every 1.36 sorties, beating everyone except Günther Scheel; Martin Becker came next at 1.43. *Wilde Sau* pilot Friedrich-Karl "Nasen" Müller matched Werner Schroer's rate of 1.73, while Paul Zorner averaged 1.83.

BIBLIOGRAPHY

Aders, Gebhard, *History of the German Night Fighter Force 1917–1945,* Jane's, London 1979. (Original edition: *Geschichte der Deutschen Nachtjagd 1917–1945,* Motorbuch, Stuttgart, 1977.)

Alexander, Jean, *Russian Aircraft since 1940,* Putnam, London, 1975.

Anon., *The Rise and Fall of the German Air Force, 1933–1945,* Arms & Armour Press, London, 1983.

Bekker, Cajus D., *The Luftwaffe War Diaries,* Macdonald, London, 1967.

Boyd, Alexander, *The Soviet Air Force since 1918,* Macdonald and Jane's, London, 1977.

Braham, John R. D., *Scramble,* Frederick Muller, London, 1961. (U.S. title: *Night Fighter*)

Caldwell, Donald L., *JG 26: Top Guns of the Luftwaffe,* Ballantine Books, New York, 1993.

Constable, Trevor J., and Toliver, Raymond F., *Horrido! Fighter Aces of the Luftwaffe,* Arthur Barker, London, 1968.

———, *The Blond Knight of Germany,* Arthur Barker, London, 1970.

Cunningham, Bob; Simons, Bob; McKinney, Jim; and Smith, Robert, *Tumult in the Clouds,* General Dynamics, Texas, 1990.

Dierich, Wolfgang, *Kampfgeschwader 51 "Edelweiss,"* Ian Allan, London, 1973.

Ethell, Jeffrey, and Price, Alfred, *Target Berlin,* Arms & Armour, London, 1989.

Faber, Harold (ed.), *Luftwaffe: An Analysis by Former Luftwaffe Generals,* Times Books, New York, 1977; Sidgwick & Jackson, London, 1979.

Galland, Adolf, *The First and the Last: The German Fighter Force in WW2,* Methuen, London, 1955. (Original edition: *Der Ersten und die Letzen: Die Jagdflieger in Zweiten Weltkrieg,* Franz Schneekluth, Darmstadt, 1953.)

Green, William, *Famous Fighters of the Second World War,* Macdonald and Jane's, London, 1975.

Hooton, E. R., *Phoenix Triumphant,* Arms & Armour, London, 1994.

Johnen, Wilhelm, *Duel under the Stars,* William Kimber, London, 1957. (Original edition: *Nachtjaeger gegen Bomberpulks: Ein Tatsachen-*

bericht ueber die Deutsche Nachtjagd im Zweiten Weltkrieg, Pabel, Rastatt, 1960.)

Knoke, Heinz, *I Flew for the Führer,* Evans, London, 1953.

Middlebrook, Martin, *The Nuremberg Raid, 30–31 March 1944,* Allen Lane, London, 1973.

Musciano, Walter A., *Messerschmitt Aces,* Arco, New York, 1982.

Obermaier, Ernst, *Die Ritterkreuzträger der Luftwaffe: Jagdflieger 1939–1945,* Verlag Dieter Hoffman, Mainz, 1966.

Parry, Simon W., *Intruders over Britain,* Air Research Publications, London, 1992.

Philpott, Bryan, *Famous Fighter Aces,* Patrick Stephens, Yeovil, 1989.

Price, Alfred, *Battle over the Reich,* Ian Allan, London, 1973.

———, *Focke-Wulf 190 At War,* Ian Allan, London, 1977.

———, *Instruments of Darkness,* Macdonald & Jane's, London, 1977.

———, *The Last Year of the Luftwaffe,* Arms & Armour, London, 1991.

Roell, Werner P., *Laurels for Prinz Wittgenstein,* Independent Books, Bromley, 1994. Shores, Christopher, *Duel for the Sky,* Blandford Press, Dorset, 1985.

Sims, Edward H., *Fighter Tactics and Strategy: A Comparative Study of the RAF, the Luftwaffe and the U.S. Army Air Forces,* Cassell, London, 1972; Harper, New York, 1972.

———, *The Fighter Pilots,* Cassell, London, 1967.

Smith, John. R., and Kay, Antony, *German Aircraft of the Second World War,* Putnam, London, 1972.

Spick, Mike, *All-Weather Warriors,* Arms & Armour, London, 1994.

———, *Fighter Pilot Tactics,* Patrick Stephens, Yeovil, 1983.

Steinhoff, Johannes, *The Last Chance,* Hutchinson, London, 1977.

Wagner, Ray (ed.), *Soviet Air Force in World War II: The Official History* (trans. by Leland Fetzer), Doubleday, New York, 1963; David & Charles, Newton Abbot, 1974.

Weal, John, *Focke-Wulf FW 190 Aces of the Russian Front,* Osprey, London, 1995.

Ziegler, Mano, *Rocket Fighter,* Arms & Armour, London, 1976. (Original edition: *Raketenjaeger Me 163,* Motorbuch, Stuttgart, 1961.)

Magazines

Air International, Air Enthusiast, RAF Flying Review, Jagerblatt (various issues)

INDEX

ROLL ME OVER
An Infantryman's World War II
by Raymond Gantter

When Raymond Gantter arrived in Normandy in the fall of 1944, bodies were still washing up from the invasion. Sobered by that sight, Gantter and his fellow infantrymen began their long bloody trek across northern France and Belgium, taking part in the historic and horrific Battle of the Bulge before slowly penetrating into and across Germany, fighting all the way to the Czechoslovakian border.

Gantter—an enlisted man and college graduate who spoke German—portrays the extraordinary life of the American soldier as he and his comrades lived it while helping to destroy Hitler's Third Reich.

Published by Ivy Books.
Available in bookstores everywhere.

JG 26
TOP GUNS OF THE LUFTWAFFE
by Donald L. Caldwell

This is the story of the pilots and campaigns of
Luftwaffe fighter wing JG 26, known as the
Abbeville Kids. *JG 26* chronicles the rise and
fall of the famous fighter wing, from its found-
ing during Hitler's military buildup through
its glory days during the first years of the war,
when its bases in northern France were to be
avoided at all costs, right up to the grim final
hours of the Third Reich.

Published by Ivy Books.
Available in bookstores everywhere.

IF YOU SURVIVE
by George Wilson

From the first penetration of the Siegfried Line to the Nazis' last desperate charge in the Battle of the Bulge, Wilson fought in the thickest action, helping to take the small towns of northern France and Belgium building by building. As the only member of Company F, 4th Infantry Division, to survive the war, Wilson bears heartbreaking testimony to the courage and honor of the men he fought with and the war they won.

Published by Ivy Books.
Available in bookstores everywhere.

RANGERS IN WW II
by Robert W. Black

From the deadly shores of North Africa to the fierce jungle hell of the Pacific, the contribution of the World War II Ranger Battalions far outweighed their numbers. They were ordinary men on an extraordinary mission, whether spearheading a landing force or scouting deep behind enemy lines. With first-person interviews and in-depth research, author Robert Black, a Ranger himself, makes the battles of the greatest war the world has ever seen come to life as never before.

Published by Ivy Books.
Available in your local bookstore.